D1031074

TOKYO
GEEK'S GUIDE

MANGA, ANIME, GAMING, COSPLAY, TOYS, IDOLS & MORE

GIANNI SIMONE

TUTTLE Publishing

Tokyo | Rutland, Vermont | Singapore

Jan 18

CONTENTS

TOKYO: THE GEEK CAPITAL OF THE WORLD

MORE THAN 30 YEARS HAVE PASSED SINCE THE WORD "OTAKU" BEGAN TO BE ASSOCIATED WITH ANIME AND MANGA. MANY THINGS HAVE CHANGED, STARTING WITH PEOPLE'S ATTITUDES TOWARD THE WORD AND ITS IMPLICATIONS. BACK IN 1983, ESSAYIST NAKAMORI AKIO USED IT IN A DISPARAGING WAY WHEN WRITING ABOUT ANIME AND MANGA FANS. BEFORE THAT, THE WORD "MANIA" HAD BEEN USED TO DEFINE SOMEONE WHO WAS MADLY IN LOVE WITH AND DEEPLY KNOWLEDGEABLE ABOUT SOMETHING, BE IT COMICS, TRAINS OR WEAPONS. BUT AFTER NAKAMORI'S COLUMN APPEARED IN MANGA BURIKKO MAGAZINE, ALL THOSE "SOCIALLY INEPT YOUNG MALES" WHO WERE GUILTY OF SEEKING REFUGE IN A FANTASY WORLD MADE OF VIDEO GAMES, TOYS AND CUTE GIRLS WERE BRANDED WITH THE OTAKU LABEL.

Of course that was a very reductive description, and recent books, articles and essays have showed what many people probably already knew: That you don't have to be a nerdy loser to be an otaku; and that the "geeky guy" label is actually quite misleading, for there are as many female otaku out there as there are men.

But people's attitudes are hard to change, and more than 20 years passed before otaku culture began to be slowly accepted, mainly thanks to the *Densha Otoko* (Train Man, 2004) phenomenon. This allegedly true story of a 20-something geek who falls in love with a girl was born on the 2channel message board, and from there spread like wildfire, eventually becoming a novel, a movie and a TV series, all of them extremely successful, and showing in the process that these otaku were not so dangerous after all, and some were actually quite cute.

While even today many Japanese have mixed feelings about this subject, foreign fans have never had any problems with the concept and have wholeheartedly used the term to describe themselves. In Europe, Japanese animation first appeared on French and Italian television in the second half of the '70s and much of the under-40 generation in those countries has been raised on a steady anime diet. In the United States, already ten years before *Densha Otoko*, many American fans who attended early anime conventions like Otakon used to proudly display the O-word on their T-shirts. And even in China—where *Astro Boy* first aired on TV in the '80s—the so-called "One-Child Generation" born at the end of last century has found ways to circumvent government's bans and restrictions on Japanese pop culture by pirating copies of popular anime and organizing their own dojin fairs.

Nowadays, of course, the words *manga* and *anime* can be found in most dictionaries, otaku culture is celebrated in countless conventions around the world, and Japanese comics and animation are widely available in

JAPANESE OTAKU ARE NOT AFRAID OF SHOWING OFF THEIR PREDILECTIONS ANYMORE.

MANGA AND ANIME CHARACTERS CAN BE FOUND EVERYWHERE, FROM KIDS' SOCKS TO POSH DEPARTMENT STORE WINDOWS (LEFT).

many languages—not only the giant robots sagas that first became popular in the West but even shojo manga and "boys' love" stories. Online communities have popped up everywhere, and in many countries we now even have dojinshi fairs and cosplay events. Some people go so far as to learn the Japanese language in order to enjoy manga and anime in their original versions.

Even highbrow culture has fully embraced the otaku world. Internationally renowned artist Murakami Takashi has cleverly exploited manga's popular appeal; the well-respected Venice Biennale has featured an otaku-themed exhibition (the 2004 Japanese pavilion was called "Otaku: Persona = Space = City"); and even the otaku concept of "moe" is now discussed by cultural critics and sociologists with the same gravity once only granted to *wabi sabi* and other exotic ideas from Japan.

In other words, today it's much easier to get your daily fix of your favorite otaku genre. However you can't really say you have fully experienced otaku culture until you have made a pilgrimage to the holy land of manga and anime. What a trip to Tokyo really makes apparent is how much otaku "sights and sounds" are part of Japanese life, from giant billboards and graffiti to the jingles in some train stations. From the moment

THE INTERNATIONAL APPEAL OF AKIHABARA'S MAIDS HAS CONTRIBUTED TO PUT OTAKU CULTURE ON THE WORLD MAP.

ABOVE UFO Robot Grendizer led the anime invasion of Europe in the summer of 1978. In France was known as Goldorak while in Italy became famous as Goldrake. RIGHT AND BOTTOM RIGHT From vending machines to bus decorations, manga and anime imagery in Japan is inescapable.

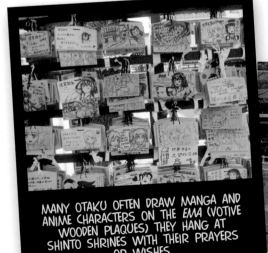

MANY OTAKU OFTEN DRAW MANGA AND ANIME CHARACTERS ON THE *EMA* (VOTIVE WOODEN PLAQUES) THEY HANG AT SHINTO SHRINES WITH THEIR PRAYERS OR WISHES.

ABOVE Otaku rooms are like small museums where fans display their huge collection of anime, manga, games and figures and decorate every available space.

DANNY CHOO (**LEFT**) AND PATRICK GALBRAITH (**RIGHT**) ARE TWO OF THE PEOPLE YOU SHOULD THANK FOR SPREADING THE WORD ABOUT OTAKU CULTURE AROUND THE WORLD.

you arrive, you just can't escape its enticing call, as now, even at Narita Airport, you can find shops selling all kinds of otaku products. Manga, anime and other pop culture icons are now so much embedded in the Japanese psyche that a few years ago the Aqua City shopping mall in Odaiba displayed a huge smoke-spewing Godzilla-shaped Christmas tree, and even Disney went so far as to produce an anime-styled spot in order to attract more people to its Tokyo Disney Resort.

Another thing worth noting is how few concessions Akihabara and other otaku districts make to mainstream Western tastes. Though local shops welcome the growing number of foreign customers, many if not most of the things they sell are for local hardcore fans, which means you will probably discover many things you have never seen—which is not necessarily a bad thing. Even as far as Western pop culture is concerned, there is precious little to be found

except what the Japanese themselves like (i.e. Star Wars and Disney). And then of course there's Tokyo itself; a city so unique and different that to many foreign travelers it looks and feels like an alien planet.

This guide has been made with the specific purpose to show you all the things you can do, see and enjoy in Tokyo, and it will no doubt whet your appetite for all things otaku. Hopefully it will be followed by a second updated edition, so if you have any suggestions, criticism, ideas, or you know a place that in your opinion should be covered here, please get in touch with me at bero_berto@yahoo.co.jp

HOW TO USE THIS BOOK

This book is about Japan. There are several shops that specialize in American toys, for instance, but I chose to focus on made-in-Japan goods and the world of Japanese comics and animation. That's why you will find precious little information on foreign-made otaku products (e.g. Star Wars or Alice in Wonderland).

In case of big chain stores with many branches around Tokyo, I have only covered what I consider their main and/or more interesting shop(s) while providing links to their websites where you can find information on the whole chain.

I have also tried to go beyond the usual places, pushing the otaku envelope a little bit and introducing a few less obvious, but in my opinion, more stimulating options.

The listings at the end of each walk are arranged alphabetically either by category or place (i.e. not following the chronology of the walk). The details were accurate at time of writing. In some cases, the sign in front of the shop is written in Japanese, in which case I have provided both the Japanese version (that's the one you have to look out for) and its alphabetic version.

Speaking of the local lingo, unless noted otherwise all the websites listed here are in Japanese. Though all otaku shops welcome foreign clients (and their money) unfortunately very few have gone so far as to add English pages to their sites.

All people's name are written according to the Japanese order, with the surname coming before the name.

Store opening time can be very tricky as some small shops don't always keep regular hours or stick to their posted opening schedule. It's always a good idea to call in advance.

WARNING: Like a living organism, Tokyo changes constantly and more quickly than any other big city in the world, with new places always being opened and others disappearing for good. This means that by the time this guide is out, a few of the stores listed here will have probably closed down.

OTAKU MUSEUMS AND LIBRARIES

The presence of manga and anime in Japanese culture is so pervasive that most people all too often take them for granted and only see them as part of something else, be it art, education (e.g. history taught through manga) or tourism (to promote a certain region). Thanks to their high level of recognition and acceptance, their services are often required by politicians (to explain their agendas) and companies (to convince consumers to buy their products).

But what is manga, really? And what separates it from other creative endeavors? For those who want to know more about their history and have a better understanding of their peculiarities and inner workings, museums and libraries offer a unique experience that at its best is able to engage both your senses and your intellect.

Considering how manga and anime are important features of Japanese popular culture, it is somewhat surprising that most related museums have been opened only in the last 20 years. For a long time even in Japan comic art was considered a rather lowbrow form of entertainment that didn't deserve a serious, academic approach. Indeed, most of these lowly magazines and comic books usually end up in the trash as soon as we finish reading them. Luckily there are places now where these publications (particularly rare and historically important titles) are collected, preserved, studied and shown to the public together with original art, manuscripts and, in case of animation,

cels and other production related props. Some places even go so far as to collect such character- and story-related materials as figures, badges, and the kind of merchandise which features manga characters (T-shirts, erasers, pencil cases, etc.).

While manga museums are a relatively recent phenomenon, they have rapidly popped up all over the country. In fact there are now about 70 manga museums in Japan. Many of them were opened by local administrations and are devoted to a particular author—in order to both celebrate their art and attract more tourists to that particular region. Kochi Prefecture, for instance, is definitely off the beaten track, but in the last 15–20 years many manga fans have traveled all the way to the island of Shikoku, where it is located, to visit a couple of museums respectively devoted to the creator of Anpanman (Yanase Takashi) and Fukuchan (Yokoyama Ryuichi).

While libraries' main purpose is to make reading and study material available to researchers and the general public, each museum's collection and organization excels at one or more of the following things:

1. Displaying art (closer to fine art museums, they mainly display the original pictures on which manga are based and generally focus on the artistic part of the medium)

2. Introducing a particular author's life and work
3. Showing manga's unique features and how they are made
4. Providing a full-immersion experience in a particular manga world or author's philosophy
5. Selling goods

Each museum listed on pages 92–93 and 132–135 has been number-coded so you will have a quick idea on what you can expect.

One more thing: otaku-themed exhibitions are by no means limited to the institutions covered here. Every year several mainstream museums and galleries (e.g. Mori Arts Center Gallery, Museum of Contemporary Art, Kawasaki City Museum, etc.) attract thousands of people especially—but not only—during the spring and summer school holidays. All these exhibitions are regularly listed online. Two useful websites are **metropolisjapan.com** and **tokyoartbeat.com**.

Manga libraries are invaluable sources of reading and study material for both researchers and the general public.

Exploring Godzilla's Tokyo

FRANCOIS TRUFFAUT'S HAUNTING FILM *THE WOMAN NEXT DOOR* ENDS WITH THE NARRATOR PROPOSING AN EPITAPH FOR THE TWO DOOMED LOVERS: "NEITHER WITH YOU NOR WITHOUT YOU." THESE WORDS SUIT GODZILLA'S TUMULTUOUS LOVE AFFAIR WITH TOKYO TO A T. INDEED, THE UNDISPUTED KING OF JAPANESE *DAIKAIJU* (GIANT MONSTERS) SEEMS TO BE IRRESISTIBLY ATTRACTED TO JAPAN'S CAPITAL, ONLY TO SMASH IT TO PIECES EVERY TIME THE TWO ARE REUNITED. SINCE GODZILLA'S VERY FIRST APPEARANCE ON THE SILVER SCREEN IN 1954, THE GIANT DINOSAUR HAS APPEARED IN 29 JAPANESE PRODUCTIONS AND TOKYO HAS BEEN MORE OFTEN THAN NOT ITS FAVORITE STOMPING GROUND. HERE'S A SHORT GUIDE TO A FEW GODZILLA-RELATED TOKYO SITES.

Tokyo Tower

Opening times *daily 9:00–23:00 (observatories)* **How to get there** *seven-minute walk from Kamiyacho Station Exit 1 (Tokyo Metro Hibiya Line)* tokyotower.co.jp/eng

Now that Tokyo has a brand-new tower (the 634-meter-high Sky Tree) everybody seems to snub this white-and-orange-striped imitation of the Eiffel Tower, but when it comes to Godzilla and other monster movies few locations measure up to the Tokyo Tower. Because let's be fair, nothing beats a crumbling, exploding 333-meter-high tower. Although Big G & Co. are rather small in comparison to the former TV and radio broadcast site, they have managed to kick the hell out of it time and time again, like in the 1995 classic *Gamera: Guardian of the Universe*, when the titular giant flying turtle blasted the already damaged tower in order to destroy the eggs that vampire bat Gyaos was hatching in that makeshift nest.

Even today the Tokyo Tower offers pretty good vistas from its two observation decks, while its four-story base houses an aquarium, several eateries, and most importantly the brand-new One Piece amusement park.

National Diet Building

Opening times *9:00–17:00 (Mon–Fri). Closed on weekends, holidays, and when a plenary session is meeting.* **How to get there** *three-minute walk from Nagatacho Station Exit 1 (Tokyo Metro Hanzomon, Yurakucho, and Nanboku Lines), six-minute walk from Kokkai-Gijidomae Station (Tokyo Metro Marunouchi and Chiyoda Lines)*

Audiences reportedly cheered Godzilla on when the Big G trampled one of this building's wings in its 1954 debut. At the time memories of the Pacific War disaster were still fresh and many were opposed to the Treaty of Mutual Cooperation and Security between the United States and Japan that was being discussed in those days. Since 1890 this has been the site of the National Diet (Japanese Parliament) but the current building (a hybrid of Western and Asia styles) was only completed in 1936. Godzilla has always had a certain anarchist, anti-establishment streak, and more than once has delightfully destroyed this center of power, most notably in *Godzilla: Tokyo S.O.S.* (2003) when the entire tower was demolished during the epic battle between Godzilla and Mechagodzilla.

You can actually visit the building on weekdays. The tour takes about one hour. The reception desk for visitors is located next to the Annex of the House of Councilors. Look for the "Tours of the House of Councilors: Entrance" signboard.

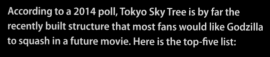

According to a 2014 poll, Tokyo Sky Tree is by far the recently built structure that most fans would like Godzilla to squash in a future movie. Here is the top-five list:

1. Tokyo Sky Tree (83%)
2. Tokyo Gate Bridge (12.6%)
3. Shibuya Hikarie (retail complex) (8.5%)
4. Kabuki Theater (6.9%)
5. Tokyo Station Marunouchi Building (6.0%)

FAR LEFT Manga artist Matsumoto Leiji-designed Himiko will add a futuristic otaku touch to your cruise down the Sumida River.
LEFT One of the fans' favorite activities is to guess what part of Tokyo will be destroyed next.

GINZA

How to get there *Ginza Station (Tokyo Metro Ginza Line)*

When Toho produced the first Godzilla movie they must have been unsure about possible sequels because that film ended up featuring some of the franchise's best locations. Ginza, for instance, is one of Tokyo's posh districts, full of upscale shops, bars and restaurants. What better idea than to unleash Godzilla's fury on Matsuzakaya, one of the area's world-famous department stores? Ginza and its surroundings have appeared in other films, like *The Return of Godzilla* (1984) and *Godzilla vs. King Ghidorah* (1991) but for sheer iconic power nothing compares to the scene in the 1954 debut when the giant monster gets rid of the clock atop the Wako store (a place every Japanese knows) before demolishing the building itself.

SUMIDA RIVER CRUISE

Opening times *9:30-17:30 (plus a few late cruises depending on the season)* **How to get there** *one-minute walk from Asakusa Station (Tokyo Metro Ginza Line)*
suijobus.co.jp (bilingual)

A nice way to see a number of Godzilla-related sites in one go (and enjoy the city from a different point of view) is by cruising the Sumida River that flows down the middle of Tokyo's shitamachi (working-class downtown). Starting from Asakusa, this route takes you under 12 bridges. The most important of them (at least for Godzilla fans) is Kachidoki Bridge, the drawbridge near the mouth of the river that had the honor of being tore down in the original 1954 film. From the boat you can also see the above-mentioned Tokyo Tower (even King Kong had a chance to climb it in a 1967 Japanese-American co-production). Most people don't go farther than Hamarikyu Garden or Hinode Pier, but you can actually cross Tokyo Bay and continue to Odaiba, the artificial island that our favorite monster visited in *Godzilla vs. Megaguirus* (2000).

Finally, if you want to add a touch of class to your otaku cruise you can skip the usual water buses and opt instead for Himiko or Hotaluna, the two spaceship-like boats designed by famous manga artist Matsumoto Leiji.

DAIGO FUKURYU MARU EXHIBITION HALL

第五福竜丸展示館

Opening times *9:30–16:00. Closed on Mon.*
How to get there *10-minute walk from Shin-Kiba Station (Tokyo Metro Yurakucho Line)*
d5f.org/

Godzilla is seen by many as a metaphor for nuclear weapons. In fact its signature weapon is its "atomic breath" or radioactive heat ray. As a matter of fact, the first Godzilla (1954) was probably inspired by an incident earlier the same year in which the crew of the Daigo Fukuryu Maru (Lucky Dragon 5) fishing boat became the victim of the US hydrogen bomb test in Bikini. The boat is preserved in a church-like hall together with other displays (old fishing tools, diaries, etc.). Special exhibitions are also held once or twice a year.

LEFT Kachidoki Bridge and the Tokyo Tower (on the far right) are among the Tokyo spots that have got Big G's rough treatment.

FAR LEFT Manga fans spend hours doing *tachiyomi* (reading while standing in shops).
LEFT Artist Hokusai's collection of sketches is among the predecessors of modern manga.
BELOW Hasegawa Machiko's *Sazae-san* is one of the best-loved characters in manga history.

THE WONDERFUL WORLD OF JAPANESE MANGA

MANGA IS CULTURE. THIS IS SOMETHING THAT MANY PEOPLE IN THE WEST FIND DIFFICULT TO ACCEPT BUT PEOPLE IN JAPAN HAVE UNDERSTOOD FOR MANY YEARS. MANGA IS SOMETHING THAT EVERYBODY CAN ENJOY AND FROM WHICH EVERYBODY CAN LEARN SOMETHING. MANGA ARE USED TO EXPLAIN MEDIEVAL HISTORY AS WELL AS HOW THE STOCK EXCHANGE WORKS, AND IN THE LOCAL PUBLIC LIBRARY SUCH WORKS AS NAKAZAWA KENJI'S BAREFOOT GEN AND TEZUKA OSAMU'S BUDDHA AND PHOENIX CAN BE FOUND BESIDE MISHIMA YUKIO'S NOVELS AND JAPANESE TRANSLATIONS OF WILLIAM SHAKESPEARE. INDEED, MANGA VERSIONS OF BOTH *HAMLET* AND THE CLASSIC *TALE OF GENJI* CAN BE FOUND IN GENERAL BOOKSTORES.

In fiscal year 2012 (between April 2012 and March 2013), about 900 million copies were sold, including both books and magazines, totaling more than 676 billion yen. Considering that Japanese population amounts to about 120 million, each person (including toddlers and centenarians) read an average of 7–8 manga in one year.

But even people who don't read comics can't escape their multiform influence. Quite literally, comic characters are everywhere, from TV commercials and food packages to corporate logos, police mascots and posters devoted to public safety.

There are several theories on the origin of comic art in Japan, and one can find early examples of comic books in the Middle Ages. The Japanese have always had an appreciation for line drawings, and even the world-famous Ukiyo-e of the 18th and 19th centuries have a certain comic quality. Modern manga, like much Japanese popular culture, was influenced by the Ameri-

can comic strips of the early 20th century, but Japanese artists have been quick to develop their own unique approach, using cinematic techniques and other clever visual conventions in order to tell their stories and subtly develop complex characters. If manga can be confusing to first-time readers, it's their very "otherness" that has won the medium scores of fans abroad.

According to manga editor and Kyoto Seika University professor Nakano Haruyuki, the seeds of manga's mass appeal in Japan were sown in the early postwar period, when kids (the so-called *Dankai no Sedai* or Baby Boom Generation) began to spend all their pocket money to buy manga, starting with *Shukan Shonen Magazine* (*Weekly Boy's Magazine*, 1959). Such was their love for the medium that they remained avid readers well beyond childhood and into their adult years, becoming ideal consumers for a rapidly-growing publishing industry that kept coming up with new titles.

In the Twentieth century many artists contributed to manga's development, from Tsutaya Kiichi (LEFT) to Tezuka Osamu and his young disciples who lived in the famed Tokiwa-so Mansion (ABOVE) near Ikebukuro.

EVEN LOCAL TRAIN LINES USE MANGA DESIGN TO INCREASE THE NUMBER OF PASSENGERS.

Those early fans and their younger brothers are the same salarymen (now in their late 60s) that puzzled foreign travelers in the 1970s and '80s, eyed suspiciously as they devoured thick manga weeklies while riding the Tokyo subway.

For decades these weeklies have been the backbone of the comic industry in Japan. Some of these cheap magazines are veritable door stoppers averaging 300–400 pages (printed on rough recycled paper) and containing several serialized and concluding stories. Today the manga-reading (or book-reading, for that matter) adults who were still a common sight in the '90s have been largely replaced by the Net-surfing generation. However manga have become a pervasive and generally accepted presence in Japanese society—one of those cultural sensations that has equally enjoyed by everybody regardless of gender, age or class differences. It is interesting to see how manga faithfully follow every development in Japanese society. The Bubble years of rampant speculation and reckless spending, for instance, were characterized by a surge

in business-related titles which delved in the lives of the corporate warriors—the hard-working, fun-loving salarymen and OLs—while sport stories show up when the national soccer and volleyball teams succeed on the international stage.

It is true that if we only judge the manga phenomenon in absolute terms the last couple of decades have seen a progressive contraction of magazine and book sales. However, as Yamanaka Chie pointed out in *Manga Myujiam e Ikou* (*Let's Go to Manga Museums*), not only every year several manga are turned into TV dramas and features films, but more and more people read them online, besides those who buy them secondhand at Book Off and other such chain stores.

What's probably more alarming is the fact that with a shrinking fan base (due to the country's rapid ageing) and tough working conditions, more and more young talent opts for different and more profitable creative outlets

like graphic design. Indeed, one thing that hasn't changed in all these years is how hard it is to break into the manga (and anime) industry. As an editor at best-selling *Shonen Jump* magazine told *The Japan Times'* Shoji Kaori, "The basic prerequisite for a manga artist are nerves of steel, a very strong stomach and the ability to work for days without sleep, cash or food." So every time we open a comic magazine or book, let's stop a few seconds and silently appreciate all the blood, sweat and tears that go into producing every manga—even popular titles like *One Piece* or *Naruto*.

Sailor Moon and other otaku characters have even infiltrated graffiti and street culture.

THE HOME OF JAPANESE ANIME

FOR MANY PEOPLE OUTSIDE JAPAN, WATCHING ANIME HAS BEEN THEIR FIRST CONTACT WITH OTAKU CULTURE AND REMAINS THEIR MAIN INTEREST. ANIME AS WE KNOW IT TODAY IS A POST-WWII PHENOMENON BUT THE FIRST ATTEMPTS AT PRODUCING ANIMATION IN JAPAN GO ALL THE WAY BACK TO THE BEGINNING OF LAST CENTURY, WHEN PEOPLE TRIED TO MAKE THEIR VERSIONS OF THE POPULAR DISNEY CARTOONS. THE FIRST MAJOR WORK TO WIN INTERNATIONAL PRAISE WAS OFUJI NOBURO'S *THE THIEF OF BAGUDA CASTLE*, MADE BY USING JAPANESE COLORED PAPER IN A CUT-AND-PASTE TECHNIQUE.

One interesting feature of Japanese animation today is the sense of intellectual freedom and ideological independence shared by many artists and best exemplified by Studio Ghibli's Miyazaki Hayao's pacifism and anti-government attitude. Yet early supporters of the anime industry included public institutions that commissioned works for PR campaigns. Then it was the increasingly authoritarian government that enrolled animators to back its nationalistic policies. The first Japanese feature-length work (Seo Mitsuyo's

Momotaro's Divine Sea Warriors, 1945) was actually a Navy Ministry's propaganda film that featured a puppy, a monkey and other animals in typical Disney style.

The American company played another important, if indirect, role in the birth of postwar animation when the president of Toei (one of Japan's major film companies) saw *Snow White* and in 1956 was inspired to create Toei Doga (today's Toei Animation, the studio where both anime giants Miyazaki and Takahata Isao began their careers). For this purpose he both sent a research team in America and invited several foreign experts to create a modern animation studio.

The first decade of the modern era was rife with problems, including financial and labor struggles, but things finally gained momentum in 1963 when Tezuka Osamu's *Tetsuwan Atom* first appeared on TV starting a huge anime boom. *Astro Boy*—as it is better known in the West—also created a blueprint for future TV anime production, as the studios, in order to make animation cheaply and quickly (to meet deadlines), began to cut the numbers of drawings (and lines in each image) and alternate animated scenes with still images while cleverly using sound effects, dialogue and other ways to simulate movement.

For nearly a decade anime remained a form of children entertainment, mainly focusing on humor, family drama, sports, science fiction, and girls with magical powers. In 1969, for instance, popular manga *Sazae-san* became a TV show and today it's the longest-running anime in TV series history. But in 1974 *Space Battleship Yamato* changed the rules of the game by introducing complex adult-oriented themes and ideas, and becoming in the process a social phenomenon that later influenced such cult shows as *Mobile*

TOP *Animerica* was one of the first professional magazines that introduced anime and manga in the US in the early '90s. TV series such as *Mysterious Joker* (ABOVE) and *Girls und Panzer* (LEFT) are a source of endless inspiration to cosplayers.

BELOW LEFT Since 1956 Toei Animation has made the anime versions of works by many famous manga artists such as Nagai Go, Ishinomori Shotaro and Toriyama Akira. BELOW RIGHT In Japan anime voice actors can greatly contribute to a title's success. Some of them even have their own hardcore fans.

ANNO HIDEAKI WHO CREATED THE *NEON GENESIS EVANGELION* SAGA, IS FAMOUS FOR HIS EXTENSIVE PORTRAYAL OF CHARACTERS' THOUGHTS AND EMOTIONS. MORE RECENTLY HE HAS SUCCESSFULLY RESURRECTED GODZILLA IN ALL ITS DESTRUCTIVE CHARM.

Suit Gundam and *Neon Genesis Evangelion*.

While in Japan the term "anime" covers worldwide animation, abroad it has exclusively become synonymous with works from Japan in recognition of Japanese animation's uniqueness and originality. Similarly to manga, Japanese anime have complex storylines that explore an extremely wide range of subjects, from the familiar to the eccentric (e.g. the surreal combination of cute girls, weapons and warfare in *Kantai Collection* and *Girls und Panzer*), including some (e.g. pornography, violence) that very few Western studios would dare to touch. Likewise, anime characters often have fully developed personalities and openly convey their feelings through subtle body language, exaggerated visual effects, and their highly expressive eyes in a way that goes well beyond the Western animation's limited arsenal of facial expressions and heavy use of dialogue.

Since the early 1990s, though Japanese studios have kept churning out new series and feature-length movies, the industry as a whole has suffered a slump partly due to a shrinking fan base at home and the competition of new forms of entertainment like cell phones. For most people involved, working in anime production remains a labor-intensive and poorly paid job (according to veteran animator Kamimura Sachiko, newbies earn on average one dollar an hour). Even *Evangelion* creator Anno Hideaki has stated that in the not so distant future Japan's lack of money and animators may lead to the local industry being outdone by up-and-coming Asian countries like South Korea and Taiwan.

However, judging by the steady stream of new titles coming out of the 430 local studios, the overall picture doesn't seem to be so bleak.

If you are here on a trip, you will probably want to spend most of the time exploring Tokyo and experiencing the otaku metropolis first-hand. However while you are in Japan, you may want to watch some anime as well, in which case you will certainly have many chances to catch a few either on TV or at the cinema (especially during the spring and summer school holidays). In 2014, for instance, 14 out of the 16 top grossing Japanese films were either feature-length animation or live-action versions of popular manga and anime works.

A NUMBER OF MUNICIPALITIES AROUND JAPAN HAVE ENJOYED SURGES IN TOURISM AFTER THEY FEATURED IN POPULAR ANIME FILM OR SERIES LIKE ANOHANA (**BELOW**).

A VIDEO GAMERS' PARADISE

FOR MANY YEARS JAPAN HAS BEEN SYNONYMOUS WITH VIDEO GAMES, AND EVEN TODAY MANY PLAYERS HAVE A SOFT SPOT FOR JAPANESE TITLES. THE EMERGENCE OF THE VIDEO GAME INDUSTRY (COMPRISING THE ARCADE, HOME CONSOLES, AND PERSONAL COMPUTER SECTORS) WAS MADE EASIER BY THE EXISTENCE OF DEVELOPED TOY AND CONSUMER ELECTRONICS INDUSTRIES, BESIDES DRAWING INSPIRATION AND IDEAS FROM MANGA AND ANIME. IN THE SAME WAY THAT TOEI ANIMATION HAD DRAWN INSPIRATION FROM DISNEY'S PRODUCTION SYSTEM, THE MAIN JAPANESE CORPORATIONS (TAITO, NAMCO, SEGA, NINTENDO) TOOK ADVANTAGE OF THEIR BUSINESS EXCHANGES WITH THE UNITED STATES BY IMPORTING THE FIRST AMERICAN GAMES BEFORE CREATING THEIR OWN CLONES. IN 1973, FOR INSTANCE, ONLY ONE YEAR AFTER NAMCO HAD BEGUN TO IMPORT ATARI'S PONG IN JAPAN, TAITO AND SEGA CREATED THEIR OWN VERSIONS: ELEPONG AND PONG TRON. HOWEVER THIS COPYCAT PHASE WAS SOON FOLLOWED BY A PROLONGED BURST OF CREATIVITY AS THE JAPANESE COMPANIES BEGAN TO BRANCH OUT IN NEW DIRECTIONS, IMPROVING ON THE ORIGINAL MODEL AND BECOMING THE UNDISPUTED GLOBAL LEADERS.

The first turning point was the arrival of Taito's *Space Invaders* in 1978. The game was such a big success that so-called Invader Houses (forerunners of today's game centers) mushroomed all over the country and every cafe added a cocktail-table cabinet to its furniture. This was soon followed by Namco's *Pac-Man* (1980) and Nintendo's *Donkey Kong* (1981).

At the same time Japanese companies began to develop home consoles. Most of the 125 items that were released between 1975 and 1983 were actually made by big TV manufacturers like Toshiba and Panasonic (for this reason video games in Japan were known as *terebi geemu* i.e. TV games), but it was Nintendo that scored the first big hit with its Color TV-Game 6 and 15 that thanks to their lower price sold a combined one million units.

As for home computers, Japanese companies had an advantage over the American competition because many of the parts used in PCs were made in Japan. The *mai-con* (micro-computer) boom arrived in the late '70s, convincing many video game producers to focus on PC games. However, when Nintendo's Famicon (known abroad as Nintendo Entertainment System, NES)

appeared in 1983, it changed the rules of the game by establishing the home console's supremacy once and for all. To give just an example of Famicon's impact on Japanese gamers (and society), until the mid-'90s, Nintendo dominated 85% of the console market, and in the mid-'80s, 30% of the toy market was related to this revolutionary machine that definitely transformed Japan into a leisure society and established game culture around the world. Nintendo's grip on the "game generation" then became even stronger with *Super Mario Bros.*, considered by many the greatest game of all time, and certainly the most influential, even going so far as to help the American video game market recover from the crash of the early '80s.

Only hardcore dojin software makers remained faithful to the PC (in the

pre-Windows era, NEC's PC-9801 was their platform of choice) and kept distributing and selling their indie games (on cassette tapes and floppy disks) via mail and at dojin events. The most famous is *Touhou Project (TP)*, a bullet hell shooter series that even today is so popular that at every Comiket TP circles far outnumber other dojin creators.

Japanese video games continued to dominate the global market through the late '90s, with such titles as *Dragon Quest*, *Zelda*, and *Final Fantasy*. However things started to change at the turn of the century and between 2004 and 2009 there was an international setback, first brought about by Microsoft's involvement in the home entertainment market with the creation of the Xbox console, which has led many Japanese developers to focus

TOP THE ONLY-SOLD-IN-JAPAN NINTENDO COLOR-TV GAME 15 DEBUTED IN 1977 AND PROMPTLY SOLD MORE THAN ONE MILLION UNITS. (**LEFT**) WITH OVER 310 MILLION COPIES OF GAMES SOLD WORLDWIDE AS OF SEPTEMBER 2015, *SUPER MARIO* IS THE BEST-SELLING VIDEO GAME SERIES IN HISTORY.

instead on the local market while the Japanese industry's share of the market has shrunk to about 13%. From the second half of the 2000s, for instance, more and more companies (e.g. Nitroplus and 5pb) have concentrated on producing visual novels (a genre little appreciated outside Japan) with strong otaku elements which are set in places like Shibuya (*Chaos;Head*) and Akihabara (*Steins;Gate*).

In fact, the Japanese game industry has always been careful to keep the Japanese and foreign markets apart, on one side coming up with products strong international (i.e. Western) appeal (e.g. *Metal Gear Solid*, *Resident Evil*), while on the other side making games for local fans. It's true that many games made in Japan are pretty much unknown abroad. Not only that, some games' localized versions are quite different from the original as the companies change or delete some features or story elements (e.g. effeminate men are replaced by women characters; references to hostess clubs, Japanese forms of gambling, are suppressed) for fear that foreign players wouldn't understand or appreciate them.

Born as a popular video game, Level-5's *Yo-kai Watch* has won many accolades even in its manga and anime versions.

MAGAZINES LIKE FAMITSU (FIRST PUBLISHED IN 1986) HAVE CONTRIBUTED TO BUILD FAMICON (NES) CULTURE IN JAPAN.

There are genres that you will hardly find abroad, like certain role-playing games (RPGs) and dating sims (romantic simulator games) that in a sense are closer to audiovisual manga. These genres feature a particular aesthetic and premises and only have a niche following in the West, but even among globally popular genres we can often see a difference in character and game design as well as animation. Compared to their Western version, some original Japanese games even seem to be more difficult and complicated, a famous example being the "bullet hell" type of shooting games where the entire screen is often almost completely filled with enemy bullets.

The current situation for the Japanese game industry seems to be quite grim, but on the upside it must be said that developers always come up with new exciting title. The hugely successful *Pokemon* franchise celebrated in 2016 its tenth anniversary, while Level-5's *Yo-kai Watch* has become the next big thing and is about to follow *Pikachu and Co.* in conquering the world. Last but not least, the rise of mobile games seems to have given a new life to Japanese companies and titles like *Puzzle & Dragons* may be the new weapons to reestablish Japan's supremacy on the gaming world.

Mobile games like *Puzzle & Dragons* (LEFT) (the first such game in history to reach $1 billion in revenue) represent the future of gaming but many fans still prefer retro games such as *Pac-Man* (BELOW).

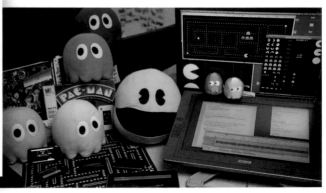

LEVEL-5'S HINO AKIHIRO

HINO AKIHIRO IS THE PRESIDENT AND CEO OF INDEPENDENT VIDEO GAME DEVELOPER AND PUBLISHER LEVEL-5 INC. FOUNDED IN 1998, LEVEL-5 HAS QUICKLY BECOME ONE OF THE MOST-LOVED BRANDS BOTH IN JAPAN AND ABROAD. WITH A 3.2% MARKET SHARE, IT IS ONE OF THE TEN LARGEST VIDEO GAME COMPANIES IN JAPAN.

When did you fall in love with video-games?

When I was about 8–9 years old, *Space Invaders* became incredibly popular in Japan, followed in 1980 by Nintendo's *Game & Watch* games. At the time many people had a somewhat negative opinion about video games, and children were forbidden from going to video arcades (much smaller affairs, closer to "video rooms" than today's huge arcades), but I secretly went anyway. Then the first home console—the so-called Mycon—came out, so I didn't even have to go out. Eventually, when I was about 12 I began to create my first computer programs.

When did you decide to turn your passion into a profession?

During my teen years I kept playing and experimenting with computers, but the turning point for me was the release of *Dragon Quest III*, when I was around 20 years old. It was the first time I played such a game, and it made a deep impression on me even though the graphics were still nothing comparable to today's standards. Like with *Game & Watch*, I was fascinated by the idea that you could hold a whole world in your hands, and I began to think I wanted to create the same thing, but professionally, and give players the same excitement I felt when I was a child.

When you come up with new game ideas, do you focus on certain themes in particular or do you just focus on the action?

More than an artist, I consider myself an entertainer. An artist has an idea he wants to express, and if he is good and lucky enough, someone will get interested in his work. For me, on the other hand, the most important thing is that the people who play with our games have fun. You could say Level-5 is like a circus, and we try to attract as many people as possible to our show. So depending on who our target users are (e.g. children or adults) we try to come up with story lines and graphics that appeal to them. Besides that, we adapt our stories according to a particular social climate. For example, in times of recession we make a more upbeat story line.

Personally I'm a big fantasy fan. More than realistic stories, I like to imagine things that don't belong to this world. Originally, Level-5 was born with the aim to create this kind of stories because after all video games are about virtual worlds into which players can lose themselves. More recently, though, we have decided to mix fantasy and reality in interesting ways. *Professor Layton*, for example, takes place in a slightly different London, a sort of parallel universe which looks familiar and strange at the same time.

How do you think the Japanese game industry has changed since you first began to work in the field?

When I started, about 20 years ago, people thought that video games were only for children—or for otaku at best. By the time the PlayStation was launched in 1994, both men and women were regular

POKEMON GO MANIA SWEEPS THE GLOBE!

Launched worldwide in summer 2016, *Pokemon Go* has revolutionized the way we play. Nintendo's smartphone game uses GPS data (available through a downloadable app) to track down and capture Pokemon characters hiding in public spaces (parks, buildings, etc.). Particularly popular among players ages 25–34, it has instantly become a huge success as in the first few weeks since its launch was downloaded 30 million times. The good and bad thing about the game is that people have to wander the streets in order to find Pokemon. Apparently the hunt is so absorbing that sometimes the players wander into off-limit areas, cause accidents and become a general nuisance. In Japan, for instance, people have been caught walking onto an expressway or driving while playing the game. In fact one month after its Japanese launch, a woman was killed by a distracted driver in Tokushima Prefecture, becoming the country's first *Pokemon Go*-related casualty. As a consequence many tourist spots and festivals have banned people from playing the game on site. Of course more than the game itself, the real problem is the players—those same people who regularly walk around with their nose buried in their smartphones, totally unconcerned about the world around them. On the upside, *Pokemon Go* seems to be good for your health and waistline, as hordes of game-loving couch potatoes lose weight while roaming the cities for hours. Some natural disaster-hit prefectures in Japan are even using the game to attract tourists.

users, and games had become an adult hobby. Now we have reached a stage in which digital culture is everywhere and games can be played on smart phones. Also, the game industry has become just a genre of the bigger entertainment industry which encompasses manga, anime, movies, etc. This makes me particularly happy because I consider myself an entertainer more than anything else.

You also create original content for the foreign market, especially the United States. What's the main difference between these two markets?
RPGs (role-playing games) sell very well in Japan, where people like to be sucked into an adventure-type story which unfolds through time. In America and other countries, on the other hand, FPS (first-person shooting) games are more popular. I'd say video games' popularity reflects each country's culture. Then, of course, there are the exceptions. *Professor Layton*, for example, is more popular abroad than in Japan, especially among women in their 30s and 40s.

In 2009 video game producer Inafune Keiji said: "Japan is over. We're done. Our game industry is finished." How does the Japanese game industry look like now?
Inafune is a good friend of mine. He likes to stir things up, and that phrase is in line with his character. He didn't really think what he said, otherwise he would have quit this job long ago. This said, there are some issues that need to be addressed, like social games and the growing smart phone market, and Inafune meant to say that we need to adapt to this constantly changing situation lest we get left behind.

Yo-kai Watch has taken the game and anime world by storm, becoming one of the most popular franchises of all time in Japan. How did you come up with this idea?
The monster game genre has always been very popular worldwide, so when I thought what to do next I hit on the *yo-kai* idea. Yo-kai are traditional supernatural monsters but I wanted to mix Japanese folklore with a contemporary story. That's how I ended up with the *Yo-kai Watch* concept—a special watch empowering the young boy at the center of the story to discover and summon mysterious yo-kai that help him solve problems in his daily life.

Why do you think *Yo-kai Watch* has been so successful?
First of all *Yo-kai Watch* is a typical example of a "media mix" project. While it started as a video game, it quickly expanded into other genres like anime, manga and toys. This synergy has made it possible to appeal to children from different points of view. Also, a lot of research went into this project. We were particularly careful to make a story that actually reflected children's thoughts and feelings, and I think they recognized and appreciated this.

Japanese Toys—An Alternate Universe

IF BEING AN OTAKU MEANS DREAMING UP ALTERNATIVE WORLDS, THEN TOYS EMBODY AND ARE THE CONCRETE, THREE-DIMENSIONAL REPRESENTATION OF THOSE DREAMS AND OUR DEEPEST DESIRES. THE JAPANESE HAVE BEEN AMONG THE FIRST TO RECOGNIZE THAT FAR FROM BEING CONSIDERED A CHILDISH ACTIVITY, PLAYING WITH AND COLLECTING TOYS IS A LEGITIMATE ACTIVITY THAT—LIKE MANGA AND ANIME—APPEAL TO MANY GROWN-UPS.

The history of toys in Japan reflects the country's ongoing cultural and technological exchange with the West. Traditionally Japanese toys mainly reflected regional folk legends and customs, and were typically made of wood and paper. However during the Meiji period (1868–1912) Japanese toy makers began to use tin and celluloid and by 1915 had overcome Germany as the main exporter to Europe and the United States. Even then, Japanese companies were highly praised for their willingness to push the envelope in search of always new products. The first tin toy robot ever produced, for instance, was made in Japan (Lilliput, 1938–41).

Japan's dominance of the international toy market was temporarily slowed down by WWII but resumed with even more force in the 1950s. This decade signaled the beginning of a golden era in which many new companies were founded (including Bandai, currently Japan's leading toy company and the world's third largest producer of toys), amazing the world with their ingenuity and technical prowess.

On the home front, toy makers were aided by the increasingly great role played by TV, manga, anime and movies in shaping popular culture. *Mighty Atom* (*Tetsuwan Atom*, or *Astro Boy* as he became known in the West) was created in 1952 by comic artist Tezuka Osamu and was the first manga and anime character to generate a whole line of merchandising. This was followed by Godzilla's frightening appearance on the big screen in 1954, giving birth to a long and successful dynasty of *kaiju* (monster) and *tokusatsu* (special effects) film-related toys.

By the mid-1950s Japanese toys dominated the global market. One of the early leaders was Marusan, a company born in 1947 that in 1951 scored a huge hit in America with the tin 1951 Cadillac. Among their technological innovations, the Japanese were the first to replace wind-up clockwork mechanisms and friction-driven mechanical toys with small electric motors powered by one or more batteries. This was particularly true for the growing robot market. Their attractively lithographed, brightly colored robots were far above the competition. Differently from their American plastic counterparts, these tin machines could walk back and forth, spin, and had other amazing features like bump-and-go action and lighted eyes.

Another important innovation that helped change the rules of the toy game was the introduction of plastic. First discovered in the 19th century, it became widely available for manufac-

BUMBLEBEE, OPTIMUS PRIME, AND IRONHIDE (FROM THE TRANSFORMERS TOY LINE) ARE A PERFECT EXAMPLE OF HOW JAPANESE TOYS HAVE BEEN ABLE TO CROSS CULTURAL LINES AND WIN NEW FANS IN THE WEST. THE RESULTING MEDIA MIX HAS SEEN THE RELEASE OF COMIC BOOKS, ANIMATED TV SERIES AND LIVE-ACTION FIILMS.

WHILE *KAMEN RIDER* FIGURES AND ACCESSORIES (**LEFT**) ARE MOSTLY COVETED BY LITTLE BOYS AND THEIR NOSTALGIC FATHERS, CUTE DOLLS LIKE AZONE'S LIL' FAIRY ERUNOE AND VEL (**BELOW**) APPEAL TO BOTH SEXES. IN JAPAN IT IS NOT RARE TO SEE MALE FANS PROUDLY SHOW OFF THEIR LITTLE BEAUTIES.

turing uses after WWII, fast becoming toy makers' favorite material. Marusan, together with Imai Kagaku, was again the leader of the pack. In 1958 they were the first Japanese company to produce a plastic model kit, the Nautilus submarine. It is a little-known fact—even among otaku model lovers—that the term "plamodel" (short for plastic model) was coined by Marusan, that registered it as a trademark in 1959.

Science fiction was the dominant theme in manga, anime and movies as the 1950s and '60s evolved into a veritable Space Age. So it wasn't by coincidence that one of the most popular TV characters of the period felt at ease as much in space as on Earth. In 1966 TV audiences were thrilled by Ultraman, a superhuman hero who battled assorted aliens and giant monster in order to protect the Earth, and Marusan quickly produced the first figures in the same year.

The '70s started with a bang when a new tokusatsu superhero debuted on TV. *Kamen Rider* is a grasshopper-headed masked biker who spends his time battling a mysterious terrorist organization called SHOCKER. Newly-founded Popy (a company owned by Bandai)

first took advantage of the new character's popularity by producing a vinyl-and-plastic replica of the Henshin Belt the protagonist uses to change into Kamen Rider. However what made Popy into a pop culture icon and toy powerhouse was the introduction of its trademark-registered chogokin toys. Named after a fictional "super alloy" from the animated Mazinger Z anime series (1972), this was a new line of die-cast metal robot and character toys. The fist-shooting five-inch-tall Mazinger sold like hot cakes and chogokin toys became the newest thing. However such heavy toys were better suited for collecting than actual playing, and by the start of the '80s PVC and ABS plastic had remained toy makers' favorite material.

By this time the Japanese toy-making industry was reeling from a double

attack coming from both inside and outside the country: On one side, in the '70s China had joined in the battle and eventually managed to dethrone Japan as the global number-one toy producer. On the inner front, in 1978 the *Space Invaders* video game had become a national sensation, preparing the way for the soon-to-come gaming revolution. However this did not stop Japanese toy makers from coming up with ever new ideas, like the new finely detailed and relatively inexpensive plastic figures that came out in the early '80s.

What these companies did not realize at the time was that they had started a revolution in figure production. Incited by the new generation of toys, many anime and tokusatsu fans began to make figures themselves, sparking off the new garage kit trend.

(**LEFT**) THE FIRST TIN TOY ROBOTS WERE MADE IN JAPAN IN THE LATE '30S.
(**LEFT BELOW**) GACHAPON (VENDING MACHINE-DISPENSED CAPSULE TOYS) CAN BE FOUND EVERYWHERE IN JAPAN, FROM TOY SHOPS TO GAME CENTERS AND SUPERMARKETS.
(**RIGHT**) VOLK'S IS ONE OF JAPAN'S PREMIER DOLL MAKERS AND DOLLFIE IS ITS BEST-KNOWN LINE.

The name of these toys comes from the fact that these figures were originally made by hardcore amateur modelers in their garage. One of them happened to work as a dental technician and produced a Mothra model by adapting the method he used to make false teeth. His method was much cheaper and more practical than traditional ejection molding, thus becoming the new standard way to make plastic toys.

Kaiyodo is the company that, more than any other, has contributed to popularize garage kits even beyond the otaku circles, thanks to its high production standards. Always looking for new ways to tap into the main-stream market, the Osaka-based company scored a huge hit in 1999 by joining forces with confectionary company Furuta. The fruit of their collaboration was the Choco Egg, a cheap egg-shaped chocolate containing a tiny but very realistic plastic toy. Kaiyodo managed to ignite a country-wide craze among both kids and adults, creating a new

LIMITED-EDITION VINYL TOYS ARE ALL THE RAGE BOTH IN JAPAN AND ABROAD. AMERICAN DESIGNER KAWS IS PARTICULARLY FAMOUS FOR HIS COLLABORATION WITH SEVERAL JAPANESE COMPANIES LIKE BOUNTY HUNTER, A BATHING APE, SANTASTIC AND MEDICOM. ONE OF HIS ART TOYS IN MINT CONDITIONS (LIKE THE COMPANION ON THE LEFT) WILL EASILY COST YOU 200,000 YEN AT NAKANO BROADWAY.

THE EXTENSIVE LINE OF KINNIKUMAN COLLECTIBLE ERASERS AND FIGURES (**BELOW**) (LICENSED IN AMERICA AS M.U.S.C.L.E) TODAY COMMANDS VERY HIGH PRICES IN THE COLLECTOR'S MARKET.

MIGHTY ATOM, KAMEN RIDER AND ULTRAMAN (**RIGHT**) REPRESENT THE HOLY TRINITY OF SHOWA-ERA HEROES. PLASTIC FIGURES OF ULTRAMAN (**BELOW**) AND HIS MANY MONSTER ENEMIES CAN BE HAD FOR CHEAP IN MANY SECOND-HAND SHOPS.

category of toys, *shokugan* (food toys), that can be only had by buying different kinds of soft drinks and junk food.

In the last few decades the world of toys has experienced a number of dramatic transformations, exploring different paths while reaching out to other apparently-distant creative fields including fine art. Freed from their humble origins as disposable play-things, toys have infiltrated many aspects of our daily lives, from furniture to appliances, and from fashion all the way up to highbrow culture. At the same time, many long time fans of Ultraman and Kamen Rider now buy toys both for themselves and their children, It goes to show that, their coming of age notwithstanding, toys still occupy a special place in many people's hearts.

THE COSPLAY EXPERIENCE

TOKYO OFFERS MANY CHANCES TO SEE LOCAL COSPLAYERS IN ACTION, PHOTOGRAPH THEM AND EVEN JOIN IN THE FUN AS ALL MAJOR OTAKU EVENTS HAVE A SECTION DEVOTED TO COSPLAYING.

TODAY MORE AND MORE PEOPLE AROUND THE WORLD ARE FAMILIAR WITH COSPLAY AND USUALLY ASSOCIATE THIS PHENOMENON WITH JAPANESE OTAKU CULTURE. HOWEVER THE IDEA OF IMPERSONATING FICTIONAL CHARACTERS WAS ACTUALLY DEVELOPED BY AMERICAN SCIENCE FICTON FANS IN THE EARLY 1940S AND WASN'T INTRODUCED TO JAPAN UNTIL THE '70S OR '80S (BY THAT TIME SOME AMERICAN COMIC FANS WHERE ACTUALLY PLAYING WITH SUCH ANIME CHARACTERS AS CAPTAIN HARLOCK). WHAT WE KNOW FOR SURE, HOWEVER, IS THAT THE TERM "COSPLAY" ITSELF WAS COINED BY WRITER TAKAHASHI NOBUYUKI IN 1983 WHEN, IN ORDER TO DESCRIBE THE MASQUERADE HE HAD SEEN AT THE ANNUAL WORLDCON IN LOS ANGELES, HE COMBINED THE WORDS "COSTUME" AND "PLAY."

Since then Japanese manga fans and gamers have wasted no time in appropriating the practice, coming up with different categories and upping the ante by introducing an unsurpassed love for the medium and attention for detail. As a result, by the late '90s Japan has begun to spread a new (some will say improved) version of cosplay worldwide. Today Japan is synonymous with cosplay, and since 2003 even hosts the World Cosplay Summit, an international event that every year attracts thousands of worldwide fans to Nagoya, a city about 450 km south of Tokyo.

Cosplaying can be divided into five main categories: regular; crossplaying (impersonating characters of the opposite sex); mecha (robots and armored characters); genderbend (turning a male character into a female or vice versa); and original (creating an original character). A smaller niche group are "dollers" (animegao or "anime face" in Japanese) i.e. people who cover their face with a manga-like mask.

For many Westerners, the ultimate experience is to cosplay in Japan. This isn't so difficult, provided you come prepared. The Japanese cosplay community is so big that Cure (Japan's biggest online forum for cosplayers) has around 1.2 million members (90% of whom are women), and every month there are 10–20 major cosplay events around the country. Some of them are cosplay-only events, but some of the biggest are general otaku festivals that feature a sizeable cosplay area, either inside the venue or outdoors.

Obviously Tokyo has a big cosplay market. In Akihabara, Nakano, Ikebukuro and other otaku districts you can find many shops selling costumes, wigs, etc. Gyakuyoga (gyakuyoga.com) is a very informative bilingual website on how to make weapons and accessories, and the materials you can get in Japan.

Crossplaying, or cosplaying as characters of the opposite sex, is a popular way to express your love for a particular manga, anime or video game.

KIRIGUMI OR DOLLERS (**CENTER**) ARE COSPLAYERS WHO GO A STEP FURTHER AND COVER THEIR FACE WITH A LATEX DOLL MASK. THEY ARE A VERY SMALL PART OF THE COSPLAY SCENE.

The Japanese take cosplaying very seriously and it's interesting to compare the different atmosphere in the cosplay areas in Japan and abroad. Here cosplayers aim to become their character of choice by striking practiced poses and taking on their personality.

One thing you will hardly see in Japan are on-stage performances and popularity contests, one notable exception being the Cosplay Collection Night, a fashion show-cum-stage performance hosted by the Cure website at the Tokyo Game Show.

If you don't cosplay but want to take pictures of cosplayers, be warned that lines can be overwhelming. Also, you are supposed to actually ask for permission before you take someone's photo.

Regardless of whether you are an active cosplayer or a *cameko* (photographer), a good way to widen your circle of friends is to prepare your own "cosplay business card" that should feature your alias and links to your website(s).

If, on the other hand you only want to experience cosplay without actually joining an event, your best bet might be a visit to Harajuku where cosplayers of different kinds (including lolitas) usually gather on weekends.

COSPLAY & HALLOWEEN

Many cosplayers have a sort of love/hate relationship with Halloween and endlessly debate on whether the traditional Western celebration can be considered a form of cosplay. Hardcore fans, for instance, point out the poor quality of most mass-produced Halloween costumes, without mentioning that many participants seem to be clueless about the characters they impersonate. To be sure, many of the people who cosplay at Halloween events have a more casual approach than otaku fans as their main purpose is to party and have fun. In any case the Japanese are famous for adopting foreign traditions, regardless of cultural differences, as long as they were fun, and Halloween is no exception. As a consequence even in Tokyo the end of October has become another opportunity to show off one's owns costumes.

The first Halloween-related events took place in the late-'90s at Tokyo Disneyland and mainly targeted kids and their parents, but in the last ten years more and more parades and events have sprung up around the country as both companies and local governments see them as a great way to attract people. In 2014, for instance, streaming video site Nico Nico and anime retailer Animate organized the Ikebukuro Halloween Cosplay Fest, a two-day festival featuring a parade, a free stage where anybody could perform (and be broadcast worldwide live online) and a Cosplay Gathering area divided by costume theme. The event was so successful that attracted 52,000 visitors including 10,000 cosplayers from Japan and other 22 countries. So if you happen to be in Japan around Halloween check out the local media!

JAPANESE IDOL MANIA

THE HISTORY OF JAPANESE IDOLS IS VERY LONG AND FASCINATING, BEGINNING IN 1964 AFTER THE FRENCH MOVIE "CHERCHEZ L'IDOLE," STARRING THEN-19-YEAR-OLD "YÉ-YÉ" SINGER SYLVIE VARTAN, BECAME A HIT IN JAPAN AND ITS THEME SONG SOLD OVER 1,000,000 COPIES. SINCE THEN THE TERM HAS BEEN APPLIED TO CUTE TEENAGE GIRL AND BOY SINGERS WHOSE POPULARITY IS MORE BASED ON THEIR LOOKS AND PERSONALITY THAN THEIR SINGING TALENT. GIRLS, IN PARTICULAR, HAVE TRADITIONALLY CONFORMED TO THE IDEALIZED IMAGE OF THE PURE, INNOCENT AND CHASTE WOMAN WHOSE ARTISTIC AMATEURISHNESS, FAR FROM BEING A PROBLEM, ENDEARS THEM EVEN MORE TO THEIR FANS.

AKB48 are the reigning queens of the Japanese idol market.

While in the 1970s a singer like **Yamaguchi Momoe** (discovered like many others through the TV show *Star Tanjo!* (*A Star Is Born*) wore frilly clothes and ribbons, sang sugary pop songs and lead a supposedly gorgeous lifestyle, the idol's image has changed in the following decades with the advent of the fresh-faced, lively girl next door who is much closer to her fans. The '80s (the so-called Golden Age of Idols) were dominated by people like **Matsuda Seiko**, the "eternal idol" and prototypical *burikko,* who alternated between innocent and sexy on her way to producing 24 consecutive number-one singles. On the other side, 52-girl strong **Onyanko Club** (1985–87) was the apotheosis of untalented everyday-ness, trailing a blaze for the many groups that have emerged since the early '90s. In the last 20–25 years,

SMAP, **Tokio** and **Arashi** have lead the way among boys (all of them managed by the Johnny & Associates talent agency), and **Morning Musume** and **AKB48** have ruled the girls' market, setting new CD-selling records while further lowering the idol's average age.

What hasn't changed since the beginning is the way agencies and TV producers control their creations while carefully manufacturing their image. Now as before, romantic relationships are hidden to the public if not completely forbidden (the only kind of pseudo-relationship allowed is between the idols and their fans) and real talent remains an option. Girls who aspire to join AKB48, for instance, must be amateurs with no formal experience in singing and dancing. Most importantly, though, the distance separating the idols and their fans has been

dramatically reduced. AKB48, for instance, regularly appear at Hand-shake Conventions all over Japan where they their fans can meet and chat with them and even have their picture taken with their favorite member) while other groups have experimented with hugging and even "whisper events" (i.e. whispering sweet nonsense in their fans' years).

The idol group model is particularly popular among otaku, and artists like **Momoiro Clover Z** and **Babymetal** can be seen at such live events as Animelo Summer Live, Tokyo Idol Festival and the @Jam Project. Some of the best places to see up-and-coming names are in Akihabara (e.g. Dear Stage, Akiba Cultures Theater) and if you are interested in the aforementioned handshakes, remember that the necessary tickets can be found inside the groups' CDs—one reason why 85% of the Japanese music market is still made up of physical music sales.

HATSUNE MIKU AND THE VIRTUAL IDOL

Since Yamaguchi Momoe got married and retired in 1980 when she was still 21 years old, many idols have called it quits for any number of reasons, including choosing real romance and a

THOUGH HATSUNE MIKU (WHOSE NAME MEANS "THE FIRST SOUND OF THE FUTURE) WAS CREATED BY DEVELOPER CRYPTON FUTURE MEDIA AS A SIMPLE SINGING SYNTHESIZER APPLICATION, IT HAS QUICKLY BECOME A GLOBAL IDOL.

simple life over the stress and obligations that come with being a celebrity. And even the others—particularly girls—have a relatively short expiration date, because getting old and being an idol don't go well together. Luckily for talent agencies and music labels, the new millennium has brought the perfect diva that neither gets old nor complains: the virtual idol.

Every otaku knows **Hatsune Miku**, the long-pigtailed pop star with turquoise-colored hair who, since her birth in 2007, has recorded hit songs, starred in her own manga and appeared in a futuristic opera. It all began when software company Crypton Future Media used Yamaha's Vocaloid voice engine to create a program that allowed users to synthesize a voice on their computer by typing in lyrics and a melody. Manga artist Garō Kei was later asked to design an avatar, while voice actress Fujita Saki provided samples of her voice. To be sure, Miku's creators have insisted that she was never meant to be an idol but only a composer's tool. However since its birth, Miku has conquered the pop world, topping the singles and albums charts and becoming one of the most loved otaku icons. In 2009 she even debuted has a "live" performer when she appeared at the Animelo Summer Festival.

To be sure, Miku has a few weapons in her arsenal that make

her special, including six different vocal tones, from Sweet to Dark, which provide her with a range well beyond any human voice. At the same time, she has become just the most successful in a long line of virtual idols whose age began in 1997 when talent agency giant HoriPro commissioned a computer graphic company to create what would become **Date Kyoko**. This first computer-generated singer was

followed by the even more successful **Terai Yuki** who went on to star in TV commercials. There is one important thing, however, that really sets Miku apart from the competition: While Kyoko and Yuki have been provided with a fabricated history and their voices are actually provided by a human singer, Miku was born as a completely artificial tabula rasa. Crypton only decided her age, height and weight, giving her fans an opportunity to shape her life and character any way they wanted. Not only that, Crypton provided her fans with the non-profit PIAPRO online community, giving them a chance to upload their own Miku-inspired compositions and make her sing their songs. This was followed by MikuMiku-Dance, a fan-made program and website where one could create and direct the videos to promote those songs. In other words, while Miku was created by Crypton, she mostly owes her success to the huge community of "prosumers," who both produce and consume her products. This ever-growing community of composers, graphic designers, and video creators has become so big that over 10,000 fans have written songs so far, and more than 100,000 have created videos, showing them worldwide through the Japanese Nico Nico website.

Miku's global success has lead to the birth of new virtual idols. The Crypton stable alone is comprised of at least four more characters: **Meiko**, boy idol **Kaito** (both of them actually born before Miku), **Megurine Luka** and the **Kagamine Rin/Len** duo who are particularly popular among cosplayers. All of them have become known as user-generated idols: Because their fans contribute so much (songs, videos, forums, etc.), they play a very active role in improving their career and, even more important, giving them life.

"GRADUATING" MEMBERS OF AKB48 (LIKE KOJIMA HARUNA, PICTURED **ABOVE**, WHO LEFT IN 2016) AND ITS FOUR SISTER GROUPS (E.G. HTK48, **LEFT**) ARE CONSTANTLY REPLACED BY NEW ASPIRING IDOLS.

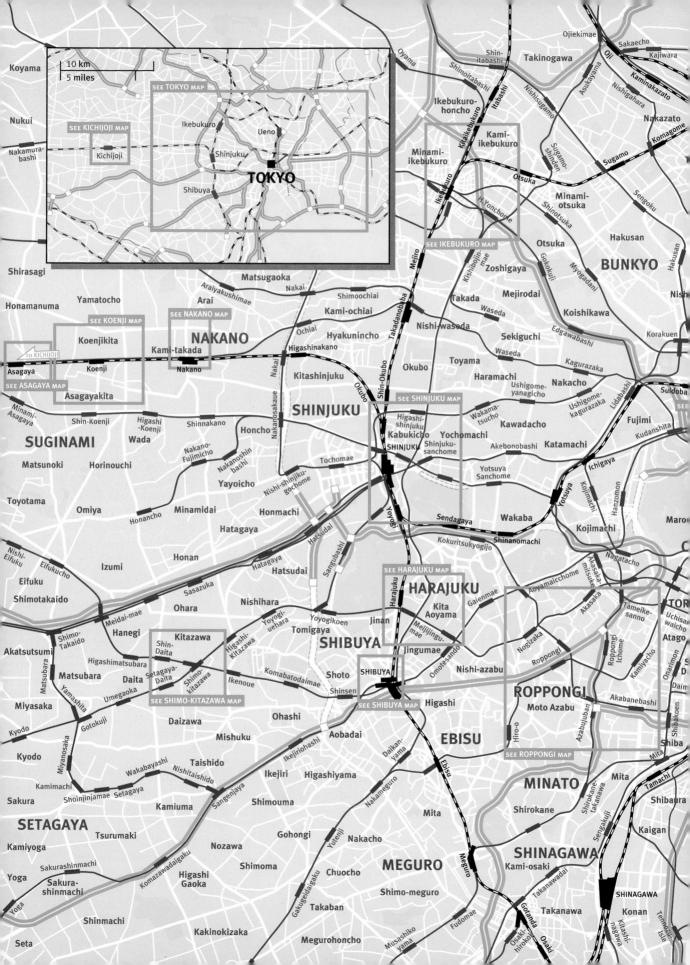

Tokyo

KATSUSHIKA

Kumanomae
ashi-ogu
Higashiogu
Sanchome
Machiya
Senjunakaicho
Kita-Senju
Yanagihara
Ohanajaya
Horikiri-Shobuen
Ohanajaya
Keiseitaka-sago
Machiya-ekimae
Machiya
Senjuohashi
Ushida
Keiseisekiya
Horikiri
Takaramachi
Tateishi
Aoto
Hosoda
Shinmika-washima
Arakawa Kuyakushomae
Minowabashi
Senjua Kebonocho
Minamisenju
Kanegafuchi
Horikiri
Keiseitateishi
Okudo
Mikawashima
Arakawa-itchumae
Minami Senju
Yotsugi
SEE KOIWA MAP
Koiwa
Higashi-nippori
Minowa
Ryusen
Kiyokawa
SUMIDA
Yahiro
Higashi-yotsugi
Okinomiyacho

SEE UENO, OKAMACHI & NIPPORI MAP
ARAKAWA
Nippori
Shitaya
Senzoku
Mukojima
Higashisumida
Highashi-Shinkoiwa
Yanaka
Iriya
Imado
Hikifune
Keisei-Hikifune
Yahiro
Nishishikoiwa
Honisshiki
UENO
Uguisudani
Taito
Nishi-asakusa
ASAKUSA
Asakusa
Narihirabashi
Kyojima
Shin-Koiwa
Matsushima
Chuo
Nezu
UENO
Inaricho
Tawaramachi
Honjoazubashi
Oshiage
Omurai
Higashi-zuma
Hirai
Hirai
Ikenohata
Ueno-hirokoji
Shin-okachimachi
Honjo
Tachibana
Yishima
Yokokawa
Kameido Suijin
AKIHABARA
Suehirocho
Akihabara
Asakusabashi
Ishiwara
Kameido
Nishikomatsu-Gawamachi
Ochanomizu
Kuramae
Kinshicho
Matsue
SEE AKIHABARA MAP
Iwamotocho
Ryogoku
Midori
Kotobashi
Kameido
Komatsugawa
Higashikomatsu-Gawa
Awajicho
Kanda
Iwamotocho
Shinni-honbashi
Bakurocho
Higashinihonbashi
Chitose
Tatekawa
Sumiyoshi
Higashiojima
Hamacho
Kikukawa
Nishi-Ojima
Ojima
EDOGAWA
Kanda
Ningyocho
Sarue
Suitengumae
Nihombashi
Senda
Umibe
Kitasuna
Funabori
Funabori
Ninoecho
Kiyosumi
Kiyosumi-shirakawa
Higashisuna
Kitakasai
Ukitacho
Yaesu
Kayabacho
Tomioka
Toyo
Minamisuna
Hatchobori
Kiba
Toyocho
Minami-Sunamachi
Nishikasai
Minato
Monzennakacho
Nishi-Kasai
Kasai
Shintomicho
Ginza-itchome
Chuo
Tsukuda
Etchujima
Shiohama
Ginza
GINZA
Higashiginza
Tsukiji
Shinkiba
Tukiji-shijo
Kachidoki
Tsukishima
Shinkaba
Seishincho
Nakakasai
Tsukiji
Shiomi
Shinkiba
Kachidoki
Harumi
KOTO
Yumenoshima
Rinkaicho
Minaikasai
SEE ODAIBA MAP
Toyosu
Tatsumi
Shinkaba
Kasairinkaikoen
Shinonome
Nishi Nagisa N
Higashi Nagisa
Odaibakai hinkoen
ODAIBA
Ariake
Kokusai-Tenjio seimon
Port of Tokyo
Tokyo Bay
Daiba
Fune-no-kagadukan
Tokyoteleport
Yurikamome Train Base
Aomi
Wakasu
Bayside

Sumidogawa River

Arakawa River

1 km
5000 ft

Tokyo

AKIHABARA

AND # JIMBOCHO

AKIHABARA: THE CENTER OF THE OTAKU UNIVERSE

IN THE 1980S, JOURNALIST VITTORIO ZUCCONI SPENT A FEW YEARS IN TOKYO AS A REPORTER FOR A MAJOR ITALIAN NEWSPAPER. AS HE LATER RECALLED IN THE BOOK HE WROTE ABOUT THIS EXPERIENCE, THE FIRST TIME HE GAZED AT THE TOKYO CITYSCAPE FROM A PLANE, HE THOUGHT IT LOOKED LIKE A GIANT TOY BOX TURNED UPSIDE DOWN. WHILE HIS WORDS WERE MEANT AS AN UNFLATTERING COMMENT ON THE CITY'S CHAOTIC URBAN SPRAWL, THEY APTLY DESCRIBE AKIHABARA. INDEED, THE DISTRICT TODAY IS NOTHING BUT A TREASURE TROVE OF "TOYS," ITS STREETS FILLED WITH PEOPLE WHO ARE CONSTANTLY LOOKING FOR OLD AND NEW MANGA, ANIME, FIGURES AND WHATEVER ELSE THE OTAKU INDUSTRY HAS COME UP WITH. HOWEVER AKIHABARA HASN'T ALWAYS BEEN LIKE THIS AND TODAY'S FUTURISTIC OTAKU CAPITAL OF THE WORLD IS JUST THE LATEST IN A SERIES OF VERSIONS WHICH HAVE ONE THING IN COMMON: INTRODUCING THE LATEST TECHNOLOGY IN ORDER TO FULFILL PEOPLE'S DESIRES.

Akihabara's history as an "Electric Town" began after World War Two, when many radio technicians who had returned from the front began to sell radio parts in the black market that had quickly developed under the elevated railway. They were joined by students from the electronic schools who began to build and sell radio sets.

The "electronic heart" of the district has survived the many transformations the area has witnessed since then. Even today, people who try to find their way at Akihabara Station are directed to the Electric Town Exit (電気街口) and both the Radio Center and Denpa Kaikan (Radio Wave Bldg.) can still be found respectively under the tracks and to the side of the Sobu-Chuo Line. If you want to devote all your precious time to manga- and game-hunting, you can easily skip this part of Akihabara, but even if plugs, LEDs and connectors bore you to tears, I suggest you stop by and pay homage to the area's oldest core where everything got started.

While the hunger for cheap entertainment was behind the postwar years' radio craze, the 1960s saw a growing demand for TVs and so-called "white goods" (large household electrical appliances) driven by the economic boom. Whole families would trek to Akihabara in order to acquire fridges and washing machines as the original hobby shops made way for stores selling these new status symbols. This trend peaked during the 1970s when as much as 10 percent of all household appliances sold in Japan were bought in Akihabara.

AKIHABARA MAY BE MAINLY KNOWN FOR ITS OTAKU AND CONSUMER ELECTRICAL APPLIANCE SHOPS (**LEFT AND TOP**) BUT RADIO CENTER (**BELOW**) AND DENPA KAIKAN STILL ATTRACT MANY DIY RADIO AND COMPUTER GEEKS.

The next big turning point in Akihabara's history came along in the early 1980s. All the major household appliance chain stores began to move to the suburbs, closer to where people lived, but the void left by these companies was quickly filled by a new kind of shops thanks to the birth of the FamiCon game console and an increased popular interest in home computers. Then in the early 1990s, the big guns began to move in, with computer giant Laox opening its main store not far from the station in 1990, while Sofmap established its first branch on Chuo-dori three years later. This process culminated in 1994 when computer-related sales surpassed other consumer electronics for the first time.

21st-century Akihabara is better known for its thriving otaku culture than computers, still in this relatively small district, there is arguably the greatest concentration of computer-related shops in the world, with brand-new PCs being sold on Chuo-dori and second-hand stuff being peddled in the small shops in the backstreets, while any kind of spare parts can be found in the narrow low-ceiling corridors near the station.

While computer hobbyists resembled the people who used to tinker with radios back in the 1950s, many of them were also into manga, anime and video games. As a consequence the new PC DIY era saw a gradual transformation of the area: with the release of a new generation of game consoles (Sega Saturn, PlayStation and Nintendo 64) more and more retailers started to sell game software, including manga- and anime-based products.

Everybody seems to agree that the single most important event behind this transition was the huge success of the TV anime series *Neon Genesis Evangelion*. First aired in 1995, subsequent reruns and the 1997 feature movie contributed to raise its cult status while the huge amount of money the title generated (an estimated 20 to 30 billion yen from books, plastic models and other goods) was a bonanza for otaku-oriented shops and contributed to attract more and more of them to Akihabara.

Since then, the thriving Japanese and international otaku communities have turned the place into their capital, so much so that since the turn of the century computer and hi-fi shops have been increasingly replaced by stores—big and small—selling manga, anime, video games and other otaku-related music and video products, including more controversial adult stuff.

Though Akihabara's association with otaku culture has brought the district huge financial gains and unprecedented global fame, mainstream Japanese society initially had a hard time accepting a community that since 1989 (the year serial killer Miyazaki Tsutomu—the so-called "Otaku Killer"—was arrested) had been seen as a bunch of creepy antisocial nerds. All this changed in 2005 with the unexpected success of the *Densha Otoko* (Train Man) book/TV drama/film saga, which signaled the popular acceptance of otaku.

The nation-wide *moe* boom that followed has contributed to shape the district's look and character as an otaku Mecca. It was also in 2005 that major electronics chain retailer Yodobashi Camera opened its mammoth Yodobashi Akiba store on the former site of an old freight depot, while at the end of the year idol girl group AKB48 debuted at their AKB48 Theater on the 8th floor of the local Don Quijote store. Since then Akihabara has become a sort of wonderland where every otaku not only has a chance to get his most outlandish desires fulfilled, but can discover things he had never dared to dream up.

TODAY COSPLAYING STREET DANCERS AND SINGERS ARE NOT AS COMMON AS TEN YEARS AGO.

LEFT Akihabara has one of the greatest concentrations of gigantic multi-story game centers in Tokyo.

SCORES OF NINTENDO DS USERS GATHER TO EXCHANGE INFORMATION THROUGH THE PASSERBY COMMUNICATION WIRELESS CONNECTION.

EXPLORING AKIHABARA

ONE GOOD THING ABOUT AKIHABARA IS THAT MOST OF THE SHOPS ARE CONCENTRATED IN A RELATIVELY SMALL AREA WEST OF THE STATION AND EVEN THE FARTHEST ONES CAN BE REACHED ON FOOT IN 5—10 MINUTES. CHUO-DORI (THE MAIN AVENUE) IS HOME TO MANY OF THE BIGGER STORES. YOU CAN USE IT AS YOUR MAIN REFERENCE POINT AND BRANCH OFF TO THE BACKSTREETS ON EITHER SIDE IN ORDER TO EXPLORE THE SMALLER, NICHE SHOPS. BE PREPARED FOR A TREMENDOUS VISUAL AND AURAL OVERLOAD, WITH GARISHLY COLORED GIANT BILLBOARDS, NEON LIGHTS AND LOUD MUSIC ASSAULTING YOU FROM EVERY DIRECTION.

Even though Akihabara's core area is only 500m x 300m wide, the sheer number of shops means that one can hardly see everything in just a few hours. So unless you can make more than one trip, you should plan your visit carefully. Be ready to climb stairs and ride elevators. This is nothing less than a treasure hunt, after all.

While on Sundays the place is crowded, it may be a good time to explore the neighborhood and take in the whole scene as Chuo-dori is closed to traffic. Even though all the singing and dancing has been outlawed, you still have a chance to catch some wandering party of cosplayers.

One last tip: For the latest updates on local events and to get maps, booklets, etc., go to the **Tokyo Anime Center** office (open 11:00–17:30 except Mon and Thu) on the second floor of the UDX Building next to the station. You can even ask for help to their English-speaking staff.

EAST OF CHUO-DORI

As soon as you step out of JR Akihabara Station (Electric Town Exit) you find yourself surrounded by otaku-oriented shops. We are going to start with one of the oldest stores in Akiba, **Tokiwa Musen**, that's been in business for more than 60 years (it's that tiny shop with the トキワムセン sign on the first floor of the massive Labi building). They only sell new games. However, as soon as an item gets "old" (sometimes after just one month) they slap a red SALE sign on it. Still on the left side is one of the area's most famous and storied buildings, the **Radio Kaikan**. Originally erected in 1950, it has been rebuilt three times. The eight-story second version, opened in 1962, was Akihabara's first high-rise structure. It was here, in 1976, that IT giant NEC opened the country's first Bit-INN Tokyo shop and began to sell its cheap PC kits (then called *mai-con* or "microcomputers"). The brand new structure you can admire today was finished in 2014. Three of its tenants are particularly worth a visit. **K-Books Akihabara** (3-4 F) is a general store selling character goods, mecha models,

ABOVE AKIBA-INFO IS A GOOD SOURCE OF INFORMATION ABOUT LOCAL EVENTS. **LEFT** CHUO-DORI AND THE ELEVATED RAILWAY ARE EXCELLENT POINTS OF REFERENCE FOR FIRST-TIME VISITORS.

RIGHT Event and new product information is attached on every available surface. Unfortunately very little of this information is in English.

CDs, video games, etc., but it's better known for stocking a staggering 2-300,000 publications of all kinds: collected manga and dojinshi, illustrated books, and more than 100 new light novels (short young adult novels mainly targeting middle and high school girls) every month.

Kaiyodo Hobby Lobby Tokyo (5F) is the popular figure and model maker's only retail shop in Japan. Kaiyodo is synonymous with beautifully crafted, highly detailed figures. Their works are so realistic that their dinosaur models, for instance, were reportedly used as material for the CG design of the monsters in *Jurassic Park*. Then there is the Revoltech series of figures featuring the company's unique "Revolver Joint" articulation system. Last but not least, the garage kits displayed every year at the Wonder Showcase (see Wonder Festival) can alsobe bought here.

Fewture Shop Akiba (7F) is a small boutique shop run by toy-maker Art Storm (of Super Festival fame) that sells beautiful garage kits and their famous EX and ES alloy models. Visiting this place is like walking into an art gallery and the impression is further reinforced by their prices. No discounts here but if you are a serious collector you may find a few treasures. On the right side of the street we find **Akihabara Gamers**. Born as a joint venture between Animate and media company Broccoli (hence its original name AniBro) and focusing on manga, anime and games, on the upper floors they often collaborate with makers (e.g. visual novel maker Nitroplus) to organize so-called Museum special events (original picture displays, card game tournaments, etc.). We finally reach Chuo-dori.

Hobby Tengoku, on the left corner, belongs to Volks, famous for producing garage and mecha kits and the world-famous Dollfie line of dolls, but this brand-new eight-story shop has

much more to offer, including a souvenir corner on the first floor and rental showcases on the basement, where people sell their treasures on consignment.

Turn right, go past the railway bridge and walk about 250 meters. There are many shops along Chuo-dori, but we are making a bee-line for **Comic Toranoana**. Stores A and B are next to each other. A visit to this place (founded back in 1994, when "otaku" still was a bad word) is a must if you are into the fan-generated comics known as dojinshi. Store A stocks mainstream manga as well, but have become universally—and deservedly—famous for its huge dojinshi catalogue (11,000 titles for a total of 1.2 million copies). If you are hunting for vintage issues or signed editions, this is the place for you. Store B specializes in CDs, DVDs and Blu-rays, including dojin audio and video works. And if you don't have the time to visit Akiba (just kidding!) they have more shops scattered around and near Tokyo (see list here: toranoana.jp/shop).

Animate, just next door, is a little smaller than the main store in Ikebukuro, but still features seven floors of everything including some goods that

TORANOANA (**BELOW**) IS PARADISE ON EARTH FOR FANS OF DOJINSHI AND OTHER INDIE AND FAN-GENERATED COMICS AND PUBLICATIONS.

can be found only here. The event space on the seventh floor hosts authors and voice actors for autographs and handshaking.

Now, if you like some song and dance, the **AKB48 Theater** is only a few meters away. Since 2005 this small venue on top of the Don Quixote discount store has been the home base of AKB48, the most popular Japanese idol group of the decade (besides hosting the other member groups of the AKB galaxy whenever they are on tour in Tokyo). The theater seats only 145 people and has a total capacity of 250, making each concert a rather intimate experience (even though two big pillars near the stage partially block your view if you happen to get the wrong seat). The bad news—especially if you are in Tokyo on a trip—is that tickets are assigned by random lottery after you have applied through their website (sorry, no English instructions). Considering the group's popularity you have between a 1:50 and a 1:200 chance to get one. Good luck!

The **Heroine Tokusatsu Kenkyujo** (Heroine Special Effects Research

MAK JAPAN (LEFT) AND G-FRONT ARE GO-TO PLACES IF YOU ARE INTO GAME CIRCUIT BOARDS, CABINETS AND ASSORTED SPARE PARTS.

From new and second-hand toy shops (LEFT) to gachapon vending machines (RIGHT) the amount of figures on sale is just overwhelming.

Center) on the next block is the door to a different, slightly darker side of Akihabara. Ever heard of such masterpieces as Zen Pictures' *Enormous Breasts Squadron Fiber Star* or *Hyper Sexy Heroine Cyber Soldier Etoile?* If you are interested in Power Rangers parodies, Sailor Moon-like and masked-girl fighters, Studio 2.5's wacky Akiba-kei action porno flicks and other low budget V-Cinema (straight-to-video) stuff, this store could change your life. They even sell the original costumes used during the shoots!

Do you want to take a break from shopping? The **Try Amusement Tower** game arcade is in the backstreet on the right (its green and white logo with the cute manga girl makes it easy to spot). Gundam has a big presence on the sixth floor while upstairs you will find a huge selection of retro games (Konami, Namco, Sega, etc.) and fighting games are on the eighth. Otherwise continue strolling up Chuo-dori and after about 200 meters, you will arrive at **Toys Golden Age.** This is the first place you should check out if you are into retro toys. This tiny, cramped shop bursts at the seams with all the classic products Japan is famous for: Godzilla, Ultraman, Kamen Rider, Mazinger Z and other sofubi and chogokin; minicars; Candy Candy and other girls' toys; tin toys; and then magazines for kids, bromides (old idol photo portraits)… It literally has things you won't find anywhere else in Akiba. Enough said. In the same building on the sixth

floor there's **Mak Japan**, one of two niche Akiba stores selling arcade circuit boards and related gear. These things don't come cheap but they have bargain sales during rainy days when business is slow. Their people are famous for being very knowledgeable and all the boards are tested before purchase.

Now turn right at the big intersection, then take the second right. On the third floor of the third building on the left is **Akiba Joshi-ryo.** Here's your chance to infiltrate a girls' dormitory (*joshi-ryo*) where the pajama-wearing "resident" girls, instead of screaming and calling the cops, are more than happy to engage you in conversation and play games. The "dorm" has several rooms furnished in different ways—one for each girl. The basic course costs 1,880 yen for 30 minutes and consists

A VISIT TO GACHAPON KAIKAN IS A MUST IF YOU ARE INTO SMALL CAPSULE TOYS.

in chatting and playing analog and/or video games with the girl of your choice. There are plenty of options as well (1–3,000 yen each) including light massages, photo-taking and even being slapped across the face!

WEST OF CHUO-DORI

A good alternative to starting from Akihabara Station is to make it your final destination: Take the Tokyo Metro Ginza Line, get off at Suehirocho Station, and slowly make your way south toward the Radio Kaikan. For starters, if you are a Morning Musume fan, the **Hello! Project Official Shop** is inside the building next to Exit 4. Here you will find a vast array of pictures, photo collections, original goods and the group's latest CDs and DVDs. There is a stage as well and events are scheduled every month, while stage costumes are on display in the exhibition space.

Around the corner there's **Friends.** You may think that this small unassuming place run by an old lady and her husband isn't worth your time. Think again, because this is a Holy Land for retro-game hunters and its ever-changing selection includes games for less

Friends (FAR LEFT) is arguably the best retro game shop in Akiba, while Cospa Gee Store (LEFT) on the second floor of the Gachapon Kaikan is a good place to check out cosplay gear, party costumes and other otaku goods.

popular consoles. Most importantly, their prices are unbeatable (they even have bins filled with loose cartridges you can get for as cheap as 100 yen) so if you find what you want here, don't bother looking for better deals. The shop is next door to **G-Front**, the other store in Akiba that sells game circuit boards, cabinets and assorted spare part. It's bigger than Mak Japan (see East Walk) but more expensive.

Now cross the intersection and walk down Chuo-dori. Dive into the first

backstreet past Mos Burger (good local fast food joint) to find **Gachapon Kaikan**, the go-to place for people who love those small toys in plastic capsules. With 430 machines to choose from (and 60 new items coming in every month) you'll go crazy trying to choose between figures, cute animals and miniature food. Prices are in the 100–500 yen range and if you are after

certain prizes you can even check the rental displays at the back where people sell their unwanted toys. The Kaikan shares the same building with **Cospa Gee Store** (2-3F) and **Cure Maid Café** (6F, see eateries) so a trip here is a great chance to enjoy the full otaku experience. Cospa is a cosplay shop with a strong otaku vibe and a good selection of costumes, wigs, contact lenses and other accessories. On the second floor they even sell party costumes, T-shirts and other anime goods.

Back on Chuo-dori and the shop on the corner of the next block is **Liberty #1** (look for the small white and green リバティー sign). Second-hand goods are

TRADING CARD GAMES

Trading card games (TCG) (also called collectible card games) are big in Japan and their popularity goes well beyond the usual world-famous titles (*Pokemon, Yu-Gi-Oh!, Magic: The Gathering*, etc.) to include many anime-based games. The main TCG-selling chains (**Yellow Submarine, Amenity Dream,** and **Big Magic**) have many branches around Tokyo and are pretty similar. They sell both sets and singles, with sets collected in binders and rare and/or popular cards displayed in showcases. They even have quite a few English cards as apparently some Japanese players prefer to use them. If you are looking for something in particular, you can make a list and give it to the staff. Just be warned that on average, singles in Japan tend to cost more than in other countries. One more tip on TCG is good manners: You will rarely see the Japanese trade cards inside shops, and actually there are some that explicitly forbid trading on the premises.

Many TCG shops have tables to play games, and on their websites you can find information on upcoming tournaments. Most of them are small events. Signing up is quite cheap and if you do well you can get some cool prizes like deck boxes, card sleeves and binders. Obviously almost all participants are Japanese, but don't worry, because they are very welcoming and curious about foreign players, and

even if you don't speak Japanese, card language is rarely a problem. For more information on playing in Japan (especially *Pokemon*) check out Finnish champion Esa Juntunen's blog (thedeckout. blogspot.jp)

TCG stores in Tokyo are typically close to each other, so if you don't like the prices or selection at one store you can always try another one nearby. One of the more convenient places is Radio Kaikan in Akihabara. The 10-story building houses six トレカ (toreka, as they are called in Japan) shops including **Yellow Submarine** (sixth floor) and **Big Magic** (ninth). And if that's not enough, in the building in front of Radio Kaikan there's another shop, **Cardkingdom**.

treated with so much care in Japan, that it is often very difficult to notice the difference between a brand-new item and a used one. So if you want to save a few yen you must try Liberty. The problem is, there are a whopping ten shops in Akihabara alone. Most stores (see liberty-kaitori.com/map.html) face Chuo-dori and are pretty close to each other. This particular branch specializes in figures while stores #4 and #5 across the street mostly sell games, CDs and DVDs. Strangely enough, they all sport different logos, which makes locating them even more confusing. Some of them are yellow on blue, others green on white. Keep your eyes open for the words リバティー (Liberty) or ホビー・フィギュアー (hobby & figures).

Trader Main Store's blue-and-yellow sign on the next corner, on the contrary, can't be absolutely missed. This chain is known as one of the best game retailers and gets high praise for having the right balance between price and selection. Game hunters have to check the first floor for new video games, the second for second-hand items and new foreign titles, and the fifth for PC games and dojin products. It is also known that Trader stocks a lot of DVDs and Blu-rays too. Check out the third floor for mainstream titles and the fourth floor for anime

THE BIG AND WELL-ORGANIZED ACOS SHOP IN AKIBA HAS PLENTY OF COSTUMES, WIGS, CONTACT LENSES AND OTHER COSPLAY ACCESSORIES.

(including related CDs), but if you are into adult flicks (including manga and games), you will have to climb all the way to the top.

The next block is dominated by giant electronics retailer Sofmap, but the best store to visit is **Akiba Sofmap #1** next to Mister Donut. If you're really in a hurry and can only hit one shop, this one is your best choice. Taking center stage in Chuo-dori, it's a sort-of otaku supermarket with a bit of everything: manga, character goods, J-Pop and idol CDs and DVDs (including a special AKB48 corner), pla-mo, cards and even light novels. The seventh and eighth floors are event spaces.

Now turn right and on the opposite corner you'll see a menacingly-looking black monolith. This "Treasure Mountain" is **Mandarake**, the largest seller of used manga- and anime-related goods. Each of its eight floors is devoted to a different genre. While their selection does not compare to more-specialized retailers, their prices are often cheaper. And if you can't come all the way to Japan, they even ship abroad. Just check their excellent English website. WARNING: If erotic stuff makes you uncomfortable, you may want to avoid the fourth "men's entertainment" floor.

If you look down the street with the Lawson on the corner you'll see **Akiba Cultures Zone**. Walk in that direction,

FLOORS 3-5 OF THE GARGANTUAN MANDARAKE COMPLEX HAVE MORE MANGA AND DOJINSHI THAN YOU CAN SHAKE A STICK AT.

but before crossing the street, turn right and go check out **Monkey Soft**. This store specializes in used DVDs and Blu-rays. From mainstream flicks to anime, idol, hentai and porno fare, they have everything you need, and then some more. The four upper floors are home to their manga cafe **Monkey Net**—a great place to indulge all your vices. Renting a private booth with reclining chair and PC (258 yen for the first 30 minutes, 103 for each 15-minute extension, 1,728 for a six-hour pack) gives you access to free hot and cold drinks, 15 different types of soft serve ice cream and junk food, and even all-you-can-eat toast and boiled eggs for breakfast. And tons of manga of course. You can even take a shower for a small fee.

Akiba Cultures Zone is home to many interesting stores—my personal favorite is **Acos** (fifth floor), a cosplay store with a much sleeker look than Cospa—but the most interesting place is actually in the basement. If you are among the many people who couldn't get hold of an AKB48 concert ticket, your best chance to catch a live performance in Akihabara is to check out the **Akiba Cultures Theater**, a 220-seat venue which holds concerts almost every day. You can buy tickets from their website, from the Ticket Pia ticket agency and even at the door, and with a rotating lineup of up-and-coming idol groups, you may be lucky enough to see the superstars of

KANDA MYOJIN SHRINE

32 See map on page 40

Looking for that elusive manga or retro game is akin to a treasure hunt. If you are superstitious and need some help from heaven, you may want to pay a visit to this beautiful shrine, one of the oldest in Tokyo, only a seven-minute walk from the station. Due to the shrine's close proximity to the

Electric Town, IT companies have come to revere the place and regularly seek out its protection by attending blessing ceremonies there. Individuals can get their share of good luck by buying their high-tech *omamori* (charm) for 800 yen. It comes in three parts: a credit card-sized card, a sticker-like strip for your PC and a thumbnail-sized sticker for your cell phone.

Kanda Myojin is one of the two main non-otaku attractions of the area (the other one is Mansei-bashi, the bridge on the south side that hundreds of years ago marked one of the entrances to the city) and it's a wonderful example of Shinto architecture. If you happen to be in Tokyo on the weekend closest to May 15 of an odd-numbered year, don't miss the Kanda Festival, in which two hundred portable shrines are carried through the surrounding streets.

tomorrow. The **@Jam Next events** take place here on the second Sunday of every month.

If you go back to Chuo-dori, you'll find **Comic Zin** just around the corner. Opened in 2009 by former Toranoana employees, this is another must for manga and dojinshi lovers. Though relatively small, it boasts that it has titles that—believe it or not—even Toraoana doesn't carry. Instead we take the street left of Akiba Cultures Zone and in a few steps reach **Super Potato**, arguably the most famous of the retro game shops in Akiba. When the area is featured on TV, chances are they are going to show this place, giving it a sort-of celebrity status. They have EVERYTHING, including Neo Geo and PC Engine games and very rare (i.e. very expensive) stuff. They even sell game-related items (strategy guides, T-shirts, Super Mario glasses, etc.). The downside is that their prices are 25–30% higher than the competition. This said, they have 2-3-day bargain sales typically during holidays (the Golden Week in early May; Obon in mid-August; and New Year). There's even a small game center on the top floor complete with glass-top cabinets for an old '70s feeling.

MARIO STANDS GUARD TO SUPER POTATO, ARGUABLY THE MOST FAMOUS (AND EXPENSIVE) RETRO GAME SHOP IN AKIHABARA.

EVEN WHILE GETTING LOST IN AKIBA'S MAZE OF BACKSTREETS, IT'S IMPOSSIBLE TO MISS KOTOBUKIYA'S GARISH GREEN FAÇADE.

Kotobukiya is only a few meters down the street (yes, it's the building with the garish green façade) and is an excellent place to check what's currently hot in Japan, as each floor has a corner dedicated to a popular line of goods. The third floor is devoted to Kotobukiya's *bishojo* figures (KanColle, Love Live!, The Idolmaster, etc.) while the fourth has lots of original plastic

models (e.g. Frame Arms). Indie sofubi (soft-vinyl figures made by small companies) and other interesting stuff like Ultraman and Godzilla can also be found on the upper floors (the fifth is also used for events and art displays).

Fancy some time at a game center? Go back to Chuo-dori, for this particular stretch has a few, starting with **Taito HEY**. This arcade is said to have the best collection of shoot 'em ups—or shmups, as shooter games are commonly called. And if you are not satisfied with "bullet hell," they even have lots of fighting games. Of course we can't talk about gaming without mentioning **Club Sega**, and Akiba is the only Tokyo district which can boast four of the 20 Clubs scattered around the city center. The main one is next to the railway bridge. You can find bigger Clubs elsewhere in Tokyo, but this one still has seven floors and, most importantly, is where all the hardcore fighters come to flex their muscles. Avoid the *UFO Catcher* on the first two floors and head instead to the upper floors dominated by Sega's famous games (e.g. *Virtua Fighter*, card-based *Sangokushi Taisen*, etc.). If you're lucky, you may even get to try one of the new games that the company tests here before releasing them.

Sandwiched between Taito HEY and Club Sega is the **Sofmap Akihabara Amusement-ka**n, another hot spot for video games. If you are lucky enough to be in Tokyo when a major title is released, you may want to join the queue here—long but slightly better than at Yodobashi Camera. But the real attraction is their wide choice of used games for TV and PC—the biggest in Akihabara.

Instead of passing under the bridge, let's take the next right and do something a little different. Akihabara may be full of fantasy mobile suits like Gundam, but here you can even buy real robots, and the building across the pachinko parlor is the best place to start. On the corner there's **Vstone**, while **Tsukumo** is a few meters to the right. They have about the same products (lots of entry-level or low-priced kits) but Vstone wins extra points for its nice English website. Besides a cute Hello Kitty robot, Tsukumo has a few interesting items on display (e.g. the popular KHR series and Robovie-X humanoids or the spider-like KMR-M6). While at Vstone you can admire some famous ROBO-ONE

FOR ROBOT FANS, VSTONE (**LEFT**) AND TSUKUMO (**BELOW**) ARE CONVENIENTLY LOCATED NEXT TO EACH OTHER.

Omnizero humanoid robots created by founder Maeda-san.

After all this walking, would you like to go for a drive? Keep following the street that runs parallel to the railway bridge. On the way to our final destination, we pass in front of yet another game center, **Tokyo Leisure Land**—the arcade which hosts the highest number of events in the neighborhood, including tie-ups with popular anime and fighting game tournaments. Cross the street at the next big intersection and go right. In the basement of the next block there's Akiba Cart, where you can rent a red go-kart—as long as you are

150–185 cm tall and have a valid Japanese or international license. Each kart has enough gas to cover 80 km, so you can actually wander away from Akihabara. Rental fees range from 2,700 yen/h, to 10,800 for one day (even less if you become a member), and if you don't feel confident enough to brave the streets of Tokyo on your own, you can even rent a "guide driver" for 1,500 yen/h. Just remember to call (03-6206-4752) or mail in advance to reserve your go-kart.

EAST OF AKIHABARA STATION

There are a few more places on the "wrong" (east) side of the station and they are definitely worth a look. So let's go check them out. From the Electric Town Exit, go left, then left again when you reach the main avenue. **Book-Off** is inside the first building past the railway bridge. Purists may scoff at the idea of shopping at this used bookstore chain (and in Akiba, of all places), as they seem to be rather clueless about the stuff they handle. It's always worth a look, though, especially if you are after video games, for they are often cheaper than other retailers. This particular branch is six stories high and even carries secondhand consoles and accessories as well as books and manga.

AKIBA SOFMAP #1 STORE IN CHUO-DORI IS A VERITABLE OTAKU SUPERMARKET WITH A LITTLE BIT OF EVERYTHING.

Continue in the same direction and take the first left. Once you pass under the tunnel you'll see **Yodobashi-Akiba** on your right. This behemoth of a building is the main reason why otaku shoppers stray into Akihabara's recently redeveloped east side. Yodobashi Camera is one of Japan's main electronics retailers and this—the crown jewel—takes up a whole block.

Compared to most shops, this is a more mainstream, family-friendly environment. Still, the sixth floor—where most otaku goods are—features an adult software corner. On this floor you will find a general selection of everything otaku, sometimes at discounted prices. Yodobashi's main draw is that you can find here otaku goods and electronic gadgets of all kinds (the store is known for its long lines of people queuing to snatch up the latest PSP and Nintendo consoles), and the sheer size and variety you will find under one roof makes for an unforgettable experience. As an added bonus, the three non-Yodobashi upper floors have other amenities. For instance, you can get a foot massage at the reflexology salon on the seventh floor, while the restaurant floor on the eighth is open until 11:30 pm.

Now walk to the end of the block and turn right at the big intersection. After passing under the elevated Expressway, you have two options: 1) Go right then take the second left. Walk about 100 meters and on the right you'll find the **Natsuge Museum**, a cool little arcade devoted to the preservation of vintage machines from the late '70s to mid-'80s. They organize events and even sell a few toys (plastic models), game music CDs and books. Don't forget it's only open Friday through Sunday; 2) Go left and walk four blocks. **Super Rajikon** is inside the gray building past the Daily Yamazaki convenience store. This store sells radio-controlled cars, train and plane models, and air guns, including all the spare parts dedicated modelers need. They even host workshops and races.

AKIHABARA NIGHTLIFE See map on page 40

23 Dear Stage

Opening times *daily 18:00–22:50 (Mon–Fri), 17:00–22:50 (weekends & holidays)*
dearstage.com
AKB84 have gone global, but there are still plenty of aspiring idols out there and this is one of the best places to check them out. It is on this cramped stage, by the way, that rising stars Denpagumi.inc had their start. The place is also famous for the rabid otaku fans who invariably launch themselves into frantic otagei cheering and dancing routines. The stage is on the 1F (500 yen cover charge including one drink) while the upper floors house a bar.

27 Game Bar A-Button

Opening times *20:00–4:00. Usually closed on Mon (check their Twitter to make sure)*
a-button.jp
If you spent the whole day hunting for retro games, you'll end up hungry, thirsty AND feeling like actually playing some of that stuff. So what better idea than paying a visit to this off-the-beaten-path bar? A favorite among both fans and game industry insiders, this place is full of games and consoles waiting for you. They even have an impressive collection of classic controllers. Booze is prized around 500–600 yen. The place is quite small so if you plan to go with a big group of people you'd better call in advance (03-5856-5475). Ah, and of course you must be over 20.

41 Pasela Akiba Showa-dori-kan

Opening times *daily 12:00–5:00 (Mon–Thu), 12:00–7:00 (Fri), 11:00–7:00 Sat), 11:00–5:00 (Sun & holidays)*
pasela.co.jp
If you are into singing, this collection of karaoke rooms is hard to beat. Each room is the result of a collaboration with a different anime or video game producer and is decorated accordingly. Some of the more popular rooms are devoted to samurai-themed game and anime series *Sengoku Basara*, fantasy *RPG Monster Hunter*, and even *Evangelion*.

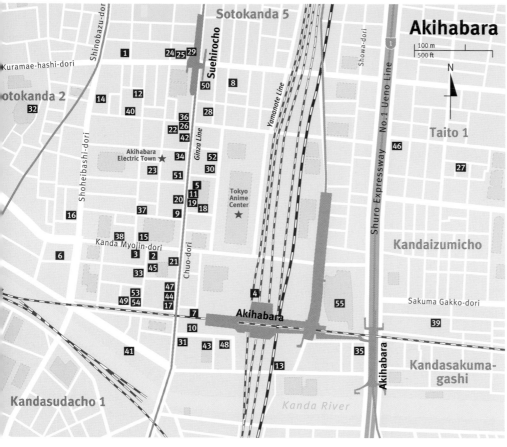

Sotokanda 5

Suehirocho

Shinobazu-dori

Kuramae-hashi-dori

otokanda 2

Shoheibashi-dori

Akihabara
Electric Town ★

Kanda Myojin-dori

Chuo-dori

Ginza Line

Yamanote Line

Tokyo Anime Center ★

Akihabara

Kandasudacho 1

Kanda River

Showa-dori

No.1 Ueno Line

Shuto Expressway

Akihabara

100 m
500 ft
N

Taito 1

Kandaizumicho

Sakuma Gakko-dori

Kandasakuma-gashi

Akihabara

ABOVE Super Potato is Akiba's most famous retro game shop.
BOTTOM Unfortunately not many stores in Akihabara have easy-to-see signs like Comic Zin.

AKIHABARA HOT SPOTS

GENERAL

9 Akiba Sofmap #1 アキバ☆ソフマップ１号店
Opening times *daily 11:00–20:00*
sofmap.com

10 Akihabara Gamers
Opening times *daily 9:00–22:00 (1F), 10:00–21:00 (2-7F)*
anibro.jp

11 Animate
Opening times *daily 10:00–21:00*
animate.co.jp

13 Book-Off
Opening times *daily 10:00–23:00*
bookoff.co.jp/

31 Hobby Tengoku
ホビー天国
Opening times *11:00–20:00 (Mon–Fri), 10:00–20:00 (Sat–Sun & holidays)*
volks.co.jp/jp/hobbytengoku/top.html/

33 Kotobukiya
Opening times *daily 10:00–20:00*
www.kotobukiya.co.jp/store/akiba/

37 Mandarake Complex
Opening times *daily 12:00–20:00*
mandarake.co.jp (English)

55 Yodobashi-Akiba
Opening times *daily 9:30–22:00*
yodobashi-akiba.com

MANGA SHOPS

18/19/20 Comic Toranoana
Opening times *Store A and B: daily 10:00–22:00; Store C: daily 11:00–22:00*
toranoana.jp

21 Comic Zin
Opening times *11:00–22:00 (Mon–Fri), 10:00–22:00 (Sat–Sun & holidays)*
comiczin.jp

43 K-Books Akihabara
Opening times *daily 11:00–20:00*
k-books.co.jp

ANIME & DVDS

30 heroine Tokusatsu Kenkyujo
ヒロイン特撮研究所 B1
Opening times *daily 11:00–22:00*
heroinetokusatsu.jp

38 Monkey Soft もんきーそふと
Opening times *daily 10:00–23:30*
monkey.co.jp/

VIDEO GAMES

24 Friends フレンズ
Opening times *11:00–20:00 (closed on Tue, or Wed when Tue is a national holiday)*
gameshop.ocnk.net

44 Sofmap Akihabara Amusement-kan ソフマップ AMUSEMENT
Opening times *daily 11:00–20:00*
sofmap.com

45 Super Potato スーパーポテト
Opening times *11:00–20:00 (Mon–Fri), 10:00–20:00 (Sat–Sun)*
superpotatoakiba.jp

48 Tokiwa Musen トキワムセン
Opening times *daily 11:00–20:00*
twitter.com/tokiwamusen

51 Trader Main Store トレーダー本店
Opening times *11:00–20:00 (Mon–Thu), 10:00–20:30 (Fri–Sat), 10:00–20:00 (Sun & holidays)*
e-trader.jp

TOYS

43 Fewture Shop Akiba
Opening times *13:00–20:00 (Mon–Fri), 10:00–20:00 (Sat–Sun). Closed on Mon (Tues if Mon is a national holiday)*
artstorm.co.jp/

26 Gachapon Kaikan ガチャポン会館
Opening times *daily 11:00–20:00 (Mon–Thu), 11:00–22:00 (Fri–Sat), 11:00–19:00 (Sun & holidays)*
akibagacha.com

43 Kaiyodo Hobby Lobby Tokyo 海洋堂
Opening times *daily 11:00–20:00 (closed irregularly for events, etc.)*
kaiyodo.co.jp/kaiyodo_HB/TK_topics/

34 Liberty リバティー
Multiple locations, most of them on or near Chuo-dori (check the URL below)
Opening times *daily 11:00–20:30 (Mon–Fri), 10:30–20:30 (Sat), 10:30–20:00 (Sun & holidays)*
liberty-kaitori.com/map.html

46 Super Rajikon スーパーラジコン
Opening times *daily 11:00–21:00 (Mon–Sat) 10:00–20:00 (Sun & holidays)*
super-rc.co.jp/shop/tokyo.html

50 Toys Golden Age
Opening times *11:30–21:00 (closed on Tue)*

53 Tsukumo
Opening times *daily 10:00–21:00*
robot.tsukumo.co.jp

54 Vstone
Opening times *daily 11:00–20:00 (Mon–Fri) 10:00–19:00 (Sat–Sun & holidays)*
vstone.co.jp (Japanese only)
vstone.co.jp/english/ (English page)

ARCADE GAMES

25 G-Front
Opening times *15:00–20:00 (Mon–Sat) 10:00–18:30 (Sun)*
gfront.com

50 Mak Japan
Opening times *11:00–19:00 (Mon–Fri), 10:00–19:00 (Sat), 10:00–18:00 (Sun & holidays)*
mak-jp.com

COSPLAY & CLOTHES

3 Acos
Opening times *daily 11:00–21:30*
www.acos.me/

26 Cospa Gee Store
Opening times *11:00–20:00 (Mon–Sat), 11:00–19:00 (Sun & holidays)*
geestore.com

IDOLS

5 AKB48 Theater
Opening times *17:00–20:00 (Mon–Fri), 12:00–19:00 (Sat–Sun & holidays)*
akb48.co.jp/theater

3 Akiba Cultures Theater
akibalive.jp

29 Hello! Project Official Shop
Opening times *12:00–20:00 (Mon–Fri), 10:00–20:00 (weekend & holidays)*
shop.helloproject.com/officialshop/shop/shop_20130324_13345.html

COSPLAY WIGS COME IN ANY IMAGINABLE COLOR AND SIZE.

GAME CENTERS

17 Club Sega
Opening times *daily 10:00–1:00*
bpnavi.jp/toru/ssc/shop/1186

39 Natsuge Museum ナツゲーミュージアム
Opening times *18:00–23:00 (Fri), 13:00–22:00 (Sat), 13:00–20:00 (Sun & holidays)*
t-tax.net/natuge
twitter.com/natuge

47 Taito HEY
Opening times *daily 10:00–24:00*
taito.co.jp/gc/store/00001703

49 Tokyo Leisure Land
Opening times *daily 10:00–1:00*
llakihabara.sakura.ne.jp

52 Try Amusement Tower
Opening times *10:00–24:00 (Mon–Thu, Sun & holidays), 10:00–1:00 (Fri–Sat)*
try-amusement-tower.com

OTHERS

8 Akiba Joshi-ryo あきば女子寮
Opening times *daily 13:00–21:30*
planetplan.net

6 Akiba Cart
Opening times *daily 10:00–20:00*
akibanavi.net

Hundreds of idol photos are on sale at Dera NanNan and the Hello! Project Official Shop.

AKIHABARA EATERIES See map on page 40

4 AKB48 Café & Bar

Opening times *11:00–23:00 (Mon–Fri), 10:00–23:00 (weekends & holidays)*

akb48cafeshops.com/akihabara/english

Are you one of the many AKB48 fans who didn't win the ticket lottery for their concerts? Don't worry! Now you can console yourself at this themed cafe featuring a 136-inch screen which shows the group's videotaped performances. All the waitresses dress in AKB-style costumes and serve dishes inspired by the idols themselves. Food goes for 800–1,000 yen while drinks are priced around 500 yen. While in some respects many bars and cafes in Japan cater to a particular sex or age group, here you will likely see a curious mix of young girls, working people on their lunch break and male fans. And don't forget to do some shopping at the souvenir store.

12 ANIMAX Café

Opening times *12:00–22:00 (Mon–Fri), 11:00–22:00 (weekend & holidays)*

cafe.animax.co.jp/

Anime TV network ANIMAX has opened a two-story cafe mainly devoted to anison and voice acting. The second floor is particularly interesting as the cafe staff (called "the cast") take turns performing on a stage (both reading scripts and singing), while the weekends are often devoted to talk shows by anime artists and creators (online reservation recommended). There is a 500 yen table charge on the second floor and on both floors there is a minimum requirement for ordering food and drink.

15 Canned food vending machines

Let's say you're going to spend the next couple of hours lining up for a new product, but still, you have to put something in your stomach. Why not head to the vending machine across the street from Akiba Cultures Zone and around the corner from Akihabara Crane Kenkyujo? The canned hot ramen and oden (traditional Japanese stew) come with a fork and are popular with local hardcore otaku.

16 Characro Café TIGER & BUNNY—The Rising

Opening times *10:00–22:20 (closed on the 3rd Wed of the month)*

namco.co.jp/characro/tigerandbunny/

Characro stands for "character cross-over" and this is one of many collaboration bars and cafes inspired by anime and video games. It was opened in 2014 after the release of the latest *Tiger & Bunny* movie and is styled after the Hero's Bar featured in the series. You must reserve your table through their website (in Japanese, sorry) and choose among five 100-minute time slots. A 300-yen table charge gets you a special sticker. Don't spend all your money on food and drink (they don't come cheap) if you want to buy their exclusive merchandize.

3 Good Smile x Animate Café

Opening times *daily 11:00–21:30*

cafe.animate.co.jp/shop/akihabara/

This spacious and well-lit cafe is another collaboration, this time between figure-manufacturer Good Smile Company and Animate (Japan's largest retailer of manga, anime and games), with changing themes every few months. Getting a seat, though, is not an easy task: You will have to 1) become a member of Club Animate; 2) make a reservation online; and 3) hope your name will be chosen, as seats are assigned according to a lottery system.

Some only-in-Akiba vending machines are famous for dishing out canned ramen and other traditional Japanese food to the hordes of hungry but busy otaku hunters.

4 Gundam Café

Opening times *10:00–23:00 (Mon–Fri), 8:30–23:00 (Sat), 8:30–21:30 (Sun & holidays)*

g-cafe.jp/

Next door to the AKB48 Cafe, this popular joint can be a pretty underwhelming experience for the casual visitor, but if you are a Gundam fan you'll love it no matter what. Besides the obligatory big screen playing videos nonstop you can admire several model kits on display. Food and drink are far from memorable but fans will surely be impressed by the staff (who are clad in Gundam-like uniforms) and the funky toilet featuring special sound effects. And the attached shop sells limited-edition goods and more food including *gunpla-yaki*, the Gundam twist on traditional *taiyaki* sweet bean paste- and cream-filled cakes.

40 Noodol (sic) Café

Opening times *13:00–21:00 (Tue–Fri), 12:00–20:00 (Sat), 12:00–19:00 (Sun & holidays). Closed on Mon.*

noodol-cafe.com/

This is the ultimate otaku experience: a chance to talk with an idol! Well, actually the pretty girls who work here are all newcomers belonging to the Platinum Production talent agency but still, for many guys it's paradise on earth. You pay 800 yen for a cup of instant noodles or bottled soft drink and the right to choose your favorite

idol ("only" 500 on weekday lunch time or if you let them choose for you), then sit down with the girl for a three-minute chat. Each idol works different shifts but you can check their schedule on their Japanese-only website (which is as bare as the cafe's stripped-down interior). There's a point system too: after you have accumulated five points you can have a photo taken with an idol. Collect ten points and they add an autograph to the deal.

*Just be warned that unless you speak the local lingo, it will be difficult to have a satisfying conversation as most Japanese are not very good English speakers.

EXOTIC DÉCOR AND ELABORATELY PRESENTED FOOD IS WHAT YOU GET ONCE YOU MANAGE TO SECURE A SEAT AT MANY AKIBA EATERIES.

41 Pasela Collaboration Cafes
pasela.co.jp/shop/akiba_multi/
Pasela is a company specializing in themed cafes and bars inspired by anime and video games. Three of them are on the second floor of its Pasela Resorts Akiba Multi Entertainment building. For more information on upcoming projects be sure to check out their home page. For anime: paselabo.tv/anime/index.html. For games: paselabo.tv/game/index.html

41 1. Final Fantasy Eorzea Café
Opening times *daily 11:30–22:00*
pasela.co.jp/paselabo_shop/ff_eorzea/
This *Final Fantasy XIV*-inspired cafe takes its name from the region where the game takes place and is modeled after its Canopy tavern (including stained windows and wooden floors). There are lots of weapons and armor on display, and even a counter with several PCs where you can actually play the game. Reservations are not obligatory, but as the place is always crowded it's a good idea to book online. You can choose among four two-hour time slots (the last one is three hours long). The 1,000-yen table charge (that you need to pay only if you reserve in advance) includes one

drink and a themed coaster. This is by far the best looking of the three.

41 2. Otomate Café
Opening times *daily 11:00–23:00*
paselabo.tv/collabotown/otomate/index.html
Otomate is a subsection of video game developer and publisher Idea Factory and this cafe is devoted to their titles (*Norn9*, *Diabolik Lovers*, etc.). Reservation and price system are the same as the Eorzea Café. If you want to buy their game-inspired goods, be sure to place your order ASAP as they sell out quickly.

41 3. Starchild Café
Opening times *daily 12:00–22:00*
paselabo.tv
Starchild is a sub-label of King Records specializing in anime music, and all the food is inspired by their titles and voice actors. This is the smallest of the three bars and its rather basic décor includes TV screens showing Starchild anime openings. Only recommended to hardcore fans of the label.

42 Queen Dolce
Opening times *14:00–22:00 (Tue–Fri), 13:00–22:00 (weekend & holidays). Closed on Mon.*
akibakotower.com/queen-dolce
The perfect mix between a maid and butler cafe, this small windowless bar is manned by a crew of danso (girls

dressing and acting as boys). They are very friendly and open to conversation (if you speak Japanese, that is) and attract a mixed clientele. They have tea, coffee and soft drinks as well but their forte is cocktails (800–1,200 yen plus a 200-yen cover charge).

MAID CAFES
2 @home café
Opening times *11:30–22:00 (Mon–Fri), 10:30–22:00 (weekends & holidays). Closed irregularly*
cafe-athome.com
Currently the most talked-about maid cafe in Akihabara, @home café has a dedicated army of 170 maids ready to entertain the honorable *goshujin-sama* (master) but only for one hour at a time. There's a 600-yen cover charge and its main location (there is another store inside Don Quijote) is divided in three floors: Classical (mainly eating and drinking in a quiet environment); Entertainment (for chatting and playing games with the maids); and Bar. Depending on the course menu one chooses, it is also possible to have your picture taken and/or play games with a maid.

7 Akiba Diner The Granvania
Opening times *12:00–23:00 (Mon–Thu & Sun), 12:00–5:00 (Fri–Sat)*
the-granvania.ciao.jp
In many respects this is a rather unique Akiba eatery. Though the maid vibe is there and they have anime-related

events, this is more a spacious restaurant than a cafe, and people actually come for their diverse menu which features roast beef and 30 brands of foreign beers, mostly from Europe. On the downside for maid photo hunters, you can't simply buy one. In order to get a picture you will have to come many times until you have filled up your point card.

14 Café Mai:lish

Opening times *daily 11:00–22:00*
mailish.jp

This small cute cafe provided the inspiration for the May Queen Nyan-nyan cafe in the *Steins;Gate* visual novel (i.e. interactive-fiction game), and is therefore a favorite destination for otaku pilgrims.. Even though it's a typical maid cafe, it has a diverse clientele (office workers, students, etc.) and it features "cosplay time" and other events (usually on Wednesday). You can't take pictures of the maids, but you can photograph the food on your table (ask the staff first). When the

AKIBA'S MAIDS ARE CONSTANTLY ON THE LOOKOUT FOR NEW CUSTOMERS.

place is particularly crowded, there's a 90-minute time limit. Otherwise you can stay as long as you want, but you have to place an order at least once every 90 minutes. They even sell maid-related good (e.g. cups, towels, etc.).

22 Cure Maid Café

Opening times *11:00–20:00 (Mon–Thu), 11:00–22:00 (Fri–Sat), 11:00–19:00 (Sun & holidays)*
curemaid.jp

The dean of maid cafes opened in 2001 and it's still going strong. Designed to resemble an old English mansion, with dark wooden furniture and lace curtains, it has a more relaxed and refined atmosphere and attracts more ladies than your typical local maid cafe. On Saturdays there are live classical music performances at dinner time. Their original organic tea is particularly recommended.

28 Heart of Hearts

Opening times *daily 11:30–23:00*
heart-of-hearts.jp

This school-themed cafe is famous for being the model for the maid cafe featured in the *Ultimate Otaku Teacher* manga series. Inside it looks like a classroom, with small desks and chairs, plus TV screens showing videos of the maids performing and a tiny stage area. You get the typical cute drawings on food and "magical" chants and gestures. Besides a 500-yen cover charge you have to order at least once every hour. Another 500 yen will get you a *cheki* (Polaroid picture) taken with a maid of your choice—which means you are not allowed to take pics yourself.

35 Maid Café Pinafore No.1

Opening times *11:00–22:00 (Mon–Thu & Sun), 11:00–5:00 (Fri–Sat)*
pinafore.jp/en

Otaku pilgrims will be happy to know that this cafe has been used as an on-set location for the movie *L: Change the World* AND two TV dramas: *Gokusen*

and the very popular *Densha Otoko*. Also, according to general consensus, the maids here genuinely seem to have fun while tending tables. 3,000 yen will get you one dish (e.g. omelet over ketchup-seasoned rice), one drink, and a maid photo, and are inclusive of cover charge. Be sure to check their website for the twice-a-month events and information on the other two Pinafore shops. **Labirinth**, in particular, is a more adult-oriented bar where you may have more chances to strike up a conversation with the maids across the counter.

36 Maidreamin Head Store

Opening times *11:30–23:00 (Mon–Fri), 10:30–23:00 (weekend & holidays)*
maidreamin.com/en

Another one of the maid cafe heavyweights, the sprawling Maidreamin empire has a whopping 12 stores in Tokyo, eight of which are concentrated in Akihabara. Their fee system is similar to rival @home café but they win extra points for having the only half-decent English homepage with details of each cafe, events, etc.

1 (Shisetsu Toshokan) Schatz Kiste

Opening times *12:00–22:00 (closed on the first Tue of the month)*
schatz-kiste.net

Quite different in many ways from your typical maid cafe, this place describes itself as a German tea house-cum-library. From the dark wooden tables and shelves (full of manga and books) to the maid outfits (long no-frills black dresses and white aprons) it exudes a certain reserved elegance. You are encouraged to sit at the two long tables that dominate the center of the room, engage other people in conversation on all things otaku, and maybe challenge them to a board game. Cover charge is 500 yen every 30 minutes but all-you-can-drink tea is included and you are not obliged to buy anything else. If you want to take photos of the place, ask a maid first. The maids themselves are verboten, sorry.

SPECIAL AKIHABARA EVENTS

Akiba Daisuki Festival

Twice a year Akiba celebrates all the things it's famous for (i.e. electronics and all things otaku) with a series of maid and idol live performances and other assorted events, including a cosplay get-together, a model train exhibition, and a gunplay-building workshop. And if at the end of the day you still have some energy left, you can even try their earthquake simulation vehicle.

Admission fee (*charges may apply to some activities*) **Dates** *Jan & Aug.* **Opening times** *11:00–18:00. Chiyoda-ku akiba-df.com*

AniCrush!!!

In the beginning there was Denpa!!!, a trailblazing event that in 2007 mixed anime and fashion with live music. Its effect on the people who attended was such that many of them were inspired to start similar projects. Today more than ever music and dance are an important part of otaku culture and AniCrush!!!'s stated goal is to introduce as many people as possible to so-called anikura (anime song club music). This event was created in 2013 by French-American expat Xavier Bensky following the International Akiba Pop Party J-Geek series of music events promoted by producer Saeki Kenzo. Since then the number of both artists and fans attending these afternoon parties has steadily grown, making it one of the more exciting events in the sometimes

reclusive anikura scene. An ever-changing lineup of guest DJs and VJs plus their regular crew of music spinners (among them idol Momochi Minami and kaxtupe of CharaAni fame) alternate anison, vocaloid, game music and J-pop tunes for the joy of both hardcore wotagei-dancing anikura fans and non-Japanese enthusiasts who make up about 20 percent of the attendees. The place where all the fun takes place is Akiba club MOGRA which, by the way, hosts a number of otaku-oriented DJ nights like Anison Matrix so you may want to check their website for upcoming events.

Admission fee *3,000 yen* **Dates** *once every 3 months (check schedule online)* **Opening times** *15:00–21:00. MOGRA, B1 3-11 Akihabara, Taito-ku. Tel. MOGRA 03-6206-8338* **How to get there** *MOGRA is a 5-minute walk from either Akihabara Station Central (Chuo) Exit (JR Yamanote and Sobu Lines) or Suehirocho Station (Tokyo Metro Ginza Line). In front of Akihabara Station you will see the Yodobashi Camera building. Go left and walk straight ahead, then take the narrow street on the right past the second traffic light. MOGRA is in the basement on the first left corner. anicrush.com (this is also a good place for information on the scene) anicrush.tumblr.com facebook.com/anicrushtokyo club-mogra.jp/*

Minami Momochi is one of the regular DJs at the AniCrush!!! events.

Mottainai Flea Market

Hardcore otaku-good hunters who are not satisfied with just prowling Akiba's shops or want to find the ultimate bargain may want to try the local flea market, part of the Mottainai recycling campaign that was inspired by Nobel Peace Prize recipient Wangari Maathai. The market takes place every month and has a lot more to offer than just toys and figures. For more information: *udx-akibaichi.jp/mottainai mottainai-fes.com*

Uchimizu

While coming to Tokyo in summer should be avoided because of the intense heat and high humidity, if you decide to come in August you will at least have a chance to see the traditional uchimizu water sprinkling routine done by scores of Akiba maids. Uchimizu is the local way to deal with the midsummer heat. People gather in the street armed with buckets. When the sprinkled water evaporates, it cools down the immediate area. Every year the Uchimizukko event takes place on a different day in August (around 10:30–11:00). Check out the Internet for details.

EXPLORING JIMBOCHO

In a neighborhood famous for its second-hand shops, Comic Takaoka prefers to focus on brand-new comic books, magazines and light novels.

TOKYO IS A CITY OF SPECIALIZED NEIGHBORHOODS, EACH ONE DEVOTED TO A PARTICULAR TRADE (MUSICAL INSTRUMENTS IN OCHANOMIZU, KITCHEN UTENSILS IN KAPPABASHI, TEXTILES IN NIPPORI, ETC). AND IF YOU ARE A SECOND-HAND, VINTAGE/RARE BOOK LOVER, YOU MUST ABSOLUTELY PAY A VISIT TO JIMBOCHO. ONCE THE HOME TO MANY SAMURAI, AT THE BEGINNING OF THE TWENTIETH CENTURY, A UNIVERSITY PROFESSOR NAMED IWANAMI SHIGEO OPENED A BOOKSTORE WHICH EVENTUALLY BECAME THE PRESTIGIOUS IWANAMI SHOTEN PUBLISHING HOUSE. OTHERS FOLLOWED HIS EXAMPLE, AND TODAY JIMBOCHO HAS ONE OF THE HIGHEST CONCENTRATIONS OF BOOK SELLERS AND PUBLISHERS IN THE WORLD, INCLUDING MAJOR MANGA COMPANIES SHUEISHA (FAMOUS FOR ITS *JUMP* MAGAZINE SERIES) AND SHOGAKUKAN. FANS OF URASAWA NAOKI'S *20TH CENTURY BOYS* (A COMIC THAT WAS ORIGINALLY PUBLISHED BY SHOGAKUKAN) WILL REMEMBER THAT THE COMPANY'S BUILDING WAS ACTUALLY FEATURED, AND DESTROYED, IN THOSE PAGES. THAT'S ONE OF THE MANY IN-JOKES THAT MANGA AND ANIME CREATORS LIKE TO SLIP INTO THEIR STORIES.

Even today the area has more than 150 bookstores ranging from big multi-story establishments selling new titles (Sanseido) to elegant antiquarian stores (Kitazawa Shoten) and tiny hole-in-the-wall sellers. Admittedly, for people who don't read Japanese it can be rather frustrating as the places that sell foreign-language books are very few. However, otaku fans looking for original materials will surely have fun exploring the shops listed below.

For the sake of our walk, instead of Jimbocho Station (Tokyo Metro Hanzomon Line and Toei Shinjuku Line) in the heart of the district, get off at Awajicho (Tokyo Metro Marunouchi Line). From exit A6 follow Yasukuni-dori keeping the wide avenue to your right. After five minutes you will see the **Shosen Bookmart** building with its huge manga billboards. The Shosen chain is famous for its wide selection of pop-culture publications and magazines, and this particular shop specializes in comics and light novels for gals. Lots of shojo and BL

manga, but also boys' comics and Teen Love stories too. They often have fairs and events like books signings. If you are into idols old and new and gravure-related goods, probably the best store in the neighborhood is in the street past the arch on the right of Shosen Bookmart (神田すずらん通り). Walk two blocks and you can't miss

IF YOU PLAN A VISIT TO KUDAN SHOBO AND KASUMI SHOBO, LOOK OUT FOR THESE SIGNS NEAR THE ENTRANCE OF AN OTHERWISE PLAIN BUILDING.

ARATAMA's read front on the right side. The first floor has DVDs, photo books (often of the naughty variety) and magazines, while the second floor has a huge stock of posters (a rare Morning Musume signed poster sells for 50,000 yen), calendars, trading cards, telephone cards, and even more magazines. Back on Yasukuni-dori, the first interesting shop we find is **Warhammer**—interesting, that is, if you are a fan of British manufacturer Games Workshop's miniature war games. Even if you aren't, it's nice to look at their detailed models of futuristic soldiers, creatures and military vehicles. Next stop is **Comic Takaoka,** which sells brand new comic books, magazines and light novels. The first floor sells manga for men, while the basement floor has works for women (including BL comics) besides reprinted classics

Jimbocho and the surrounding area is one of the few remaining places in Tokyo where you can find older buildings dating back to the Showa period.

BESIDES VINTAGE MANGA, NAKANO SHOTEN SELLS OTHER GOODS SUCH AS ANIME CELS.

by famous authors like Tezuka Osamu and Nagai Go. After crossing Jimbocho's main intersection (where Jimbocho Station is), we arrive at **Nakano Shoten** on the second floor of the Kanda Used Books Center (神田古本センター). If you only have time for one place, this is it. The most famous old-style vintage manga store in the district is a paradise for serious collectors. For instance, this is the store where you have the best chance to find Tezuka Osamu's first editions. *Lost World* and *Treasure Island* will likely be prized around 100,000 yen. On the other hand, they have old Garo and COM issues going for as cheap as 400–800 yen depending on their rarity and condition. They used to be the two best alternative comic anthologies in the late '60s-early '70s and are definitely worth your yen. This shop sells anime cels too and a lot more. Just a few meters down the street and we see **Bunken Rock Side**'s bright red front. Its specialty are music magazines but if you dig around you will find many idol and anime magazines as well. There are still two more shops to check out on this side of Yasukuni-dori: **Vintage** covers about the same genres as Bunken, while **@Wonder** is only worth a visit if you are into Western (mainly American superhero) comics.

Now go back to Warhammer. Cross the street where McDonald's is. Walk three blocks and turn right past Luncheon. Go straight past an ENEOS gas station. After 150 meters you will see the small くだん書房 sign near the entrance of a small derelict building on the right. That's **Kudan Shobo**. From comic books and magazines to dojinshi and kashihon (rental books), this tiny messy shop is all about girls manga and well worth a visit. **Kasumi Shobo** next door stocks an interesting mix of books and magazines on anime, tokusatsu, SF and music. On the way back to the station, don't miss the tiny sign at the entrance of the red-bricked building on the right, just a few meters from Kudan Shobo. The sign reads 古本・かんけ書房・2F and belongs to **Kanke Shobo**. Slightly bigger and much tidier than Kudan, This shop carries a small but interesting selection of boys and girls manga, old Garo and COM issues and other vintage delights.

JIMBOCHO HOT SPOTS

1 @Wonder @ワンダー
Opening times *11:00–19:00 (Mon–Sat), 11:00–18:00 (Sun & holidays)*
atwonder.blog111.fc2.com

2 ARATAMA
Opening times *11:00–20:00 (Mon–Sat), 11:00–19:00 (Sun) aratama.com*

3 Nakano Shoten Manga Store 中野書店漫画部
Opening times *10:00–18:30 (Mon–Sat), 11:00–17:30 (Sun & holidays). Closed on the first, third, and fifth Sun. nakano.jimbou.net*

4 Comic Takaoka コミック高岡
Opening times *11:00–21:00 (Mon–Fri), 11:00–19:30 (Sat), 12:00–18:30 (Sun & holidays) comic-takaoka.jp*

5 Kanke Shobo かんけ書房
Opening times *11:00–16:30 (Mon–Sat), 11:00–14:30 (Sun & holidays). Closed on the third Sun. homepage2.nifty.com/kanke*

6 Kasumi Shobo スミ書房
Opening times *13:00–18:00. Closed on Sun. ne.jp/asahi/kasumi/syobo*

6 Kudan Shobo くだん書房
Opening times *11:00–19:00 (Mon–Sat). Closed on Sun & holidays kudan.jp*

7 Shosen Bookmart Shosenブックマート
Opening times *10:30–20:30 (Mon–Sat), 10:30–19:00 (Sun & holidays) shosen.co.jp/mart*

8 Bunken Rock Side ブンケン・ロック・サイド
Opening times *10:30–19:30 (Mon–Sat), 11:00–19:00 (Sun & holidays) homepage2.nifty.com/bunken*

9 Vintage
Opening times *11:00–19:00 (Mon–Sat), 12:00–19:00 (Sun & holidays) jimboucho-vintage.jp*

10 Warhammer
Opening times *13:30–20:00 (Mon–Tue, Thu–Fri), 12:00–20:00 (Sat), 12:00–19:00 (Sun). Closed on Wed. games-workshop.com*

CHAPTER 2

HARAJUKU, AND SHIMO -

SHIBUYA KITAZAWA

Exploring Harajuku

Walking through youth fashion central these days, it's hard to believe that during the feudal period ninja were quartered here and even had their own shrine (Onden Jinja, 5-26-6 Jingumae), while the local farmers cleaned rice and milled flour at the local watermill on the Shibuya River. Today JR trains run under the Harajuku bridge instead of water, but the real action happens on the bridge itself, with tribes of lolitas (both cute and gothic), French maids and other assorted cosplayers vying for attention. If quirky, loud, cute fashion is your thing, then forget other Tokyo districts and quickly head here. The area east of Meiji-dori in particular (Jingumae 3- and 4-chome; the very same area the ninja had turned into a maze of narrow winding streets in order to make life hard to possible invaders) is now internationally known as Ura-Harajuku (Harajuku backstreets) and is full of small independent fashion shops.

THE EASIEST ACCESS TO HARAJUKU IS THROUGH ITS EVER-CROWDED JR STATION.

Takeshita-dori (TOP) is an unavoidable stop for Harajuku pilgrims, while doll lovers make a bee line for Volks Tenshi no Mado (NEXT PAGE).

On the other hand, more orthodox otaku treasure hunters may be a little disappointed as several shops and cafes have either moved to Akiba (e.g. Blister, Hello! Project) or Ikebukuro (Evangelion) while others have closed for good (Edelstein). But if toys and figures are what you are after, Harajuku is still worth a visit as the district has established itself as a serious toy collector's Mecca.

From Harajuku Station (JR Yamanote Line) cross the street keeping the Gap store to your left and enter the backstreet with the Gindaco shop on the corner. We soon arrive at **Johnny's Shop Harajuku**. While female idol heavyweights AKB48 and Hello! Project fight for prominence in Akihabara, boy idol kingpin Johnny Kitagawa has opened his official store in this quiet backstreet location. Here you will find countless photos and all the SMAP, Arashi and Tokio merchandise you have ever dreamed about. A few meters in the same direction and we discover one of those Tokyo oddities, a strange building in a Western neo-classical style. Welcome to **Volks Tenshi no Mado**, Tokyo's biggest Super Dollfie (SD) store. This is a sort of temple devoted to Volks' famous dolls and their owners. On the first floor there is an SD display corner while a dress and wig shop is on the second and the basement floor is a rental space where doll fans can organize parties, ceremonies and photo shoots. Follow the path on either side of the Volks showroom and go left when you reach Omotesando, the district main avenue. Cross the big intersection and see the multi-mirrored entrance to Tokyu Plaza Omotesando Harajuku. If you have landed at Haneda Airport but have missed its **Tokyo's Tokyo** gift shop, another one is inside here on the fifth floor. This store sells books and anime-inspired toys, clothes and accessories. You may walk out with a bag full of *Doraemon* mugs, *Sailor Moon* magic wands, *Cardcaptor Sakura* stickers, or even Studio Ghibli figures.

50

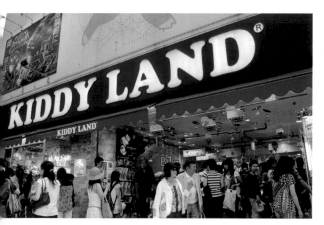

Harajuku Bridge (real name Gorin Bridge) is where cosplayers and other exotically-clothed youth gather in the weekend.

Now you have to decide what to do next: If you cross to the other side and go left you'll reach one of the district's most popular toy shops. When **Kiddy Land** opened, more than 60 years ago, it was the first big toy shop in Tokyo. While not particularly big by today's standards, its five floors are packed with toys, stationery, clothes and any kind of character goods. The first floor showcases what's currently trendy in Japan (e.g. over-the-top yuru-kyara Funasshi) while the second floor is a riot of kawaii character goods. Things gets even more interesting on the third floor with toys, figures and dolls for boys, girls and even adults, while on the top floor you'll find the Hello Kitty shop. In the Japanese site you can see a

Tokyo's oldest toy shop Kiddy Land still faces the beautiful Omotesando avenue.

complete floor guide (kiddyland.co.jp/ harajuku).

If you prefer to give Kiddy Land a pass for the time being, keep to the left side of Omotedando and turn left past the Seibu Bank. This narrow street takes you to **6%DOKIDOKI**. More than 20 years have passed since artist and designer Sebastian Masuda dropped its version of "kawaii anarchy" in the middle of the unsuspecting Harajuku crowd. Many things have changed since then (most notably Masuda's collaboration with Kyary Pamyu Pamyu) but his pink and yellow (!!!) boutique is still the go-to place to find outrageously cute clothes and accessories.

Keep walking in the same direction past the Barbie store and go right when you reach the end of the street, then take the second left. The white building enveloped in black steel pipes that you see after about 100 meters is the **Design Festa Gallery**. Like **Design Festa** itself, this is not an otaku-only venue, but among its 21 show rooms and 50 individual display sections, you will surely find some amazing art

including manga- or anime-inspired works. Plus it's free.

The street now bends to the left. When you reach the end, the building you see in front of you is **Secret Base**'s new address. This is a paradise for indie sofubi lovers, and even sells posters, original T-shirts and other gadgets. And if this is not enough, there is another Secret Base not far from here (B1F 3-22-8 Jingumae). When you are finished getting drunk on PVC figures, go back on the street and turn right. When you reach the main street (Meiji-dori), you have arrived at the **Moshi Moshi Box**. Strategically located at the junction between Takeshita-dori and Meiji-dori, this colorful place mainly works as a tourist information office (you can even use their PCs and charge your smart phone for free; exchange your money; and ship things home via FedEx) but they have a neat souvenir shop too, in case you want to pick up some kawaii Harajuku goods.

Now cross the street. We are almost at the end of our walk, but in order to reach our last destination you will have to get through Takeshita Street (the entrance is on the left of the traffic light) and, if it's a weekend, brave the hordes of tourists and local youth. When you finally reach the exit, turn right and find the **Tamagotchi Department Store**. When Bandai released the handheld digital pet in 1996, it became an instant success. Though the Tamagotchi craze of the 1990s is long gone, it's still a very popular pastime, and its new app has already garnered millions of downloads. This TamaDepa resembles the one featured in the anime series. Here you can buy tons of goods (dolls, toys, accessories, etc.) and even its character-shaped donuts. This is the main store, while a smaller branch is located in Tokyo Character Street inside Tokyo Station.

HARAJUKU ACCORDING TO CHOCOMOO

EVERY TIME CHOCOMOO VISITS HARAJUKU FROM HER NATIVE KYOTO, SHE PAYS A VISIT TO HER FAVORITE SHOPS, SPIRAL (**TOP RIGHT**).

Chocomoo one of the new rising stars of Harajuku's youth culture. The Kyoto-born artist has already turned 31 but she still looks 23—the same age when she turned her lifelong passion for drawing into a career. Inspired by Jean-Michel Basquiat and Andy Warhol on one side and traditional calligraphy and wood-block prints on the other, her streetwise punk sensibility first raised the interest of Japanese pop singer AI, who asked her to design some goods for her next tour. Since then she has collaborated with such brands as Milkfed, Override, Ravijour, and has designed tour goods for "Japan's Lady Gaga," Kyary Pamyu Pamyu.

On a sunny warm June afternoon, Chocomoo takes me on a tour of her favorite spots in the neighborhood. Our first destination is **Laforet Harajuku**. Opened in 1978, this historical place has contributed more than any other store to shift the center of Japanese youth fashion from Shinjuku to Harajuku. Our visit is perfectly timed as on the third floor we can admire Chocomoo's latest and biggest collaboration yet: a new collection for

influential LA-based brand **Joyrich**. Back on Meiji-dori, Chocomoo points out the Gallerie shop on the corner. That's where Spinns 02 Harajuku stood until recently. Chocomoo had illustrated both its front and interior, but both the shop and the murals are gone now. Spinns' original location just down Meiji-dori (B1F 6-5-3 Jingumae, Shibuya-ku) opened in 2010 and has fast become one of the favorite brands of the hip Harajuku crowd. Branch #2 may have closed but there are three more branches left in the area. So we dive into the first backstreet between Gallerie and a crepe shop. After about 40 meters the road bends to the left but we take the narrow pedestrian street on the right instead and follow the long winding path to the very end where we see the brand-new **Spinns 2.5** store. The "2.5 fashion" sold here presents an exciting mix of street culture, anime characters and other otaku themes. As Chocomoo points out, compared to other countries where one fad usually follows another, in Japan you can see several different trends and styles at the same time, and people are not afraid to experiment and freely mix them all together.

Going down the slope we reach the ever-crowded Takeshita-dori, turn right and go past yet another Spinns. We cross

Meiji-dori, take the street to the right of the **Moshi Moshi Box** (see page 51) and enter so-called Ura-Harajuku, the area where most street fashion is made and sold. This is a relatively quieter area where the boutiques share space with small shops, cafes and residential buildings. At the end of the street we pass under the Harajuku Arch and take the first right. Our next destination is **Mishka Tokyo**, the sister store of Mishka New York. Mishka is a small but stylish store packed with hats, T-shirts and jackets as well as the designer's toys collection. The shop is worth visiting for the interior decorations alone. The designer is a good friend of Chocomoo and they share a love for weird toys. She often goes to flea markets, and even when she returns from her travels abroad her suitcase is always full of toys. By the way, there's a great toy store in front of Mishka. So we head to **Spiral**. According to some people, this little shop may be the mother of Tokyo's toy stores for girls. Whatever the case, don't be fooled by its diminutive size. It's a treasure trove of kawaii goods, and all the available space is taken by toys and anime-inspired figures. They have a lot of vintage dolls and American collectibles like Doughboy, Popples, Smurf, Troll, etc.

THE NOW-CLOSED FASHION STORE SPINNS 02 FEATURED CHOCOMOO'S DISTINCTIVE ART.

Harajuku

200 m
1000 ft

N

Jingumae 1

Jingumae 3

Jingumae 4

Jingumae 5

Jingumae 6

Harajuku

Takeshita-dori

Takeshita-dori Shopping Street

Ota Museum of Ukiyo-e Prints

Watari-Um Museum

Meiji-jingumae

★ Harajuku Shopping District

Omotesando-dori

OMOTESANDO CROSSING

Galen-nishi-dori

Omotes...

HARAJUKU EATERIES

5 Kawaii Monster Café
Opening times *daily 11:30–22:30.*
kawaiimonster.jp
Art Director Sebastian Masuda of 6%DOKIDOKI fame has come up with yet another outrageous idea to further expand his own peculiar kawaii agenda. This somewhat twisted version of Alice in Wonderland is divided in four different zones and is patrolled by five Monster Girls. Primary colors abound everywhere including the rather expensive food. There's a 500-yen charge per person if you don't fill all the seats in your booth or table, and a 90-minute time limit.

HARAJUKU HOT SPOTS

1 6%DOKIDOKI
Opening times *daily 12:00–20:00*
dokidoki6.com

2 Design Festa Gallery
Opening times *daily 11:00–20:00*
designfestagallery.com/index_en.html

3 Johnny's Shop Harajuku
Opening times *daily 10:00–19:00*
johnnys-net.jp

4 Joyrich c/o Laforet Harajuku
Opening times *daily 11:00–20:00*
joyrich.com

6 Kiddy Land
Opening times *11:00–21:00 (Mon–Fri),*
10:30–21:00 (Sat–Sun & holidays).
Closed irregularly
kiddyland.co.jp/en/index.html

7 Mishka Tokyo
mishka-tokyo.com

8 Moshi Moshi Box
Opening times *daily 10:00–18:00*
moshimoshi-nippon.jp/box

9 Secret Base
Opening times *daily 11:00–19:00*
secret-b.com

10 2.5 Spinns
Opening times *daily 12:00–19:00*
25spinns.amebaownd.com

11 Spiral おもちゃや *Spiral*
Opening times *12:00–20:00*
spiral-toy.com

12 Tamagotchi Department Store
Opening times *11:00–19:00 (Mon–Fri),*
10:00–19:00 (Sat–Sun & holidays)
tamagotch.channel.or.jp/tamadepa

13 Tokyo's Tokyo
Opening times *daily 11:00–21:00*
omohara.tokyu-plaza.com/en

14 Volks Tenshi no Mado
天使の窓
Opening times
11:00–20:00
Closed on Wed and the third Tue.
volks.co.jp/jp/tenshinomado

STREET FASHION AND TOYS SHARE SPACE AT MISHKA TOKYO.

EXPLORING SHIBUYA

THOUGH SHIBUYA WARD IS NOT PARTICULARLY FAMOUS AS AN OTAKU SPOT, IT ACTUALLY HAS A LOT TO OFFER TO TREASURE HUNTERS AND URBAN EXPLORERS ALIKE. MANY THINGS HAVE HAPPENED SINCE THE 17TH CENTURY, WHEN THE DISTRICT WAS A STRATEGICALLY IMPORTANT CASTLE TOWN TASKED WITH THE DEFENSE OF EDO. ITS COMPLETE DESTRUCTION BY US AIR RAIDS DURING WWII WAS THE STARTING POINT FOR RAPID DEVELOPMENT BY THE TOKYU CORPORATION THAT TURNED ITS STATION INTO ONE OF TOKYO'S MAIN TRANSPORTATION NODES.

AT SHIBUYA 109 YOU CAN GET SOME FANCY HELLO KITTY NAILS.

Even today, in order to access Otaku Shibuya you only need to step out of JR Station's Hachiko Exit. The area in front of the station, including its world-famous scramble crossing has been featured in countless stories, probably starting with 1985 OVA *Megazone*. More recently the district has been featured in the *Ghost in the Shell: Stand Alone Complex* series, episodes of *Tokyo ESP* and *Sengoku Collection* and most importantly in the visual novel *Chaos;Head*. On the other side of the scramble, another anime regular is the Q-front building. A visit to the big **Tsutaya** store inside will give you a good idea of what manga are currently hot in Japan as they prominently display all the new popular titles, while from the ever-busy Starbucks you can enjoy the same view of the crossing that was used in the Sophia Coppola movie *Lost in Translation*.

WIth kaiju, Shibuya has been a late addition. But Godzilla and company have wasted no time in giving the neighborhood the royal treatment, beginning with *Gamera 3: The Revenge of Iris* (1999), when our favorite giant flying turtle disposed of a couple of Gyaos but only after destroying Shibuya Station, the Hachiko statue and Shibuya 109, and killing in the process twenty thousand people. Then one year later, in *Godzilla vs. Megaguirus*, the district is literally flooded during the fierce battle between the Big G and its foe.

Speaking of **Shibuya 109**, the iconic tube-shaped fashion mall on the left of the station was completed in 1979 and is the single major reason why the

HACHIKO (**ABOVE**) AND THE SCRAMBLE CROSSING (**LEFT**) ARE TWO OF SHIBUYA'S BETTER KNOWN LANDMARKS.

district has become a major trend setter. With 120 boutiques distributed on ten floors, this is a temple to the kind of flashy, colorful clothes, shoes and accessories which are popular with teen girls. Even many anime characters can't resist the desire to pay it a visit, as it happens in episodes of *The Idolmaster* and *Oreimo*. However, apart from the tiny **sanrio vivitix SHIBUYA** on the eighth floor selling Hello Kitty goods, there is precious little to be found in terms of otaku fashion.

From the Hachiko Exit cross the scramble crossing and take the street on the right of Tsutaya. On the right side of the street you will see a building with an OIOI symbol. That's **Marui**. Though this department store is mainly devoted to men's and ladies' fashion, its top two floors feature a few otaku shops worth your attention. Most people of course come here for the **One Piece Mugiwara Store** on the seventh floor (mugi-wara-store.com). The Guinness World of Records recognized Oda Eiichiro's mega hit manga as the

ABOVE A LIFE-SIZE STATUE OF LUFFY WELCOMES YOU TO THE ONE PIECE MUGIWARA STORE.

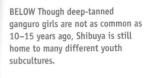

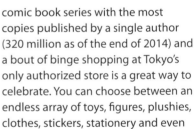

BELOW Though deep-tanned ganguro girls are not as common as 10–15 years ago, Shibuya is still home to many different youth subcultures.

comic book series with the most copies published by a single author (320 million as of the end of 2014) and a bout of binge shopping at Tokyo's only authorized store is a great way to celebrate. You can choose between an endless array of toys, figures, plushies, clothes, stickers, stationery and even character-shaped snacks and chocolates. Next to One Piece we find a **Namco CharaPop Store** (Namco キャラポップストア) (namco.co.jp/chara_shop) and the **I.G Store** (ig-store.jp/about/english). **CharaPop** mixes anime- and game-themed original goods (T-shirts, stickers, postcards, etc.) with lotteries and other game attractions. I.G Store is Production I.G's official shop and sells merchandise from the anime studio's famous works (*Kuroko's Basketball*, *Haikyu!!*, *Psycho-Pass*, the *Ghost in the Shell* franchise, the *Joker Game* series, etc.) including some special exclusives.

RIGHT ABOVE The brand-new production IG Store inside Marui features an impressive model of the Logicoma from *Ghost in the Shell: Arise*.
RIGHT Like the One Piece shop, even Namco CharaPop Store has moved to Marui department store.

GALAXXXY INTERNATIONAL IS ARGUABLY THE COOLEST SHIBUYA BOUTIQUE FOR OTAKU-INSPIRED FASHION.

They also have an exhibition space where they show a few impressive items, such as a model of the Logicoma from *Ghost in the Shell: Arise*. The eighth floor features a few event spaces (often devoted to anime and manga characters) and **The Chara Shop** (**THE キャラ SHOP**), a sort of collaboration store selling limited-time merchandise inspired by newly released anime and video games.

Now cross the street at the traffic light just in front of Marui and keep to the left of the uphill road (Koen-dori) walking past the curiously-shaped Disney Store. If you are a fan of the iconic clothing brand A Bathing Ape, turn left just before Parco: you will find a **BAPE** store on the left. Instead we keep climbing Koen-dori and turn left at the intersection. The megastore on the corner at the end of the slope is **Tokyu Hands**. DIY-inclined otaku (cosplayers, manga artists, etc.) should check out this amazing "creative life department store," because they literally have everything—and even many things you didn't even suspect existed. Anything connected with paper, leather, wood, textiles, etc. can be found here. They sell toys too. There are six more branches in central Tokyo alone but this nine-story building is their home base.

Turn left at the Tokyu Hands corner and the second block on the right is the BEAM Bldg, another hotbed of otaku activity. Here you will find the most atmospheric of Tokyo's three **Mandarake** stores—at the bottom of two dark flights of stairs. The slightly sinister atmosphere is broken by some loud anime music coming out of the PA system. With its meandering corridors and dim lights, this place can be rather confusing but you'll have a lot of fun checking out all the goods. This place is particularly famous for its huge stock of used manga and dojinshi of any kind. They even have a small stage where the cosplaying female staff take turns singing. Apparently you can do the same as long as you spend at least 1,000 yen. When you are finished here, don't forget to explore the rest of the building that, apart from Mandarake, houses an **Animate** store on the third floor, a **RECOfan** branch on the fourth selling thousands of new and used CDs (including lots of anime soundtracks), and a stylish manga cafe on the fifth.

Back in the street, go right toward the station and when you reach the futuristic-looking police box, take the street on the right with a Family Mart on the corner. The next small intersection has a **Club Sega** (**4** see map on page 58) on the left and another Village Vanguard on the right. The Village

Vanguard Shibuya Udagawa Store is the biggest branch of this funky chain. Here, among other things, you can find Shibuya Girls Pop's sexy kawaii fashion and accessories. On your right there is a very good **Book Off** branch (**2** see map on page 58) branch with lots of cheap second-hand manga, DVDs, CDs and video games. However we are going straight instead. Turn right when you reach the main street with a Citibank in front of you. When you reach the traffic light with a big **Don Quijote** on the left, you have two options: if you turn left you'll reach the **galaxxxy International Store**. galaxxxy is the proof that "otaku" and "cool" are not mutually exclusive concepts.

Besides its popular DINO character, the Shibuya-based fashion brand excels in design collaborations with an ever expanding lineup of popular titles like Hello Kitty, Dirty Pair, Creamy Mami, Inferno Cop, Papillon Rose and manga artist Azuma Hideo. Anyone who has ever dreamed of owning a Dreamcast controller-shaped backpack will definitely have to pay a visit to its stylish boutique. If you go right instead, take the narrow street past the Tokyu department store and after about 200 meters you'll see **Project 1/6** on the right. This is Medicom's original flagship store (a second one can be found on the fourth floor of Tokyo Solamachi). Medicom is deservedly famous among toy and figure lovers for its ever-expanding Kubrick and Be@rbrick collector series, and most people come here to drool over their weirdly cute original designs. But there's a lot more, including other character-based toys (Doraemon, Peanuts, Pixar, Disney, Evangelion, Hello Kitty), each one showcased in its beautiful museum-like display.

THE PRINCE OF TENNIS AND 2.5-D MUSICALS

For centuries the Japanese have been enthusiastic theatergoers, equally enjoying kabuki and noh, modern theater, and the only-in-Japan all-female Takarazuka troupe. Musical is another extremely popular genre, with major productions regularly selling out and enjoying long runs. This doesn't really come as a surprise because many of the above-mentioned genres mix drama and music to great effect. What is rather surprising, though, is the clever way in which manga, anime and video game story lines are being adapted to the musical form, creating a new kind of entertainment that is uniquely Japanese. Called 2.5-D musicals, these productions have successfully mixed 3-D stage acting and 2-D illustration-like gimmicks.

The originator and by far the most popular of these works is *The Prince of Tennis Musical*, a stage adaptation of Konomi Takeshi's hit manga of the same title. After a slow start in 2003, *Tenimyu* (short for Tennis Musical), as it is affectionately called by local fans, has proved increasingly popular, particularly among girls who make up most of the audience at every sold-out performance. Though the manga ended its run in 2008, the stage version (composed of 22 different musicals) has lasted until 2010,

requiring in the process double casting of characters and live streaming in multiple theaters in order to satisfy the growing demand. It was followed by a second series in 2011–2014, while a third one premiered in 2015.

The story of a teenage boy who first fights his way into his junior high school's prestigious tennis club and then leads his team to the national title would seem an odd choice for a musical, but it has proved the right mix of drama, quirky humor, songs, and dance numbers.

At the heart of each performance are the choreographed tennis scenes where the actors (a parade of cool *ikemen* i.e. handsome boys, hence the franchise's popularity with girls) jump around the almost empty stage while hitting an imaginary ball. Then they suddenly stop to create surreal and highly dramatic freeze-frame effects, turning the frantic on-stage action into a manga-like tableau. It is this mixture of 3-D performance and 2-D sensibility that makes these 2.5-D musicals so engaging. Of course this being a musical, each scene is accompanied by over-the-top tunes and exciting songs that are later collected in high-selling CDs (you will likely find them in many Otome Road shops in Ikebukuro).

This novel formula has proved so successful (*Tenimyu* has sold more than two million tickets so far) that the ad-hoc created Japan 2.5-Dimensional Musical Association has since come up with a seemingly endless stream of new productions, adapting to the stage such otaku heavyweights as *Sailor Moon*, *Naruto*, *Haikyu!!*, *Sengoku Basara* and *Death Note*. Many of them are staged at the brand-new AiiA 2.5 Theater Tokyo located near Yoyogi National Stadium between Shibuya and Harajuku. One of the place's best features for people who don't understand Japanese is its subtitle system which displays English, French, Chinese and Korean subtitles on an eyeglass device.

AiiA 2.5 Theater Tokyo
2-1-1 Jinnan, Shibuya-ku
aiia-theater.com
Prince of Tennis Musical
tennimu.com
2.5-D musical lineup
j25musical.jp

SHIBUYA NIGHTLIFE

Nerv:Shibuya (Joysound Shibuya)

9 **Opening times** *daily 11:00–6:00*

shop.joysound.com/eva/ nerv-shibuya/

Like its sister location in Nakano, this karaoke box features two Eva Special Rooms (#901 and #902) with an Evangelion-themed décor.

MANDARAKE'S SHIBUYA UNDERGROUND STORE AMAZES VISITORS WITH AN EYE-CATCHING ENTRANCE AND MANGA-PAINTED STAIRS.

SHIBUYA SHOPS

7 BEAM Shibuya
shibuya-beam.com

5 galaxxxy International Store
Opening times *daily 13:00–21:00*
galaxxxyrocks.com (English)

7 Mandarake Shibuya
Opening times *daily 12:00–20:00*
mandarake.co.jp/en/shop/sby.html

8 Marui department store
Opening times *daily 11:00-21:00 (until 20:30 during national holidays)*
0101.co.jp/013

10 Project 1/6
Opening times *daily 11:00–20:00*
medicomtoy.co.jp/official_shop/more.php

12 Tokyu Hands
Opening times *daily 10:00–20:30*
shibuya.tokyu-hands.co.jp/en/index.html (English)

13 Village Vanguard Shibuya Udagawa Store
Opening times *daily 10:00–24:00*
village-v.co.jp

SHIBUYA EATERIES

1 Alcatraz E.R

2F 2-13-5 Dogenzaka, Shibuya-ku
Opening times *17:00–23:30 (Mon–Thu & Sun), 17:00–4:00 (Fri & Sat)*
alcatraz-er.net

Fans of horror anime and games will have a ball at this "medical prison" (one of the oldest theme restaurants in Tokyo) where they will be hand-cuffed and locked in a cell by the cute and naughty nurses (they will even slap you in the face—on request). If you have ever dreamed of tasting penis- or bowel-shaped sausages, blue curry in a kidney dish or brain juice while sipping cocktails served in syringes and test tubes in a raucous atmosphere, this is the place for you.

11 The Lockup

B2F 33-1 Udagawa-cho, Shibuya-ku
Opening times *17:00–1:00 (Mon–Thu), 17:00–4:00 (Fri), 16:00–4:00 (Sat), 16:00–1:00 (Sun & holidays)*
lock-up.jp

Quite similar to Alcatraz (see above) in setting, atmosphere and menu (typical Japanese pub food), your dinner will be interrupted by blackouts and staged jailbreaks, with weirdly masked prisoners visiting your cell. Shibuya is probably the most popular location but there are similar branches in Shinjuku, Ikebukuro and Ueno (see website for details).

MAID AND BUTLER CAFES

6 Maidreamin Digitized

B1F 30-1 Udagawacho, Shibuya-ku
Opening times *15:00–23:00 (Mon–Thu), 15:00–5:00 (Fri), 11:00–5:00 (Sat), 11:00–23:00 (Sun & holidays).*
maidreamin.com/shop/shibuya_denno

Born out of collaboration with the teamLab multimedia studio, and arguably the most stylish of the many Maidreaming cafes around Tokyo, this store features digitized walls and lights that change color and emit sounds according to the way people move around. The obligatory mini stage is in the middle of the room, and there's even a small trampoline that emits noises whenever the maids jump on it.

3 Butlers Café

5F 11-6 Udagawacho, Shibuya-ku
Opening times *12:00–16:30, 18:00–23:00 (Tue–Fri), 12:00–23:00 (Sat), 12:00–21:00 (holidays). Closed on Mon.*
butlerscafe.com

If Japanese women see butler cafes as romantic places, for many of them the ultimate fairy-tale experience is to be waited on by a handsome foreign guy. And this is what you get here. The local ladies are treated like princesses and encouraged to speak in English. Maybe not very exciting if you are a foreigner yourself, but on the upside you won't have problems placing your orders (a minimum of two during your two-hour stay). Plus there's no table charge. Reservation required. WARNING: A few foreign ladies have posted less than stellar reviews of this place. You may want to check them out before going.

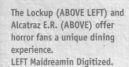

The Lockup (ABOVE LEFT) and Alcatraz E.R. (ABOVE) offer horror fans a unique dining experience.
LEFT Maidreamin Digitized.

FUNKY SHIMO-KITAZAWA

WHILE TECHNICALLY LOCATED IN SETAGAYA WARD, THIS LAIDBACK BOHEMIAN DISTRICT IS JUST A THREE-MINUTE TRAIN RIDE FROM SHIBUYA AND ABSOLUTELY WORTH A DETOUR. THIS NEIGHBORHOOD, AFTER ALL, IS REGULARLY VOTED BY LOCAL YOUTH AS ONE OF THE TOP-THREE PLACES WHERE THEY WOULD LIKE TO LIVE IN TOKYO. THIS IS THE PLACE, BY THE WAY, WHERE ALL THE CHARACTERS IN THE *SOMEDAY'S DREAMERS* MANGA ANIME SERIES LIVE. SHIMO-KITAZAWA IS SOMEWHAT SIMILAR TO URA-HARAJUKU BECAUSE MANY OF THE STREETS SURROUNDING THE STATION ARE SO NARROW ONLY PEDESTRIANS ARE ALLOWED. BUT WHILE HARAJUKU IS AN ATTENTION-GRABBING WORLD STAGE WHERE PEOPLE GO TO SEE AND BE SEEN, SHIMO-KITAZAWA BELONGS TO AN OLDER COUNTER-CULTURAL ERA WHEN STUDENTS AND INTELLECTUALS WERE MORE INTERESTED IN STAGE THEATER AND LIVE MUSIC. EVEN TODAY THE AREA IS FAMOUS FOR ITS MONTH-LONG THEATER FESTIVAL, HELD IN FEBRUARY AT THE HISTORIC HONDA GEKIJO AND SEVEN OTHER SMALL VENUES JUST A FEW MINUTES FROM THE STATION. INDIE MUSIC IS STILL BIG TOO, AS CAN BE SEEN BY THE MANY LIVE HOUSES (SMALL CONCERT HALLS) AND SECOND-HAND RECORD SHOPS DOTTING THE AREA. AND IF YOU HAPPEN TO VISIT IN JULY, YOU WILL BE ABLE TO ENJOY THE LOCAL MUSIC FESTIVAL, WITH MOST OF THE ACTION HAPPENING IN THE STREETS. BUT EVEN IF YOU ARE NOT INTO STAGE PERFORMANCE, LIVE MUSIC OR SMOKY CAFES, THIS IS DEFINITELY A NEIGHBORHOOD WORTH CHECKING OUT. THRIFT AND VINTAGE CLOTHES STORES ARE OTHER FAMOUS FEATURES IN THE NEIGHBORHOOD, AND AMONG THEM YOU WILL FIND A FEW OTAKU-FRIENDLY PLACES SELLING NEW AND OLD MANGA, TOYS, FIGURES AND CHARACTER GOODS.

WELCOME TO TOKYO'S BOHEMIAN DISTRICT, WHERE FUNKY BUILDINGS ABOUND AND EVERYBODY SEEMS TO CHILL OUT.

Finding your way around Shimo-Kitaza-wa can be rather tricky, especially when you visit for the first time, as the place is a maze of narrow winding streets. But that's part of the fun. After leaving the station at the North Exit (北口), we go left. At the end of this street, on the left corner, we find **Swing Toys**. Strictly speaking this shop doesn't belong in this guide as we only cover made-in-Japan products, but if you are into Marvel, South Park, Disney, Gremlins, etc., you may want to check it out. Here you will find Star Wars and Simpsons tote bags, Batman candy trays, Minion cushions and glassware sets, troll dolls, and lots of Toy Story items. Turn right at the T-junction, away from the station. This is a typical Shimo-Kita neighbor-hood with several cafes and vintage clothes shops on both sides of the

BELOW THE SUZUNARI IS ONE OF SHIMO-KITA'S MANY SMALL INDEPENDENT THEATERS.

streets. Walk straight for 10 minutes. When you reach an intersection with a Lawson on the right corner, turn left. Look for a nondescript gray building on the left side of the street with the sign コミケットサービス on the second floor. That's **Comiket Service**. It's true there are a number of shops where you can buy the dojin goods sold at the biannual Comic Market, but if you want to go to the source, this is it. This place is very small and looks even smaller because of all the boxes jammed in the aisles between the shelves. Still, they stock 200,000 items (mainly second-hand dojinshi) including indie anime, games, novels and much more. The shop is sometimes closed irregularly so you may want to check their website or call in advance.

Among other things, Shimo-Kita is famous for its countless vintage and used cloths shops.

Keep walking about 150 meters in the same direction and just before you reach the intersection with the big arch you can see a small shop on the right whose door sports the word 悪童処 written in big yellow characters. That's **Warugaki Salon**, arguably one of the weirdest, funkiest shops in Shimo-Kita. If you can read Japanese, you will find the place's description on the door which says *mayonaka no dagashiya* i.e. "late

night *dagashi* shop". Dagashi of course are cheap old-style sweets and junk food (they are often featured in older manga and such anime as *Chibi Maruko-chan* and *Sazae-san*) and the "late-night" bit means that the shop

does not open until the sun goes down. So if you happen to visit the neighborhood earlier in the day, you can save yourself the long track from the station. On the other hand, if you are a nighthawk, this shop definitely

COOL CAFES **(LEFT)** AND UNUSUAL OTAKU GOODS **(ABOVE)** ARE TWO OF THE AREA'S MAIN ATTRACTIONS.

TOY LOVERS CAN FIND BOTH FOREIGN DOLLS AND FIGURES
AND MADE-IN-JAPAN GOODS.

Our next destination is located south of the railway. Cross the tracks, walk under the arch and go straight. You will see the **Village Vanguard** red neon sign on the right. **VV** calls itself an "exciting book store," but this chain actually sells a lot more, from otaku goods (toys, character T-shirts, anime, etc.) to wigs, clocks and junk food. Their stock is so random you can find Gothic paraphernalia sharing space with lava lamps. There are about 30 **VV** branches in Tokyo alone (each one with a slightly different stock and atmosphere) but the one in Shimo-Kitazawa is particularly recommended, with a larger-than-average collection of new and vintage manga that runs the gamut from a boxed set of Miyazaki Hayao's *Nausicaa of the Valley of the Wind* to several books by comic maverick author Maruo Suehiro. In the same neighborhood there's also a **VV Diner** (6-3-1 Daita).

deserves a visit as it sells old-fashioned toys as well (dolls, playing cards, badges, stickers, tabletop games, etc.), starting with a wide selection of Doraemon figures and dolls. The owner, Higashikujo-san, is a natural-born storyteller and horse-racing expert, and if you speak Japanese you may find yourself spending the night listening to his tall stories.

Next we retrace our steps, go past Lawson, and take the third street on the right. After passing Mos Burger, there's a shop called Zappas on the right. **Natsukashiya** is on the second floor. This place literally smells of old. In business since 1981, its name means "nostalgic shop" and all its cabinets and shelves are packed with toys and other cultural detritus from the past. Most of the space is taken by old tin and plastic toys, mainly from the '50s and '60s (including a fair share of monsters and dolls like Pekochan) but there's a lot more, and you will be endlessly fascinated by its eclectic collection of posters, magazines, clocks and funky ashtrays.

Shimo-Kitazawa

SHIMO-KITAZAWA SHOPS

1 **Comiket Service**
コミケットサービス
Opening times *13:00–20:00. Closed on Mon. and irregular days*
comiketservice.com

2 **Dorama**
Opening times *daily 10:00–1:00*
dorama.co.jp/store.shtml

3 **Natsukashiya** 懐かし屋
Opening times *14:00–19:00. Closed on Tue.*
shimokita1ban.juno.bindsite.jp/shop/1/natsukashiya.html

4 **Omu-rice** オムライス
Opening times *12:00–19:00. Closed on Tue.*

6 **Sunny**
Opening times *11:00–21:00 (Mon–Tue, Thu–Sat), 11:00–20:00 (Sun & holidays). Closed on Wed.*
hobbyshop-sunny.co.jp

7 **Swing Toys**
Opening times *daily 11:00–21:00*
swing-toys.tumblr.com

8 **Village Vanguard**
Opening times *daily 10:00–24:00*
village-v.co.jp

9 **Warugaki Salon** 悪童処
Opening times *daily 18:00–5:00*
blog.livedoor.jp/dagasiya63

Keep going in the same direction and take the first right. Pass under the other train line and walk straight ahead until you see a couple of **Dorama** shops on your right. This chain of used video games, trading cards, CDs and DVDs has several branches in Shimo-Kita. Two of them are specialized in secondhand books, magazines, and comics, and three more are game arcades full of *UFO Catcher* (check the website for details). In the first backstreet on the right past Dorama, you'll find **Sunny**. From the outside this two-story shop looks very small but inside it's packed from floor to ceiling with toys. The first floor is mainly about model kits (tanks, planes, etc.) while the second floor has lots of figures and other toys (both foreign and Japanese products like new Bandai releases), all neatly packaged in their boxes.

Now back to the Dorama street, turn right and follow that road as it winds through the neighborhood until you reach a fork. Go left, then right at the Youkaen flower shop. 20 more meters and you'll reach **Omu-rice**, our last destination. In business since 1988, for some reason (maybe because it's a little off the beaten track?) this vintage toy store is less known than Natsukashiya, but it has a lot (I mean a lot) more stuff for sale. There is a little bit of everything, and its prices are quite good.

SHIMO-KITAZAWA EATERIES

Shiro-hige's Cream Puff Factory (Shimo-Kitazawa)
5 **Opening times** *10:30–19:00. Closed on Tue (the day after if Tues is a holiday)*
shiro-hige.com

Only one station away from indie culture Mecca Shimo-Kitazawa, there is this little-known but not-to-be-missed Ghibli-themed bakery. Their Totoro-shaped cream puffs are not only delicious; they are so cute most people hesitate a few seconds before sinking their teeth into their crunchy heads. Regular choux are filled with custard cream or chocolate while other fillings (strawberry, peach, green tea, etc.) are only available in certain periods (check the website for details). They sell Totoro-, leaf-, acorn- and mushroom-shaped cookies too. The same food can be also enjoyed at the Tolo Café on the second floor. Last but not least, the whole building is decorated with Ghibli artifacts and drawings (maybe authored by Miyazaki Hayao himself?).

CHAPTER 3

SHINJUKU,
AND WEST

NAKANO TOKYO

EXPLORING SHINJUKU

SHINJUKU DOESN'T ENJOY NAKANO'S PEDIGREE AND FEW PEOPLE WOULD DARE TO PUT IT ON THE SAME LEVEL WITH TOKYO'S MAIN OTAKU CENTERS. TO BE SURE, THIS BUSTLING DISTRICT IS MORE FAMOUS AS A BUSINESS AND ENTERTAINMENT CENTER THAN FOR ANY MANGA- OR ANIME-RELATED CONNECTIONS. IN REALITY SHINJUKU HAS A LOT TO OFFER TO OTAKU HUNTERS AND FUN SEEKERS ALIKE. ON ONE SIDE, IN THE LAST FEW YEARS SEVERAL SHOPS HAVE OPENED IN THE AREA EAST OF THE STATION, AND THOUGH THEIR NUMBER IS STILL FAR SMALLER THAN AKIHABARA OR IKEBUKURO, THERE ARE ENOUGH INTERESTING PLACES TO KEEP YOU BUSY FOR A WHOLE DAY. HOWEVER, WHAT REALLY SETS THE PLACE APART FROM THE COMPETITION IS THE SHEER NUMBER OF OTAKU BARS AND CAFES. FOR MANY YEARS NOW THE KABUKICHO DISTRICT ON THE OTHER SIDE OF YASUKUNI-DORI HAS BEEN SYNONYMOUS WITH NIGHTLIFE, AND IT IS HERE THAT YOU WILL FIND A SURPRISINGLY HIGH NUMBER OF GAME- AND ANIME-THEMED BARS THAT STAY OPEN ALL NIGHT.

There are many ways to reach Shinjuku. The most fascinating one would be to take the JR Yamanote Line, take on the huge crowds headfirst and try to get out of the world's busiest transport hub in one piece (just kidding) but for this walk we are taking the Tokyo Metro Marunouchi (or Fukutoshin, if you prefer) Line. Choose Exit B2 and when you reach ground level, go left and cross the street at the police box. Go left again and after 20 meters you reach the **Shinjuku Marui Annex**. This place has plenty of interesting things to offer. Its sixth floor, for instance, features an **Animate** collaboration cafe (cafe.animate.co.jp/shop), an Alice-inspired Lolita-style boutique (babyssb. co.jp), and female-oriented video game maker **Otomate**'s one and only official store (otomate.jp/otomate_store). On the seventh floor you will find the **Animega** all-genre shop (bunkyodojoy. com/shop/pages/animega_t_shin-juku0101.aspx), craft and model shop **Mokei Factory** (mokei-factory.com), yet another ultra-kawaii Lolita-style boutique (angelicpretty.com), and the **Village Vanguard** and **Namco Char-aPop** stores. Then don't forget to check out **FewMany** on the third floor (fewmany.com) (eclectic collection of stationery, original art, cute figures and quirky Medicon toys) and the event space on the first floor often used to promote new animation movies.

Still hungry after this otaku binge? Then go back to the intersection you crossed earlier and walk about 300 meters past the big department stores until you see the Kinokuniya bookstore across Shinjuku-dori (look for the 紀伊國屋書店 blue sign). Kinokuniya is one of the most revered bookstores in Japan. The best place for English books is its newer, bigger location near the JR station's South Exit (6F 5-24-2 Sendagaya, Shibuya-ku), but for all things otaku you want to go to the Forest annex behind the main store (adhoc Bldg.). The M2 floor mainly sells CDs and DVDs, while the manga, art books, magazines, video game guides, and other publications are upstairs. The store is even decorated with signing boards from visiting artists. And while you 're there, don't forget to

West Shinjuku features Tokyo's most stunning collection of high-rise buildings and a few iconic anime locations.

ABOVE A building-block-made Pac-Man advertises the movie Pixels (2015) in the streets of Shinjuku.

LEFT The egg-shaped Artnia shop is a little out of the way but definitely worth a visit. ABOVE Marui Annex has two floors full of otaku shops.

check out the Sanrio gift shop on the first floor and the Grand Cyber Café Bagus on the third. Sanrio Gift Gate is especially worth a visit. There are many similar shops in Japan (11 just in central Tokyo; see the website for details), but this particular branch is perfect for taking commemorative photos, as its entrance is guarded by the biggest Hello Kitty statue in the world.

If you are into cosplay and costume making, from the adhoc building go left and then take the first right when you see the Book Off sign; then walk straight ahead for about 150 meters until you see the **Okadaya** sign next to Labi. This store is popular with students from nearby fashion design schools. One six-story building has nothing but textiles, while the seven-story shop next to it sells all the accessories you may need. Cosplayers may be particularly interested in the stage make up and costume accessories on the second floor.

Going right from here, you can see the bright red and yellow **Don Quijote** sign (ドン・キホーテ) across Yasukuni-dori. The craziest, tackiest, and messiest discount chain store in Japan sells everything, from food and clothing to cosmetics, electronics, toys and costumes. And finding what you want is part of the fun. Tokyo has plenty of branches, but as Shinjuku is a place that comes alive at night, why not try this particular shop that's open 24 hours? Besides, this location is the ideal starting point to explore the neighborhood's many otaku bars (see Shinjuku Nightlife).

There's actually one more store left: **Artnia**. This is Square Enix's official shop. From the outside it looks like a slightly squashed egg; inside like a jewelry-cum-museum. They even found enough space for a cafe. The gift shop (selling the company's popular character goods) is rather small but this place is so stylish it's worth a visit. Unfortunately it's quite out of the way. So unless you want to walk one more kilometer, you'll better hop on the subway (Marunouchi or Toei Shinjuku Line) and get off at Higashi Shinjuku Station, Exit A3.

IF YOU ARE AFTER CUTE PLUSHIES AT AFFORDABLE PRICES VILLAGE VANGUARD IS WORTH CHECKING OUT.

WHY SETTLE FOR A PLAIN BOX OF SWEETS WHEN YOU CAN GET THEM IN A DORAEMON CONTAINER?

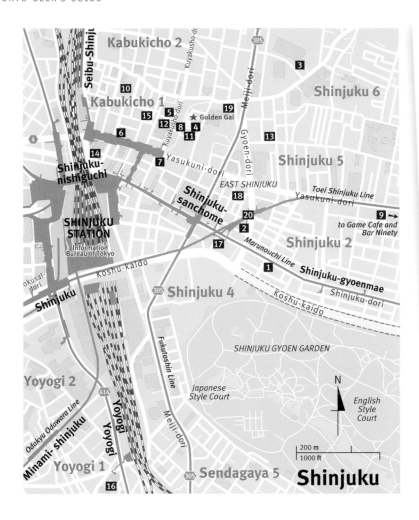

GODZILLA HOTEL GRACERY SHINJUKU

10 *shinjuku.gracery.com (English)*

After visiting Shinjuku three times in the past—*Godzilla* (1984), *Godzilla vs. King Ghidorah* (1991), *Godzilla 2000 Millennium* (1999)—the Big G officially became a resident of this ward on April 9, 2015. To celebrate the event, Hotel Gracery opened a special twin room on the eighth floor with a dramatic layout featuring trick walls, black lights, wall artwork and more. If you can't afford the steep price (49,800 yen a night, 59,800 on weekends), you can still book a single "Godzilla View Room" (18,800 yen, 25,050 on weekends) from which you can see its huge 12-meter-high head perched on the terrace. Otherwise you can always admire it from the street for free. For reservations check out the hotel's Japanese website.

SHINJUKU HOT SPOTS

3 Artnia
Opening times *daily 11:00–22:00*
jp.square-enix.com/artnia/en

6 Don Quijote
Opening times *daily 24 hours*
donki.com/en

7 Forest Kinokuniya
Opening times *daily 10:00–21:00*
kinokuniya.co.jp/c/store/Shinjuku-Main-Store/shopinfo.html

14 Okadaya
Opening times *daily 10:00–20:30. Closed irregularly*
okadaya.co.jp/shinjuku

7 Sanrio Gift Gate adhoc Shinjuku
Opening times *10:00–21:00 (Mon–Fri), 10:00–20:00 (Sat–Sun & holidays). Irregularly closed*
sanrio.co.jp/english/store (English)

17 Shinjuku Marui Annex
Opening times *11:00–21:00 (Mon–Sat), 11:00–20:30 (Sun & holidays)*
0101.co.jp/stores/guide/storetp/limited/00003detail.html

LEFT and BELOW Otaku events such as Re:animation feature an exciting mix of dance music, anison and cosplay.

SHINJUKU FESTIVALS AND EVENTS

CharaAni

Similar to Akiba's AniCrush!!!, CharaAni is an all-genre DJ event. Lots of anison but the resident DJs and VJs like their techno, EDM and J-Pop too. The main difference with AniCrush!!! is that this is an all-night dance party. Check the Unique Laboratory schedule for a revolving lineup of anikura, vocaloid, idol, anison disco and other otaku-friendly DJ events.

Other interesting events around town are **Anison Disco** (3–4 times a month) (ameblo.jp/anisondisco) and **Haru no Utage** (twitter.com/miimanoutage) while at Anieve-Z (anievez.com/c) you can check anison events around Japan. **Admission fee** *guys: 2,000 yen (including one drink); gals: 500 (drinks not included).* **Dates** *every month on the third Sat.* **Opening times** *23:00–05:00. Unique Laboratory, K-Plaza B2F 2-1-1 Hyakunincho, Shinjuku-ku.* **How to get there** *2-minute walk from Shin-Okubo Station (JR Yamanote Line). Cross Okubo-dori and go right under the railway. The K-Plaza building is right before the Mini Stop convenience store* chara-ani.com

Re:animation

Their slogan says it all: animation meets club music and rave. Re:animation appeared out of the blue in 2010 when some 800 otaku and other passersby occupied Kabukicho's theater plaza in Shinjuku one cold December afternoon. Since then the event has gradually expanded, with one to three meetings every year, reaching almost 2,000 ravers in 2013. In the last couple of years the dancing circus has moved in front of Nakano Station while a few special events have been held in clubs, amusement parks and even at Haneda International Airport for two dates of all-night dancing.

Most editions (special events excluded) are free, start around noon and last until 18:00 or even later depending on the place. The DJs typically mix anison and anime soundtracks with house and techno but compared to classic anison events there is more emphasis on club music. If you want to have a better idea

OTAKU DJ EVENTS CAN BE ENJOYED IN MANY CLUBS AROUND TOKYO.

of what actually happens at these raves, you can watch past editions online at Vimeo: vimeo.com/reanimationjp/videos. **Admission fee** *see website.* **Date and opening times** *see website for schedule.* reanimation.jp *(the website is in Japanese but they provide a Microsoft translator at the bottom of the page)*

SHINJUKU MANGA CAFES

In many countries Internet cafes have been part of the urban landscape since the early 1990s. While people use them for different reasons (in some Asian countries, for instance, they engage in hardcore gaming and even conduct business), most places look the same everywhere. In Japan, though, things are a lot different. The Japanese are famous for tinkering with other people's ideas and coming up with even better versions, and the local joints—called manga cafes (漫画喫茶 manga kissa)—offer a lot more than a simple Internet connection. That's why in the age of smart phones these places are still going strong and can be found everywhere.

A typical manga cafe is, more than anything else, a place for relaxation and entertainment. Besides a PC, unlimited Internet access and free WiFi, some things you will find everywhere (for no extra fee) are thousands of manga, books and magazines, DVDs, and unlimited soft drinks and coffee. Many cafes even have all-you-can-eat soft-serve ice cream; sell instant and junk food; and even let you charge your phone and print things out from your PC.

When you arrive at a manga cafe, you will be offered a range of time and seating options. Most people choose the private booth which comes with either a reclining chair or a flat mat. In the 2000s, with local economy going down the drain and a sharp increase of working poor, many people in their 20s and 30s began to use these cafes as alternative lodgings becoming so-called "net cafe refugees." Since then the authorities have countered this phenom- enon with new laws (e.g. you can't be admitted unless you prove you have a legal address) but now many places offer "night packs" (e.g. six- or nine-hour all-night stay), free luggage storage and even showers (for an extra fee), so that people who have lost

the last train home can crash there for the night. Most cafes are very clean, and this is definitely an only-in-Japan kind of experience you may want to try. Just remember that only a thin five-foot-high plastic wall separates you from the other cubicles, so in some cafes you may not be able to sleep a lot, what with ambient lighting you can't turn off, muffled but constant background noise, and the occasional snoring.

A few good chains are:
Bagus
bagus-99.com/internet_cafe/shops
Media Café POPEYE
media-cafe.ne.jp
Manga Kissa GeraGera
geragera.co.jp/store

SHINJUKU EATERIES

See map on page 68

5 Capcom Bar

Opening times *14:00–23:30 (Mon–Fri), 11:30–23:30 (Sat–Sun & holidays)*
paselabo.tv/capcombar (link to English page at the bottom)
Try the latest Capcom games while tasting their themed food and drinks. Particularly well done is a *Resident Evil*-inspired Brain Cake (actually a Mont Blanc capped with raspberry sauce). The deep blue interior is closer to a night club but the line-reciting waiters bring the overall atmosphere back to otaku level. As usual, be sure to go with your pockets full because they sell more *Sengoku Basara*, *Monster Hunter* and *Ace Attorney* goods than you can shake a stick at.

19 Tokusatsu Café & Bar Pondisheri Purantan 特撮 Café & Bar

ぽんでぃしぇりぷらんたん

4F 5-18-11 Shinjuku, Shinjuku-ku
Opening times *daily 14:00–5:00*
pondisfx.jp
The good folks at Pondisheri run both this Tokusatsu-themed bar (lots of figures you can actually play with) and a maid-staffed massage parlor (pondi.tokyo) on the second floor.

20 Ufotable Dining

Opening times *11:30–16:00, 18:00–24:00. Closed on Wed.*
ufotable.com/dining/
See Ufotable Café (page 80). Opening time is subject to change depending on each theme. See the schedule for details.

五感で味わえ、
ゲームの世界を

CAPCOM BAR
CAPCOM × PASELA ENTERTAINMENT BAR

The infamous Brain Cake (LEFT) at Capcom Bar (ABOVE) actually tastes much better than it looks.

TAKADANOBABA

Just a couple of Yamanote Line stations north of Shinjuku, Takadanobaba was until 15 years ago a minor otaku Mecca of sort, with several small shops selling used video games and CDs for a few yen. Nearly all the shops are gone now, but you may want to pay a quick visit anyway to admire the beautiful mural in front of the station's main (North) exit, underneath the tracks, portraying many of Tezuka Osamu characters. Tezuka Productions used to be based here—like Dr. Tenma's laboratory where, according to the *Tetsuwan Atom* manga, *Astro Boy* was born in 2003. On the west side of the station, each post on both sides of the main street (Waseda-dori) is decorated with a banner featuring *Astro Boy*, *Black Jack*, *Kimba*, *Ribon Knight*, and *Three-Eyed One*.

How many cities in the world go so far as to devote whole murals to the world of manga and anime?

SHINJUKU NIGHTLIFE

See map on page 68

2 8-bit Café

5F 3-8-9 Shinjuku

Opening times *19:00–2:00 (Mon, Wed–Thu, Sun), 19:00–5:00 (Fri–Sat). Closed on Tue.*

8bitcafe.net

One of the oldest game bars in Tokyo is also one of the most popular, even among the local expat community. This place is like its website: geeky, elegant and retro in equal measures. Mainly dedicated to 1980s subculture (the so-called Famicon/NES generation), there are tons of new and rare games and consoles and even a tabletop arcade game and a 1.5-meter-tall giant Nintendo Game Boy on which you can actually play original games you will find nowhere else. They often hold music DJ events too (techno, electronica, etc.). Most drinks and food are in the 500–900 yen range, and there's a yen charge of 500.

1 16 Shots

Opening times *20:30–4:00 (Mon–Thu), 20:00–5:00 (Fri–Sat). Closed on Sun.*

16shots.jp

Three blocks away from 8-bit Café (see above), 16 Shots is much easier to find but harder to get in as it only seats nine. Better reserve a seat in advance, especially on a Friday. The owner prefers groups of up to three people. More than a playing room, this is a typical bar (albeit decorated with game-related paraphernalia) where people enjoy some game talk. They don't even lend games anymore (out of respect for makers' copyrights) but you can bring yours. Apparently most of the customers work in the gaming industry.

4 Bar Uramen

Opening times *daily 19:00–the morning after. Sometimes closed on Sun & holidays*

971.jp/

Once upon a time, there was another tiny bar called Qunai Bros. It was hidden under street level in the famous Golden Gai bar area and boasted a collection of hundreds of Famicon games. Well, that bar is still there, only its name has changed. And according to its very minimal website, the collection is now up to 500–600 games. Drinks from 400 yen, plus seat charge of 800 yen.

Sleazy Kabukicho (ABOVE) and boozy Golden Gai (BELOW) would seem to be unlikely places to enjoy some innocent otaku fun. Look harder because many small anime- and game-themed bars are hidden in those streets.

8 GAmE Bar Shinjuku

5F 1-2-7 Kabukicho, Shinjuku-ku

Opening times *daily 19:00–8:00*

Across the street from Neo Black Sigma and the Capcom Bar there is a building with massive fake Greek columns. On the fifth floor you will find a strange hybrid place that looks like a hostess bar (there's plenty on them in that building), instead the hostesses let you play with Sega Saturn, Playstation, Super Famicon and Wii. You decide what's better. The 1,000 yen charge is a little steeper than other game bars, but this joint is decidedly better looking.

9 Game Café and Bar Ninety

ゲームカフェ・バー **Ninety**

2F 16-16-2 Arakicho, Shinjuku-ku

Opening times *17:00–24:00 (Mon–Sat), 13:00–22:00 (Sun & holidays)*

interhits.co.jp/ninety

Yet another refuge for people who are

EVERY NIGHT KABUKICHO'S BRIGHT LIGHTS ATTRACT SCORES OF FUN SEEKERS.

Golden Gai is home to at least two otaku bars but there are many more joints devoted to music, movies and even more esoteric and eccentric subjects.

into nostalgia from the 80s and 90s, this cafe has a sizeable collection of video and analog games, manga, and baseball and pro wrestling cards. Playing is okay (you can even bring your own games) but the owner stresses that this is more a place where people chat about their passions while eating and drinking. This said, Monday is Portable Games Night while Wednesday and Thursday are devoted to trading card games and Sundays are for TRPGs (tactical role playing games). Most food and drinks are priced around 600–700 yen, and there's a 500 yen table charge.

11 M2S
Opening times *daily 20:00–5:00*
goldengai.net/shop/b/06
While a distinct minority, anime and figure otaku can be found in the Golden Gai bar area too. Decorated with signatures from famous anime singers and voice actors, this bar sits about ten. Customers can even try their hand at anison karaoke while tasting the owner's original drinks (priced 500–800 yen) like the cassis-based Lupin III or the Lamu (with green tea liquor). There's a 1,000 yen table charge.

12 Neo Black Sigma
ネオ・ブラックシグマ
B2F Miyata (ミヤタ) *Bldg. 1-4-12 Kabukicho*
Opening times *daily 19:00–early morning*
blacksigma.jp
Join the Black Sigma crew in their karaoke all-nighters and be part of their secret plan to conquer the world through anime and tokusatsu songs! For 1,200 yen (600 for gals) you can sing your heart out for either 90 or 60 minutes, depending on whether you enter their underground secret base before or after midnight. Soft drinks cost 600 yen while alcohol starts from 700.

13 New Type Shinjuku
サブカルカフェ＆**BAR New Type** 新宿
Opening times *18:00–2:00 (Mon–Thu), 18:00–5:00 (Fri–Sat), 18:00–23:30 (Sun)*
ces-n.com/nt
Similar to other subculture bars in the area, this one is relatively bigger and

even has a second floor that can be rented for private events. You can borrow one of their costumes if you are in a cosplay mood.

15 Robot Restaurant

Opening times *16:00–23:00. Closed irregularly (see their website for schedule details)*

shinjuku-robot.com (English)

First of all forget the food. Though this place calls itself a restaurant, people are mainly attracted by its three daily performances (four during the weekend). It's easy to understand why the place is extremely popular with tourists. Featuring scantily-clad cuties, cow-riding pandas, boxing robots, and bright flashing lights, the mad mish-mash of tradition (taiko drumming!) and futuristic technology is probably what Japan looks like in the eyes of many foreign travelers. It's very kitsch, very loud, and very entertaining in a silly way. Then it's up to you to decide if the show is worth the 7,000 yen entrance fee (6,500 if you pay online by credit card). Luckily for you the mediocre food (1,000 yen) is an optional. You can either make reservations online or by phone (03-3200-500). If you have tattoos you will have to cover them.

16 Robota 秘密基地酒場ROBO太

1-28-1 #101 Yoyogi, Shibuya-ku

Opening times *18:00–23:00 (Mon–Tue, Thu–Sat), 18:00–22:00 (Sun). Closed on Wed.*

yoyogirobota2004.blog.jp

Secret Base Bar Robota (that's the original Japanese name) is guarded by a statue of the great Mazinger which doubles as a sign to help newcomers locate the place. This apartment-turned-bar sits more than 20. Inside it looks like a toy shop: figures are everywhere, and on request they will even let you try on their collection of *Kamen Rider* belts. Drinks are priced around 500 yen while food starts from 300.

18 Star Club Shinjuku

スタア倶楽部

Opening times *20:00–4:00 (Mon–Sat), 20:00–1:00 (Sun & holidays)*

bar-starclub.com

If you are wondering what happened to the Muteki (Invincible) Mario shot bar, well, it's still in the same place, still run by the same video game developer from Osaka, still devoted to Nintendo's most popular character. Only its name has changed (for copyright issues?) and "Muteki Mario" is now just one of their original cocktails. Inside is small and dark, with a rather chic atmosphere. Booze: 700–800 yen. Food: 500. Cover charge: 500.

ROBOT RESTAURANT (**BELOW AND RIGHT**) IS A CRAZY TACKY FUN HOUSE THAT ENCAPSULATES ALL THAT IS GOOD, BAD AND UGLY ABOUT TOKYO.

STAR CLUB SHINJUKU IS ONE OF THOSE COZY LITTLE BARS WHERE OTAKU FANS AND PROFESSIONALS COME TO SHARE THEIR PASSIONS.

EXPLORING NAKANO

IF AKIHABARA IS THE OFFICIAL, ATTENTION-HUNGRY SIDE OF OTAKU TOKYO, NAKANO IS ITS OPPOSITE, BOTH GEOGRAPHICALLY AND TEMPERAMENTALLY. IT'S QUIETLY GOING ABOUT ITS BUSINESS WITHOUT FANFARE, YET ATTRACTING THOUSANDS OF DEDICATED MANGA AND ANIME FANS BY THE MERE STRENGTH OF ITS OFFERINGS. NAKANO IS JUST A FIVE-MINUTE TRAIN RIDE FROM SHINJUKU, YET IT COULDN'T BE MORE DIFFERENT FROM ITS GLITZY, NAUGHTY NEIGHBOR. ACTUALLY THERE WAS A TIME WHEN NAKANO WAS CONSIDERED TRENDY AND MANY CELEBRITIES CALLED IT HOME. IN THE '60S AND '70S, THE WARD BECAME THE CENTER OF A REVITALIZATION PROJECT THAT TRANSFORMED IT INTO A FANCY DISTRICT. 1966 SAW THE COMPLETION OF NAKANO BROADWAY, A LUXURY APARTMENT COMPLEX WITH A FOUR-STORY SHOPPING MALL AND SIX MORE FLOORS OF APARTMENTS. THE BUILDING COST A THEN-RECORD-BREAKING SIX BILLION YEN AND FEATURED A GARDEN AND POOL ON ITS ROOFTOP. THEN IN 1973 PRIME MINISTER TANAKA KAKUEI HIMSELF INAUGURATED NAKANO SUN PLAZA, A 21-STORY CULTURAL AND AMUSEMENT COMPLEX FEATURING A CONCERT HALL, A HOTEL AND A WEDDING HALL.

In order to reach Nakano Broadway you have to walk through Sun Mall, very worth a visit if you have some time left.

However the good times were not meant to last, as in the '70s and '80s Nakano was gradually overshadowed by hipper areas like Kichijoji further down the Chuo train line. It was around this time that avant-garde anime circles began to move into the area, with bookstore **TACO ché** distributing cutting-edge comic magazine Garo along with underground literature. Meanwhile, in 1980 former Garo contributor Furukawa Masuzo opened in Nakano Broadway a second-hand manga store called **Mandarake**. This tiny shop (only 6.6 square meters wide) proved so successful that more and more otaku outlets followed Furukawa's example, turning Nakano Broadway into one of Japan's major centers of otaku activity, probably second only to Akihabara.

NAKANO BROADWAY

The JR Chuo Line conveniently divides the area in two parts: the sleepy residential south side and the fun-loving north side which is where you should head. Cross the plaza in front of the station and go into Sun Mall, a 240-meter-long glass-covered shopping arcade whose 100 plus stores sell everything, from food and booze to clothes, shoes and watches. As soon as you exit the mall you'll see the entrance to Nakano Broadway (nbw.jp) in front of you. Don't be fooled by all the non-otaku shops on the first and basement floors that sell clothes, watches, medicines, electronics, food, etc. Most of the fun awaits you on the second-to-fourth floors. At this point you have two options: If you don't have a lot of time, plan your visit in advance and zero in on a few shops. Otherwise you can just leisurely roam the aisles, take in the unique atmosphere and discover

unexpected delights. The mall's layout is rather haphazard and the hallways have been arranged with the apparent purpose of making you lose your way. However if you are not in a hurry your visit will become the strangest shopping expedition of your life. Just try to avoid weekends and holidays when its aisles and stores become seriously crowded. Also, remember that most otaku shops (unless otherwise noted) are closed on Wednesdays.

Even if your interests go beyond browsing and shopping, Nakano's

NAKANO BROADWAY SHOPS

6 Alf (2F)

Opening times *12:30–20:00 (Mon–Tue, Thu–Sat), 12:30–19:00 (Sun & holidays)*
alf-ec.com

Choro-Q, Tomica, Ebbro, Tamiya… If the sound of these names makes you drool, don't waste any time and run to this shop. They specialize in Japanese mini-cars (the cute Choro-Qs are typically 3–4 cm long) and stock foreign stuff like German Minichamps too. Particularly recommended if you are looking for a rare model. Just be prepared to empty your wallet.

6 Aloha Toy アロハトイ (2F)

Opening times *daily 12:00–20:00*

This female-oriented shop is packed with manga-, anime- and game-related toys and goods (dolls, figures, badges, posters, key chains, cards, etc.). If you are into otome games, BL manga and light novels, etc., this is a real Aladdin's cave.

6 Alphaville アルファヴィル (3F)

Opening times *daily 13:00–19:00. Irregular holidays*

The keyword here is *bishojo* (beautiful young girls). This is a veritable bishojo gamer paradise, with tons of PC games (from mainstream titles to more maniac stuff, both new and second hand) but also DVDs, adult and PC magazines, game instruction books, etc. all piled up in a relatively spacious but messy store. They pride themselves in carrying products you will hardly find anywhere else.

6 Amenity Dream Nakano アメニティードリム中野店 (3F)

Opening times *daily 12:00–20:00*
amenitydream.co.jp/

Amenity Dream is one of the Big Three trading card chain stores in Japan and has eight more shops in and around Tokyo (see website for details). They carry all the popular series, from *Vanguard* and *Yu-Gi-Oh!* to *Weiss Schwarz*, *Gundam War* and *Magic: The Gathering*.

6 Anime Shop Apple Symphony (4F)

Opening times *daily 10:00–19:00*

If you have been mourning anime cel shops, Commit's demise don't worry because it's still there, only the owner and name have changed. Hundreds (thousands?) of those beautiful hand-drawn and painted cels are either

advantage is that everything is close to the station and concentrated in a very small area. Most of the bars, cafes and assorted entertainment listed in this book, for instance, are on either side of the Sun Mall/Nakano Broadway axis. The area east of Sun Mall is especially worth exploring because its shop- and bar-filled narrow streets (sleepy during the day, quietly alive at night) have retained a nostalgic retro atmosphere that will give you a fairly good idea of how Showa-era Japan looked and felt.

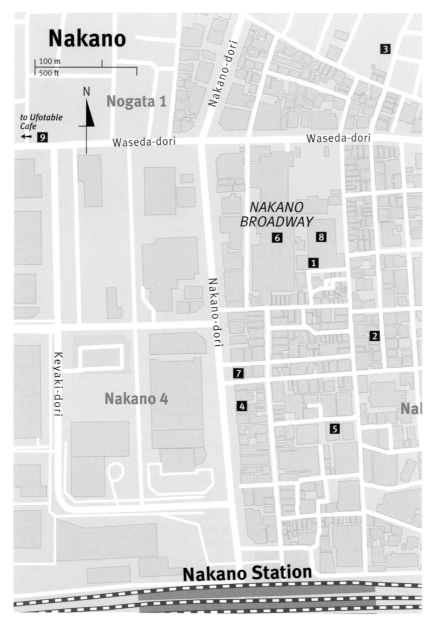

collected in binders or displayed in bins. Here you will find both prohibitively expensive rare items (Studio Ghibli, Dragon Ball, Sailor Moon, Gundam, etc.) and equally beautiful but much cheaper cels from less famous anime.

6 Anime World Star (2F)
Opening times *daily 12:30–20:00*
anime-world-star.com (Japanese)
anime-world-star.com/docs/2000/cel.htm (English)
Differently from rival Anime Shop Apple Symphony (see above) this store doesn't only sell cels (they claim to have 100,000 pieces in stock) but anime-related goods too (badges, coasters, plastic folders, postcards, cell phone straps, etc.). Simple line drawings can be had for 500–2000. If you can't make the trip to Japan, now you can even buy through their website.

Nakano Broadway covers just about every otaku genre including all you need to make your own dolls.

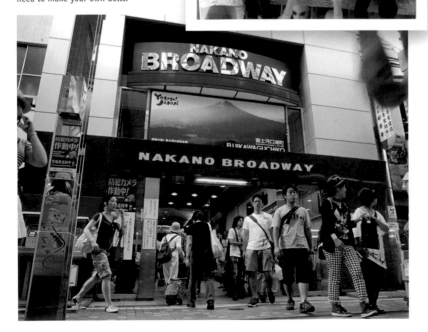

6 Candy One (2F)
Opening times *daily 12:00–20:00*
candy-one.com
This is the ideal shop for people who are new to cosplay and don't want to commit too much money to their first purchase, as Candy One's cheapest costumes only cost 5,000 yen. Made-to-order outfits, on the other hand, start from 20,000 yen. Their vast stock of accessories include their originally designed pura-ishi (プラ石) or decorative "plastic stones."

6 Decotrand (4F)
Opening times *daily 13:00–20:00*
decotrand.ocnk.net/
For all the gals out there who fancy looking like Sailor Moon or some other ultra-cute anime character, this tiny shop sells original accessories and gadgets and plush toys. Hotcake-shaped pendants and brooches anyone? How about triangular hairpins with *Naruto* decorations, or teddy bear-ice cream bracelets?

6 Gaocchi (3F)
Opening times *daily 12:00–20:00*
Showa-period ('50s-'70s) retro bonanza is the name of the game here. The list is endless: dolls, *menko* playing cards, character masks, *shokugan* (food toys), monster sofubis, Sanrio and Sailor Moon toys. And then Gundam-, Kinnikuman- and Super Car-shaped erasers, Bikkuri Man stickers, etc. are only a few of the nostalgia-inducing things you can buy. They make for nice souvenirs too.

6 Hal Shop (2F)
Opening times *daily 11:00–20:00*
twitter.com/hal_shop
It may not be as famous as Akiba's Gachapon Kaikan, but this place has more than 100 machines, surely enough to satisfy your gachagacha cravings.

6 Mandarake (1-4F)
Opening times *daily 12:00–20:00*
mandarake.co.jp/shop/index_nkn.html
While second-hand otaku goods chain Mandarake has a cool underground store in Shibuya and an eight-floor Complex in Akihabara, Nakano is its home base. Indeed, with 25 different shops spread on four of Nakano Broadway's five floors it's an inescapable presence. Luckily each store is devoted to a different genre so you won't lose your sanity having to go through one million total items. This is one of the few places in Tokyo that goes so far as to include among its staff people who can actually speak English

THIS FUJIKO FUJIO'S MAGAZINE FROM 1957 AND OTHER RARE COLLECTOR'S ITEMS AVAILABLE AT MANDARAKE WILL COST YOU A SMALL FORTUNE.

and other languages. Here's a brief description of some of its 25 branches

門 **(Mon)** (1F): Studio Ghibli goods.

Live-kan (2F): ladies dojinshi.

Galaxy (2F): video game software and hardware

Deep-kan (2F): dojinshi for men.

∞ **(Infinity)** (3F): Boy idols- (Johnny's) and voice actors-related goods

Anime-kan (4F): anime scripts and cells, signed sketches.

変や**(Hen-ya)** (4F): novelty goods, vintage and antique toys.

Mania-kan (4F): vintage manga magazines and books (including Tezuka Osamu's original editions), records (anime, tokusatsu), movies scripts.

Plastic (4F): dolls (Volks, Blythe, Licca-chan), doll wigs and other accessories.

Special 1-6 (2-4F): each store is devoted to a particular genre of figures and models.

6 Murakami Takashi's galleries.
Art superstar Murakami Takashi is a very media- and market-savvy guy and knows where the money is. So it's no wonder that he opened not one but three galleries and a bar inside Nakano Broadway to showcase his and other up-and-coming artists' otaku-inspired works besides anime and video game

The stunningly looking Hen-ya (ABOVE) is one of the 25 Mandarake shops you will find inside Nakano Broadway.

Pixiv Zingaro is one of the three galleries where famous artist Murakami Takashi showcases anime-related and inspired art.

original art. All the galleries (each one with a different character) are open 12:00–19:00 but only whenever they have an exhibition ongoing.

pixiv Zingaro (2F) pixiv-zingaro.jp/
Hidari Zingaro (3F) hidari-zingaro.jp
Oz Zingaro (4F) oz-zingaro.jp/

6 Parabox Shop (3F)
Opening times *daily 12:00–19:00*
parabox.jp/tenpo.html (Japanese website)
parabox.jp/eng_new/ (English website)

This shop has everything you need to make your own custom doll: from bodies, heads and eyes to clothes, shoes, wigs and other accessories. They come in different sizes, from 1/6 to 1/3 scale. They provide advice and a maintenance service as well. Their main shop is in Kawasaki, a 20-minute train ride from Shibuya, but their smaller branch inside Nakano Broadway is more convenient. And if you want to get an idea of the strange and wonder-

ful things they sell and do, you can start by having a look at their excellent English-language site.

6 Plabbit プラビット (1F)

Opening times *daily 11:00–20:00*
plabbit.ocnk.net/

Let's say you love those gorgeous Gunplas but you are too lazy to build

The weird signboard in front of TACO che' reflects the shop's unorthodox offerings.

them yourself. No problem! The good folks at Plabbit have a great selection of pre-built models on sale (for 20,000–30,000 yen). They also excel at customization. Do you want a new paint job, or maybe you want to add some accessories or some other custom modification? Just ask. But remember that custom work takes time (between one and four months, depending on what you want), so it's not good if you are in a hurry or just visiting Tokyo for a few days.

6 TACO che' (3F)

Opening times *daily 12:00–20:00*
tacoche.com

While Otakudom has its own version of the indie world (dojinshi and the like), what about the off-off scene—the cutting-edge artists whom no mainstream shop dares to carry on its shelves? TACO che' is the perfect

starting point for your exploration. Apparently they have more than one million publications in stock (small-press books, alternative comics, zines) plus DVDs (mostly of the weird variety), CDs (grindcore, noise, and what-the-hell-is-that music), T-shirts, badges and illustrations by such underground masters as Umezu Kazuo, Maruo Suehiro and Tawaraya Tetsunori. From time to time they even hold exhibitions and other events.

6 Trio 1-3 (2-3F)

Opening times *daily 12:00–20:00*
trio-broadway.com/tenpo.html

You can overdose on old and new idols (both guys and girls) and J-Pop singers even in Akihabara, where Trio has two more shops inside Radio Kaikan and Akiba Cultures Zone, but we prefer these three stores filled to the brim with photos, picture fans, posters, magazine back issues and other idol-related goods.

NAKANO NIGHTLIFE

See map on page 76

1 & 2 Anison Karaoke Bar Z #1 & #2

アニソンカラオケバーZ
Opening times *daily 18:00–23:30*
anisonkaraokebar-z.com/access.html

With a mini stage and a cute Cheerleading Army, these karaoke bars give you a chance to become the star of the show. Guys pay 2,300 yen for the first hour (including an all-you-can-drink menu!) and 1,100 yen for each 30-minute extension, while gals get a 600-yen discount. And they have a 500-yen discount for first-timers. For an extra 220 yen, then, you can get the bar's cosplaying girl unit to cheer you up while you are singing.

7 Nerv:Nakano (Joysound Nakano)

5-8F (reception 6F) 5-67-3 Nakano
Opening times *daily 11:00–6:00*
shop.joysound.com/eva/nerv-nakano/

Karaoke box chain Joysound has come up with a new way to attract otaku fans. The fifth floor of this particular location features three special rooms devoted

to *Evangelion*, each one with a different decor (you can check them out online by clicking on their number). Two more special *Evangelion* rooms are available at their Shibuya branch. Groups of at least four people need to reserve these and other rooms online.

NAKANO EATERIES

See map on page 76

1 Anison DJ Café Bar Raizeen アニソン DJ Café Bar 雷神

Opening times *daily 19:00–23:00. raizeen.com (click on MAP for directions)*

If you can speak some Japanese this is a good place to kick back with a beer (there's no cover charge) and share your love for all things otaku with fellow anime fans and the friendly staff. This bar is particularly famous for its DJ booth that anybody can rent on weekday afternoons (1500 yen/h including one drink) when there are no events scheduled (check the calendar online). Assorted figures and models and a big screen showing anime complete the decor.

6 Bar Zingaro

Opening times *11:00–21:00 (Mon–Thu & Sun), 11:00–23:00 (Fri–Sat & holidays)*
bar-zingaro.jp

Not content with having not one but three galleries inside Nakano Broadway, hip artist Murakami Takashi teamed up with Fuglen (a small chain of bars and cafes from Norway) to open his own joint. When you get tired of shopping you can take refuge in this stylish bar and sip one of their interesting coffee and tea concoctions surrounded by Murakami's colorful and manga-like paintings.

3 Dai Kaiju Salon 大怪獣サロン

1-14-16 Arai, Nakano-ku
Opening times *daily 15:00–23:00*
picopicoshimbun.web.fc2.com/salon.html

If Akiba is Otaku Central, Nakano goes one step further into uncharted territory. This bar, for instance, manages to be cute and weird at the same time. Created by *kaiju* (monster) artist Pikopiko and adult video director Nakano Takao, it's arguably the only place in Tokyo devoted to Japanese monsters. Even its resident hostess Mucho is a kaiju! The place is a cafe until 18:00 and turns into a bar in the

THE WAITRESSES WORKING AT SEIYU CAFÉ & AUDITION STAGE VOIDOL ARE ASPIRING VOICE ACTRESSES.

evening. There's no cover charge but they have the usual one-order-per-hour system. And for 500 yen, Pikopiko will teach you how to make your own cute monster (reservation required).

5 Hobby Bar Professor TK Hobby Bar プロフェッサーTK

3F Tsuchiya Bldg., 5-60-14 Nakano
Opening times *daily 19:00-2:00*
twitter.com/gunoya

Every Gunpla lover should check out this bar whose already limited space is mostly taken by model boxes stuck floor-to-ceiling (they are for sale) and glass cases full of finished robots, some of them very rare, built by the owner himself—a member of one of Japan's major Mecha-building circles. As most clients are regulars, the bar not only offers the traditional Japanese bottle-keep service (each patron buys a whole bottle and gets it stored for future visits), but even a Gunpla keep (the bar keeps everybody's kits and tools as they use the place as a working space). However non-regulars are also welcome and can either buy soft drinks (500 yen) or Japanese spirits (800).

Newcomers are advised to go on a Wednesday or Thursday, when the bar is less crowded, and you should check its Twitter page beforehand in case the place is closed for a private event.

8 Seiyu Café & Audition Stage Voidol 声優カフェ&オーディションステージボイドル

1-2F 5-54-3 Nakano
Opening times *14:00–21:30. Closed on Mon. ameblo.jp/voidol-nakano/*

The waitresses in this cafe are aspiring voice actresses. After waiting tables on the first floor they have a chance to perform radio dramas, songs and other routines upstairs. Even the auditions are open to the public. Clients pay a 500-yen cover charge for 30 minutes or 1,500 yen for two hours and are expected to place one order every 60 minutes.

9 Ufotable Café

Opening times *11:30–23:00. Closed on Mon. ufotable.com/cafe/ (click on the featured anime or game)*

Animation studio Ufotable (*God Eater, Fate/stay night, Tales of Symphonia*) must have realized that the food/

anime/game combination can be quite lucrative, as they currently run two eateries in Tokyo (the other one is in Shinjuku, and three more in south Japan. Every month or two they devote their menu and interior decoration to a different anime or video game, and the Nakano cafe even has a big screen showing screenshots of the featured work and a couple of small galleries where you can admire related posters and other illustrations. Food orders come with a cool placemat while a drink will get you a coaster. Then of course you can buy tons of merchandise (straps, tumblers, stickers, badges, etc.). Don't forget that a reservation is usually required. You might get a seat anyway on a weekday, but do it at your own risk.

1 Jojo Bar Dio ジョジョ風 Bar Dio
2F World Kaikan 5-55-6, Nakano
Opening times *daily 18.00 ~*
Located inside the same World Kaikan building housing Raizeen and Anison Karaoke Bar Z #1, this bar is completely devoted to the *JoJo's Bizarre Adventure* saga, including the decorations and the extensive menu whose names have been changed to reference charac-

ters' names and famous lines from the story. Food and drinks from 500 yen, and there's a 500-yen cover charge.

MAID AND DANSO CAFES

4 Danso Bar Prince
男装バープリンス
Opening times *17:00-23:00 (Mon, Wed–Thu and Sun), 17:00-4:00 (Fri–Sat). Closed on Tue.*
bar-prince.net
If you are tired of maid cafes and their cute & gaudy atmosphere, you may want to check out more classy places like this one, with chandeliers, leather sofas and deep-red heavy curtains.

SOME GAME BAR PATRONS PREFER BOARD GAMES TO THE USUAL VIDEO GAMES.

Kuroneko is probably the only maid cafe left in Nakano.

Their cross-dressing girl butlers are an interesting bunch and are always ready to entertain you with their witty chat. They have a 500-yen table charge but there's no time limit and on Friday and Saturday they are open all night. Soft drinks 600–800 yen; spirits 700–900; food 700–1000.

6 Kuroneko Maid Mahou Café
黒猫メード魔法カフェ
Opening times *15:00–23:00 (Mon–Thu), 15:00–5:00 (Fri & day before holiday), 13:00–5:00 (Sat), 13:00–23:00 (Sun & holidays)*
necomimi.info/
This is Kuroneko's original cafe (there are two more inside Nakano Broadway; see website for info). The décor and cat-ear-wearing cutie maids are typical for this kind of place. The *mahou* (magic) feature that sets it apart from the competition is their selection of spirits. They even have a *nomiho-dai* menu: 30 minutes (20 after 19:00) of all-you-can-drink booze for 1,000 yen.

Dai Kaiju Salon is a friendly place devoted to those only-in-Japan weird monsters.

EXPLORING KOENJI

THE VAST SUBURBAN AREA WHICH LIES WEST OF SHINJUKU HAS TRADITIONALLY BEEN HOME TO AN ECLECTIC GROUP OF CREATIVE PEOPLE (WRITERS, MUSICIANS, ETC.), INCLUDING MANY MANGA AND ANIME ARTISTS WHO, ESPECIALLY IN THE PAST, USED TO LIVE HERE, PROBABLY BECAUSE APARTMENTS WERE CHEAPER. THE WESTBOUND CHUO AND SEIBU SHINJUKU TRAIN LINES ARE PARTICULARLY IMPORTANT FOR THE HISTORY OF MANGA. A NUMBER OF PEOPLE WHO WERE INVOLVED IN SEMINAL AVANT-GARDE COMIC MAGAZINE GARO, FOR INSTANCE, LIVED IN ASAGAYA. AS FOR ANIMATION, ALMOST 100 OF THE 400 PRODUCTION STUDIOS IN JAPAN ARE LOCATED IN SUGINAMI WARD AND MUSASHINO CITY, IN THE AREA ROUGHLY INCLUDED BETWEEN KOENJI AND MITAKA STATIONS. OVER THE LAST FEW YEARS, MORE AND MORE OTAKU-ORIENTED STORES, BARS AND RESTAURANTS HAVE OPENED, ATTRACTING AN INCREASING NUMBER OF FANS AWAY FROM THE USUAL CENTERS OF ANIME AND MANGA CONSUMPTION. WHILE MANY OF THESE PLACES ARE SCATTERED AROUND WESTERN TOKYO AND REQUIRE A FAIR AMOUNT OF TRAIN TIME, NEIGHBORHOODS LIKE KOENJI AND ASAGAYA HAVE A SLIGHTLY HIGHER NUMBER OF OTAKU SPOTS AND DESERVE TO BE EXPLORED PROPERLY.

Koenji is one of the first places you should hit if you are into used clothes.

For people who only know Tokyo through mainstream press and TV programs, Koenji may be—together with Shimo-Kitazawa—one of the city's best-kept secrets. Like Shimo-Kita, Koenji has long nurtured a local community of artists and intellectuals who have given the district a particular vibe. The main difference between the two places may be that Koenji arguably features a wider palette of cultural and musical influences and a stronger tradition of anti-establishment political activism (e.g. it was the starting point to the anti-nuclear protests which followed the 3/11 disaster in Fukushima). At the same time, this is still a typical Japanese neighborhood, with plenty of temples and old-fashioned shopping streets, and every summer hosts the Awa Odori traditional dance festival (last weekend of August) which attracts about 10,000 performers and one million people.

Koenji is particularly famous for two things: used clothes and music. From the JR Chuo Line South Exit, go right and find the entrance to the covered

A trip to Koenji is a chance to discover all the cool little shops, cafes and bars both sides of the station.

THE AWA ODORI FESTIVAL IS ONE OF TOKYO'S BIGGEST SUMMER EVENTS.

PAL shopping street. Walk the whole length of the arcade and at the end you will find Look Street (ルック商店街). Koenji is said to have about 100 used-clothes shops, and one fourth of them are concentrated along this street, sharing space with cool coffee shops and a few pre-war buildings that were spared by US aerial bombings.

As one of the main centers of alternative youth culture, Koenji is the go-to place to enjoy indie music of any kind. While it is particularly famous as the birthplace of the local punk rock scene, the many live venues and music bars cater to different genres, from folk to glam rock, jazz and experimental music.

It's no surprise, then, that Koenji abounds in retro and thrift stores and other quirky shops, including of course those of the otaku variety. While nearly all these places are located south of the train line, let's first visit the lone store on the "wrong" side of the tracks. Cross the square in front of the North Exit and head for the red arch on the far left. Walk the whole length of the

Ichibanboshi (BELOW) is a treasure trove of figures like this army of Ultramen (LEFT).

shopping street and turn left (there's a bakery on the corner). At the end of that short street you will see a shop called **Star Case** on the second floor. That's our building. Star Case is considered one of Tokyo's best Star Wars shops and is definitely worth a look if you are into it, but we actually want to go to the store next door, **Ichibanboshi**. This vintage toy shop is

KOENJI HOT SPOTS

1 **2000 Collectable Toys**
Opening times *12:00–21:00. Closed on Wed.*
2000collectabletoys.com

2 **Gojira-ya**
Opening times *14:00–21:00. Closed on Tues & Wed.*
1.plala.or.jp/GODZILLAYA

2 **Bar Gojira-ya**
Opening times *14:00–18:00, 20:00–4:00. Closed on Sun.*
1.plala.or.jp/GODZILLAYA

3 **Ichibanboshi** (一番星)
Opening times *14:30–19:00 (Tue–Fri), 12:00–19:00 (Sat–Sun & holidays). Closed on Mon.*
1ban-boshi.com

4 **MT Base** (MT 基地)
Opening times *daily 20:00*
mt-kichi.com

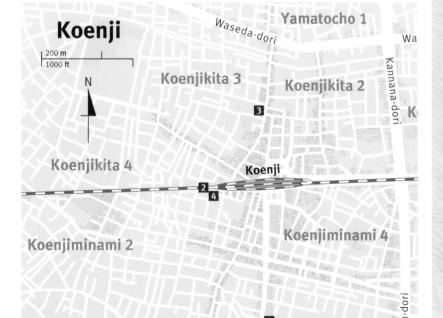

PRODUCTION I.G ANIME STUDIO

ITALY-BORN FRANCESCO PRANDONI IS IN CHARGE OF INTERNATIONAL OPERATIONS IN ANIME STUDIO PRODUCTION I.G.

Can you briefly introduce Production I.G?

Production I.G started in 1987 as a tiny studio with five people in one rented room, located near JR Kokubunji Station, in the outskirts of Tokyo. Today the studio has 120 full-time employees, and fortunately more room to accommodate them. The company's name comes from the initials of the two founders, producer Ishikawa Mitsuhisa and animator Goto Takayuki, who are still at the head of the studio today. Collaboration with director Oshii Mamoru proved instrumental to raising the studio's profile, and Production I.Gryiad started gathering attention with the two *Patlabor* movies (1989 and 1993), and especially with *Ghost in the Shell* (1995), which became influential to Hollywood creators such as James Cameron and the Wachowskis. The studio's first full digital production, *Blood: The Last Vampire* (2000) became one of the main reasons Quentin Tarantino contacted I.G for creating the animation sequence in *Kill Bill: Vol. 1*.

Tell me about your artistic philosophy and market strategy.

Japan is a highly competitive market for animation, and every studio has to carve its own slice of the pie. There are big studios outputting character-driven, merchandising-centered, long-running franchise shows. There's a myriad of micro-facilities forming a sea of subcontractors. Production I.G went in a different direction, actively investing in its projects, and establishing itself as a studio with a limited number of high-end and edgy productions every year. Creators are our competitive edge, our greatest asset, and

Ghost in the Shell 2: Innocence (2004) is the anime/computer-animated sequel to *Ghost in the Shell* (1995). They were both directed by Oshii Mamoru.

a hard-to-find one, therefore we would like to keep a working environment that can be attractive for the best talents around. Although we have increased the volume of TV series productions since 2005, and we do work on popular mainstream properties, today Production I.G is still one of the few studios in Japan focusing on high-quality, director-driven animated feature films. Making films was one of Ishikawa's dreams since the company inception, and this has not changed throughout the years. One difference from the output of the 1990s and early 2000s is perhaps that in recent years, the SF/action projects most people associated

Directed by Hara Keiichi, *Miss Hokusai* (2015) is based on Sugiura Hinako's manga *Sarusuberi* and takes place in Edo-period Tokyo.

I.G with have been paired with family and/or drama-oriented stories, such as *A Letter to Momo*, *Giovanni's Island* and *Miss Hokusai*, which all became internationally award-winning films.

What's Japanese animation's current situation and the role played by Japanese studios in the foreign markets?

Today most anime shows aired on Japanese TV are being simulcast in a remarkable number of countries, and feature films screen at major international film festivals, where they are often greeted with recognitions. However, animation in Japan has always been primarily intended for the domestic audience. This is also the main reason for Japanese animation's uniqueness, as it has never tried to meet "international" standards by adapting to marketing rules and storytelling algorithms. This uniqueness eventually turned out to be the strongest appeal when Japanese productions were "discovered" at different points in time, by non-Japanese audiences. You could compare Japanese animation's position in the international market to ukiyo-e. Woodblock printing was an astounding technique, yet by the end of the 19th century had become obsolete. In the same way, hand-drawn animation is a technique that all the world except Japan has abandoned in favor of CG, making this country a sort of Galapagos

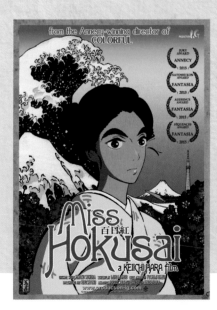

within the industry. Visitors from the United States—as well as Singapore or Taiwan—are amazed at the sight of Japanese animators drawing with pencil on paper. Professionals and journalists find it hard to believe we did not use CG for the visual effects in *Jin-Roh* or motion capture in *A Letter to Momo*. It is a fact that today's animation industry in Japan, like the whole entertainment business throughout the world, needs to adapt to quick and drastic changes in distribution and business models. However, there's no point in trying to be competitive with Hollywood studios by imitating what they do, as no Japanese production will ever manage to raise such budgets. Besides, *ukiyo-e* still look beautiful today, don't they?

How did a foreigner end up working for a Japanese animation studio?
At the time the animation segment for *Kill Bill: Vol. 1* attracted global attention on Production I.G, and *Ghost in the Shell 2: Innocence* was heading for the Cannes Film Festival, the studio's executives realized it was wise to have English-speaking staff with some degree of international operations expertise. I.G had already a rep office in Los Angeles, but surprisingly there was nobody with that specific role in Tokyo. I had already been in the industry for more than a decade, although in acquisitions and distribution. I went for an interview, and they took me. As a matter of fact, I.G has a long history of non-Japanese employees. We currently have people from Korea, China, France and Italy, and none of them are in the animation department. I really cannot say I am an exception here. What most people sending e-mails to our HR department tend to forget, however, is that being proficient in both spoken and written Japanese is not simply a plus, but a sine qua non in order to work in a Japanese company like this, because that will be the only language your co-workers will be using and understand.

Like Ichibanboshi, Gojira-ya is chockfull of gorgeous vintage toys and rare figures.

mainly devoted to figures (Godzilla, Astro Boy, Ultraman, Kamen Rider, you name it). Inside, all the available space is taken by glass cabinets full of soft vinyl toys, while others hang from the wall inside their plastic cases. Ichibanboshi is also famous for its collaborations with indie sofubi maker Real x Head.

Now let's retrace our steps. Once you pass under the red arch, go straight and pass under the rail tracks next to McDonald's, then turn right and follow the Chuo Line for about 200 meters until you see **Gojira-ya**'s sign. The shop (one of Tokyo's oldest toy collector's stores) is on the second floor and besides lots of Godzilla merchandize, covers about the same genres as **Ichibanboshi**. There are glass cases chock full of rare vinyl figures and die-cast toys, and then books, dolls, model kits, movie posters, etc. Downstairs, **Bar Gojiraya** is an ideal stop for a drink and a full immersion in 1970s retro atmosphere.

On the way back, you may want to stop at another bar on the right side of the narrow street, next to Bar Alba: **MT Base** (MT 基地). MT is for Moso (delusion) Tohi (escapism) or "escape into a fantasy" and this "cosplay and anime bar" claims to be the best place where otaku can "join forces and fight against reality." An army of military-clad girls (hostesses?) are here to chat and share their interest in manga, games, etc. with you. There's a 3,000 yen all-you-can-drink 60-minute plan. For karaoke lovers, one song costs 200 yen, but on Tuesdays it's free.

The last stop in our otaku tour of Koenji is an optional for **2000 Collectible Toys** only sells American and European toys from the 1980s and 90s, so if you are only after made-in-Japan goods you may want to skip this one. However this is another amazing store and for once in a while each category (Ghostbusters, pro wrestling, Gremlins, Star Wars, etc.) is neatly displayed in its own showcase. Also, this is the rare store where the staff can actually speak English, and they are very knowledgeable about the things they sell. If you are not too tired to walk an extra 500–600 meters, go back to the station and take the first main street on the right. The store is on the left side past the fourth street light. You will easily recognize the colorful windows.

Shopping aside, Koenji is a genuinely interesting place to explore, and you'll have fun hunting for the locations featured in the Sunrise anime series *Accel World* or—if you are so inclined—getting lost in its backstreets while trying to recapture the atmosphere created by Murakami Haruki in his novel *1Q94*.

A VISIT TO A GAME CENTER

IN *AIKATSU!*, PLAYERS HELP ASPIRING IDOLS PASS AUDITIONS.

Video game arcades—or game centers, as they are called in Japan—used to dot the cities and shopping malls around the world. Most of that scene has now disappeared, replaced by home consoles, PC software and portable devices. Only in Japan time seems to have stopped as many people still enjoy their weekly (sometimes daily) commute to those loud, crowded and mesmerizing temples of electronic fun. The secret of their longevity is the clever way in which game producers and arcade owners have managed to create a kind of experience that goes beyond the games themselves and can only be enjoyed in the arcade environment.

Japanese game centers can be either one-floor mazes or multi-story fun palaces, but their basic layout is about the same anywhere you go. Let's take as an example a medium-sized, three-story Taito arcade in suburban Tokyo. The first floor is crammed with *UFO Catcher* (crane and claw game), a couple of *Taiko no Tatsujin* (Drum Master) (a particularly popular game that attracts players of any age and

sex) and a few kid's games such as card-based games. These cabinets are strategically placed near the entrance because they are more likely to attract casual passersby, young couples and families. Originally *UFO Catcher* was the name of a prize game that arcade industry giant Sega created in 1985 and derives its name from its UFO-shaped claw. It has proved so successful over the years that even today, all crane games (including those made by other companies) are called like this. Anyway, whatever the type, you better avoid them like the plague, because they are nothing but coin suckers. Though deceptively easy, your chances to get one of those cute stuffed toys (unless you are blessed with beginner's luck) are close to naught. It's not by chance that revenues from *UFO Catcher* can be as much as 40 percent of all game revenues at arcades in Japan.

Going upstairs, the second floor (in bigger arcades even the third and possibly the fourth) features what many consider the

heart of a game center. It is here that you will find the typical games that most people identify with arcade fun: shooting games; fighting games; and dedicated cabinets. These genres have evolved dramatically since the first hit games appeared in the late 1970s (remember *Space Invaders*?). Shooting games, for instance, have always been the dominant arcade games, but recent STGs (as they are known in Japan) can be so complicated that they only attract the more dedicated players (someone would call them maniacs) as it takes a lot of time and money to memorize their

LEFT and RIGHT Music- and rhythm-based games are relatively new additions but have proved to be a big hit while attracting a new breed of fans. BELOW Some game centers have notebooks where everybody can write messages or draw their favorite characters.

amazingly intricate patterns. As for fighting games, constant innovation on 3-D technology has made them increasingly appealing and today the likes of *Street Fighter*, *Tekken* and *Virtua Fighter* share pride of space with the STGs. When it comes to virtual brawls, one of the more interesting features in Japanese arcades is that many if not most cabinets are connected to common motherboards. In this particular game center, for instance, two rows of four cabinets each are placed back-to-back. This way each person can challenge one of the players on the opposite row. It's completely anonymous yet the fact that you are actually playing against someone who is in the same room adds a thrilling note to the already exciting situation. The downside, needless to say, is that if you are unlucky enough to be challenged by a master player you will likely walk out of the game center with empty pockets and a bruised ego.

If you want to avoid this embarrassment, you can always take refuge in one of the many dedicated cabinets (i.e. games housed in specific casing) that offer a quintessential arcade experience. These driving, flying and gun-shooting games offer a degree of sensorial immersion and emotional involvement that cannot be duplicated at home.

While the above-mentioned games have been around forever, we have to go upstairs to see the hottest fun in town. It is on the semi-dark third floor, in fact, that we find the huge variety of music-based games. This genre is relatively new but has proved extremely successful in luring new customers to the Japanese arcades. Games are roughly divided in three groups: dance games, music simulators, and rhythm games. Dance games used to rule in the late 1990s, with people sweating it out while trying to match maddeningly intricate steps, but recently have lost a lot of their appeal. Guitar and drum sims, like DJ games, continue to attract a core fan base, but the real winners in recent years have been *Groove Coaster*, *Jubeat* and the *Sound Voltex* series, all of them games where you manipulate knobs and hit buttons in order to match a certain rhythmic or musical pattern.

You will notice that some people pull out a smart card every time they play a game. These so-called e-Amusement cards cost 300 yen and are part of an online service that players use to save progress

THE FIRST THING ONE SEES UPON ENTERING A GAME CENTER ARE *UFO CATCHER*.

between games, keep track of their statistics and ranking, and access exclusive features like special songs. Also, in this particular arcade they let card holders try new games for free. Just swipe your card on the reader and get a one-time free game!

These are the main arcade features. A typical game center has even more to offer but it's either games of chance (e.g. electronic mahjong and pachinko... not terribly exciting stuff) where you must know the rules and luck matters more than skills, or card-based games to enjoy which you obviously need the cards on top of understanding what the hell is going on.

Much better to finish your full arcade immersion with a visit to the Purikura or photo-sticker booths (you can find them either on the first or top floor) that let you choose backgrounds, scribble digital notes, add decorations to the pictures and even retouch your face and body so that you can look like a model. Just be warned that in some places men are not allowed unless accompanied by a female.

SHOOTER GAMES LIKE *GUNSLINGER STRATOS* (**ABOVE**) HAVE LONG BEEN POPULAR AMONG GAME CENTER PATRONS.

EXPLORING ASAGAYA

THOUGH ONLY A TWO-MINUTE TRAIN RIDE SEPARATES K'OENJI'S SUBCULTURAL MELTING-POT FROM ASAGAYA, THIS IS A MORE SOPHISTICATED, HIGHER-END RESIDENTIAL AREA WHOSE TYPICAL SOUNDTRACK IS JAZZ RATHER THAN PUNK ROCK OR NOISE MUSIC (THE LOCAL JAZZ STREET FESTIVAL LIVENS UP ITS SMALL VENUES AND BACKSTREETS EVERY YEAR ON THE LAST WEEKEND OF OCTOBER). THE DISTRICT IS ALSO KNOWN FOR ITS LITERARY CONNECTIONS, AS DAZAI OSAMU, YOSANO AKIKO, IBUSE MASUJI AND OTHER FAMOUS WRITERS CALLED IT HOME FOLLOWING THE 1923 GREAT KANTO EARTHQUAKE. HOWEVER, EVEN A PLACE WITH SO MANY HIGHBROW CONNECTIONS CAN HARDLY ESCAPE A PERVASIVE OTAKU AND POP CULTURAL PRESENCE. FOR INSTANCE, AN INCREASING NUMBER OF MANGA, ANIME, AND MANGA-BASED LIVE-ACTION MOVIES AND TV DRAMAS HAVE BEEN SET IN THE DISTRICT, INCLUDING THE TWO *RING* J-HORROR FILMS, THE HUGELY POPULAR *DEATH NOTE* FRANCHISE AND, MORE RECENTLY, THE *AQUARION LOGOS* ANIME SERIES.

ASAGAYA PEARL CENTER TOKYO.

DOLLER IDOL MOMOCHI MINAMI CAN BE OFTEN SEEN DJING AT OTAKU EVENTS AROUND TOKYO.

On the other side, though for many years Suginami-ku has been a hot bed of anime creativity, in the last few years the area has lost part of its appeal as other prefectures have lured production companies away from Tokyo with tax cuts and other benefits. In order to reaffirm the district's connection with both otaku fans and creators, in 2014 a 120-meter-long stretch under the JR rail tracks was turned into a shopping area, **Asagaya Anime Street (AAS)**, which is particularly good news for dedicated fans for nearly all the local otaku stores and cafes are now concentrated in one area. To reach AAS, take the station's South Exit. Just in front, you can see the roofed entrance to a covered shopping street. That's the Pearl Center. This 650-meter-long arcade appears in *Aquarion Logos* but it's particularly famous because every August it becomes the crowded, messy, colorful center of the **Asagaya Tanabata Festival**. First celebrated in 1954, this is but one of many Tanabata festivals that are held around Japan in summer, but this particular location is worth checking out because besides the usual streamers and lanterns, it features big papier-mâché anime and manga characters hanging from the roof of the arcade.

But we are here to visit AAS. From the station, cross the street on the left and follow the narrow passage along the rail tracks for about 250 meters. Take the second left and you'll see the AAS logo. More than a street, AAS is a long (and rather dark) corridor directly under the Chuo Line. This is a family-friendly place, so you won't find any kind of adult content here. As we enter AAS, we find the **GoFa Labo**, a cafe-cum-gallery by the same people who run the Gallery of Fantastic Art in Shibuya, and a small space with 16 Bandai gachapon machines. Next there are two cosplay shops, **Cosmania** and **Copin**, the latter one being a specialized store for girls impersonating male anime characters. On the left side, after Cosmania we find two anime goods shops, **Pikatto Anime** and **Asagaya Camp**. The camp is manned by Momochi Minami, a very friendly "animetic" idol/anison DJ/MC who always covers her face with an anime mask. On the right side there are two cafes, **Baroque Café** and **Shirobaco**. Baroque's main feature is the home theater in the back where you can watch anime movies on a giant projector screen while sitting on special surround-sound seats. Shirobaco has an all-white interior and its floor and kitchen staff are aspiring voice actors who take turns

Asagaya Pearl Center is one of Tokyo's longest shopping streets.

performing on a mini stage in front of the customers. They also have other anime-related live events and a small exhibition space. All in all, AAS is an interesting place to explore. Probably not a must-see destination, but you may combine it with a visit to Koenji's toy shops.

If, instead of these cafes, you prefer something stronger, go back to the station, turn right at McDonald's, under the railway bridge, then go left and take the Star Road (スターロード) on the right of the bus terminal. Follow this backstreet until you see the sign for **44 Sonic**. This is another small bar where people can watch anime, sing their favorite anime songs, and share their love for manga, idols and tokusatsu movies. Seat charge is 800 yen. Food and booze from 500 yen.

ASAGAYA HOT SPOTS

1 44 Sonic
Opening times *19:00–24:00. Closed on Wed.*
44sonic.net

2 Asagaya Anime Street
Opening times *daily 11:00–18:00 (with some exceptions)*
asa-st.com

EXPLORING KICHIJOJI

A 15-MINUTE RIDE FROM EITHER SHINJUKU OR SHIBUYA (EXPRESS TRAIN), KICHIJOJI IS COMPARATIVELY LIVELIER THAN KOENJI AND ASAGAYA, BUT IT OFFERS THE SAME BLEND OF RESTAURANTS, CAFES (THE ATMOSPHERIC HARMONICA YOKOCHO CLUSTER OF ALLEYS CONTAINS OVER 100 EATERIES), SHOPS AND GOOD VIBES. IT'S SO POPULAR WITH THE LOCALS THAT IS CONSISTENTLY VOTED AMONG THE BEST TOKYO NEIGHBORHOODS.

Toy Cats Showcase in Kichijoji specializes in less-known toys such as Microman (ABOVE) and Micronauts.

Some of the area's most famous landmarks are south of the Chuo Line (e.g. the beautiful Inokashira Park, one of the best places to admire the cherry blossoms in spring, and the Ghibli Museum) but our walk will focus on the north side, a very busy shopping area full of big department stores (Isetan, Parco, Bic Camera, etc.) and small shops. As for otaku spots, Kichijoji used to have a lot more to offer. Unfortunately in the last ten years, a number of interesting toy stores have closed (Wave B-Jay, Post Hobby, Volks). Among the survivors are small branches of both the **Animate** (animate.co.jp/shop/kichijoji) and **Lashinbang** (lashinbang.com/store/kichijoji) chains besides the usual **Book Off** and **Dorama** (dorama-kaitori.com/shoplist). Still, Kichijoji continues to attract many fans as it is often chosen as an anime location (*Shirobako and Great Teacher Onizuka*, just to name a couple). The station's

At Character Park Kichijoji you can find popular Japanese brands like Rilakkuma.

North Exit faces a big plaza full of bus stops. Keep on the left of the plaza and go straight into the covered Sun Road shopping mall (you'll see a McDonald's on the left). When you reach the first traffic light, turn left and keep going until you see the Coppice banner. On the sixth floor of this department store there is **Character Park Kichijoji**. Devoted to cute character goods and toys and run by Harajuku-based store Kiddy Land (see page 51), here you can find Hello Kitty, Rilakkuma, Kapibara-san and other Japanese and foreign brands. Out in the street again, now go back to where you came from, but this time keep walking until you reach the Yodobashi Kichijoji building (past **Book Off** on the right side, in case you want to check it out). Go left, then take the first right. You'll see a yellow building at the end of the street. **Toy Cats Showcase** is next door on the right. Among the many toy shops in Tokyo, this one distinguishes itself by specializing in little known Microman, Micronauts, and Henshin Cyborg collectibles. The Cyborgs, for instance, are 12-inch action figures made by Takara that were only sold in Japan between 1972-74, while the smaller Microman/Micronauts were among the most successful toys in Japan in the mid-70s. This shop has lots

Opened by Studio Ghibli in 2001, the Ghibli Museum showcases the anime studio's world-famous stories and characters and is devoted to the art and technique of animation.

of *Dragon Ball* and gachapon toys too. When you are finished, go left past the Aland love hotel. Take the first left, then the second, right, and left again when you reach the elevated railway. You'll see **Café Zenon**'s big glass-windowed front right away. This spacious well-designed cafe regularly devotes its space to a particular manga or anime, with a story-inspired special menu and assorted merchandise on sale. Compared to similar places, though, both its extensive menu and general look are less otaku-centric. The cafe also serves as an exhibition rental space.

Kichijojihoncho 3

Gotenyama 1

Inokashira
Park Zoo ★

INOKASHIRA PARK

Kichijoji-dori

Kichijoji-dori

Inokashira
Pond

Kichijoji
Minamicho 1

200 m
1000 ft

N

Inokashira 4

Inokashirakoen

Inokashira 5

Inokashira 3

KICHIJOJI EATERIES

1 Cafe Zenon

2-11-3 Kichijoji Minamicho, Musashino City
Opening times *11:00–24:00 (closed irregularly)*
cafe-zenon.jp

CAFÉ ZENON IS LESS OTAKU-CENTRIC THAN OTHER EATERIES BUT STILL WORTH CHECKING OUT IF YOU ARE IN KICHIJOJI.

KICHIJOJI SHOPS

2 Character Park Kichijoji

6F Coppice Kichijoji 1-11-5 Kichijoji Honcho, Musashino City
Opening times *daily 10:00–21:00*
coppice.jp

4 Toy Cats Showcase

B1 1-26-4 Kichijoji Honcho, Musashino City
Opening times *daily 12:00–20:00*
toycats.no-mania.com
toycats.net (old website)

KICHIJOJI MUSEUMS

3 (3•4•5) Ghibli Museum

As stated on their website, the Ghibli Museum is a portal to a storybook world. In this sense, more than just a celebration of Ghibli's animation, this is a place where one can understand the story-making process itself. Ideally after walking through the five rooms which comprise this amazing house, you will get a better understanding of the ideas and inspirations that go into making anime and movies in general. Miyazaki Hayao has always strived to be different from other anime people, and the museum reflects his personality. The Saturn Theater, for instance, shows original short animated features that can only be seen here; a library has been set up to give TV- and video game-obsessed children a chance to experience the pleasure of reading; and even at the cafe almost everything comes from organic farms. Of course there is a shop, but besides the usual stuff you can even buy hand-painted cels and woodblock prints of film scens. The labyrinthine building itself looks and feels like the houses you would see in a Ghibli movie, with that typical faux European touch that is a trademark of so many of Miyazaki's films.
Admission fee *1000 yen (13–18 years old 700; 7–12 yrs 400; 4–6 yrs 100). Entrance only by advance purchase of a reserved ticket. In Japan buy it at Lawson's. For information on how to buy it from abroad check the website.* **Opening times** *10:00–18:00. Closed on Tuesday and for periodic maintenance*
Inokashira Park West Side, 1-1-83 Shimo-Renjaku, Mitaka City. **How to get there** *15-minute walk from Kichijoji Station (JR Chuo and Tokyu Inokashira Line). From the South (Minami) Exit, go right and turn left at the intersection. Follow Kichijoji-dori all the way to the museum, keeping left after you cross the bridge. The museum is in the park on the left.*
www.ghibli-museum.jp/en (excellent English site with plenty of information)

KICHIJOJI FESTIVALS

Kichijoji Anime Wonderland

With several studios clustered around Mitaka and Kichijoji Stations, Musashino City is one of West Tokyo's hot spots for anime production. So it was only a matter of time before the city came up with its own special festival devoted to the medium. Centering on Kichijoji, Anime Wonderland is also one of the longest otaku events in Tokyo as it stretches for 9–10 action-packed days (sometimes even longer) as opposed to the usual 2–3. The festival's main feature is the juried competition whose main object—according to its creator, editor and manga artist Takekuma Kentaro—is to showcase small projects by up-and-coming animators. Non-screening time is then filled by stage events, workshops (e.g. plastic model classes) and toys and goods sales at the Parco department store. An added nice touch is that some of the celebrations take place in Inokashira Park, one of the best tourist spots in the neighborhood, where a number of companies set up their booths.
Admission fee *Some events are free. See schedule for the rest.* **Dates** *from the first Sat to the second Mon in Oct (sometimes longer).* **Opening times** *See schedule.* Tel. *0422-22-3631.* **How to get there** *Kichijoji is a 15-minute ride from Shinjuku (Chuo Line). 216 yen one way.*
www.kichifes.jp/wonderland/home.html

Museums and Libraries in West Tokyo

THE SHOJO MANGA-KAN HOUSES THOUSANDS OF GIRLS MANGA MAGAZINES AND BOOKS.

THE SUGINAMI ANIMATION MUSEUM OFFERS A HISTORICAL OVERVIEW OF JAPANESE ANIMATION WITH ENGLISH LANGUAGE EXPLANATIONS.

(1•2•5) Ome Akatsuka Hall

Akatsuka Fujio is one of Japan's most popular and beloved manga artists. His story is closely tied to that of other would-be famous mangaka, as he was part of the gang of youngsters who lived with Tezuka Osamu at Tokiwa Mansion in the early '50s (lovingly reproduced in this museum). During his career he created many characters but the ones for which he is best remembered are the proto-magical girl Secret Akko-chan (first appeared in 1962 in Ribbon magazine) and Bakabon (a gag manga that debuted in 1967 in *Shonen Magazine*). The museum starts from "the end" as the entrance is taken up by the shop selling Akatsuka's manga and DVDs together with toys, T-shirts, food, etc. On the first floor we find big-sized reproductions and statues of Akatsuka's characters, some of their famous words and page art from his manga highlighting the author's wicked sense of humor. There is also an exclusive photo sticker machine. The museum proper is upstairs, with many colorful artworks taking up much of the space. Akatsuka had a very public persona (he became a sort of TV personality) and several photos present this side of his life. Another room is devoted to the many cute and bizarre toys and big-toothed dolls produced under his name, while at the end we find a collection of his books and weekly magazines that featured his work in the '60s and '70s.

Admission fee *450 yen (children 250 yen).*
Opening times *10:00–17:00. Closed on Mon (Tues when Mon is a national holiday).*
How to get there *5-minute walk from Ome Station (JR Ome Line). Cross the square in front of the station and go straight until you reach the main street, then turn left. The museum is on the right side.*
ome-akatsukafujio-museum.com

Though rather small, the Suginami Animation Museum (ABOVE LEFT and RIGHT) houses a screening theater and a library.

Shojo Manga-kan (library)

Opened in 1997 by a group of shojo manga lovers and currently run by a married couple, this cute little archive in the middle of nowhere houses 55,000 magazines and books from the 19th century to this day. Here you will find complete collections of such classics as *Weekly Margaret* and *Ribon* as long as much rarer and out of print publications that people from around Japan have donated to the library. Neither borrowing nor photocopying is allowed but they will let you take pictures of whatever you want. And of course you can spend all day reading on the second floor. It's by no means easy to reach, but if you are a hardcore fan or are researching the subject, the trip is surely worthwhile.

Free admission. **Opening times** *13:00–18:00. Open only on Sat between Apr & Oct, and on Nov 3rd (Manga Day). Otherwise you have to call in advance to arrange a visit. Tel. 042-519-9155 (only when the library is open)*
How to get there *the library is about 2 km from Musashi Masuko Station (JR Itsukaichi Line). Take the road that runs perpendicular to the station and turn left at the first traffic light, then go straight for about 1 km. When you see a bridge ahead, take the road on the right instead and cross the smaller bridge Follow this road*

Ome Akatsuka Hall will teach you everything you want to know about manga artist Akatsuka Fujio.

until you reach a parking lot and a group of houses on the right. The library is painted a light blue so it shouldn't be hard to find. nerimadors.or.jp/~jomakan/

(1•3) Suginami Animation Museum

Without a doubt, this is one of the best museums in Tokyo, and it's free! It shows from different angles (history, entertainment, theory and practice) anime's unique features and how they are made. The historical and artistic sides are explained through a corner devoted to the development of Japanese animation and a temporary exhibition space celebrating important works, creators and characters. On the other side, the museum offers the opportunity to experience anime production first-hand, like making your own page-flipping kind of anime (that you can even save on a CD-R or USB); using a PC to understand the process of digital animation; and trying your hand at voice recording and post-production dubbing. There is also a well-stocked library (borrowing and photocopying are not allowed though) and last but not least, you can even watch anime works, either in the movie theatre or by requesting a DVD from the library and enjoying it in the privacy of a booth. Did I mention all this was free?

*Free admission. **Opening times** 10:00–18:00. Closed on Mon (Tues when Mon is a national holiday). **How to get there** 5 minutes by bus from Ogikubo St. North (Kita) Exit (JR Chuo Line and Tokyo Metro Marunouchi Lines). Take the Kanto Bus at #0 or #1 stop and get off at Ogikubo Keisatsu-mae (Ogikubo Police Station). On foot it takes about 15 minutes. Follow the main street to the left past the police box. When you get to the big police station, turn left at the signal. The museum faces a big shrine across the street. sam.or.jp*

Tachikawa Manga Park (library)

People in Tachikawa seem to take their kids' well-being seriously. At the end of 2012 the City opened the Children's Future Center with the goal of supporting child-raising. As manga have traditionally been regarded in Japan as learning tools, the Center decided to turn the second floor of their Good Design-awarded building into a manga paradise where for a small fee you are free to explore the incredibly diversified world of manga. Faithful to the Center's original goal, a lot of educational manga can be found, ranging from cooking and history to sports and science. Their target, though, are not only children. There is something for every age and taste, and aside from kinky stuff, no genre is left uncovered. When the place opened, its sturdy bookshelves—each one organized by genre—carried about 30,000 volumes but their target is to eventually reach 50,000 titles. There is also a 500-volume strong picture-book corner for younger kids. During the weekends the Center even organizes regular manga-drawing classes and flea markets. More than a library, the aptly-named "manga park" invites people to get comfy while enjoying a good read. The whole area is covered with tatami mats for comfort which means you can lounge on the floor, take your books to the cafe corner or out on the balcony. They have even provided closet-like spaces for extra privacy. Speaking of which, you may want to avoid the weekends and the spring and summer school breaks as the place get packed with kids and their parents.

*Admission fee 400 yen (200 yen under 15 years old, free for preschoolers). **Opening times** 10:00–19:00 (Mon–Fri), 10:00–20:00 (weekends & holidays). Admission until one hour before closing time. **How to get there** 7-minute walk from Nishi Kunitachi Station (Nanbu Line), 13 minutes from Tachikawa Station South (Minami) Exit (Chuo Line), 12 minutes from Tachikawa-Minami Station (Tama Monorail). From Tachikawa, there is a big square-shaped overpass in front of the station. Keep left and go down the stairs near the Tsutaya and Big Echo signs. If you see a 7 Eleven on your right and a Mr. Donut on your left you are on the right way. Keep walking straight for about 750 meter. The Manga Park is soon after a big intersection. Tachikawa Children's Future Center official site: t-mirai.com*

AT THE TACHIKAWA MANGA PARK YOU CAN EVEN ENJOY YOUR FAVORITE BOOKS IN THE PRIVACY OF CLOSET-LIKE SPACES.

Tachikawa Manga Park (FAR LEFT and LEFT) has in stock tens of thousands of manga of any kind and hundreds of picture books that you can enjoy for just a modest fee.

CHAPTER 4

IKEBUKURO

EXPLORING IKEBUKURO

SOME PEOPLE CAN'T HELP SMIRKING WHENEVER THEY TALK ABOUT IKEBUKURO. IT COULD BE THE DISTRICT'S PERCEIVED GRITTIER, SLEAZIER CHARACTER; OR MAYBE THE FACT THAT THE AREA ATTRACTS ALL THE PEOPLE FROM THE UNCOOL PREFECTURES NORTH OF TOKYO. WHATEVER THE REASON, IKEBUKURO IS OFTEN OVERLOOKED IN FAVOR OF MORE FASHIONABLE OR GLAMOROUS PLACES LIKE SHINJUKU, GINZA OR SHIBUYA IN SPITE OF ITS EFFORTS TO GET NOTICED FROM TWO OF THE COUNTRY'S BIGGEST DEPARTMENT STORES (TOBU AND SEIBU), THE CITY'S THIRD TALLEST BUILDING (240-METER TALL SUNSHINE 60), AND A TOP-NOTCH CULTURAL CENTER THAT SOMEHOW IS BETTER KNOWN FOR HAVING THE WORLD'S LONGEST ESCALATOR.

When it comes to anime and manga, few areas in Tokyo can boast a better pedigree than Toshima Ward, where Ikebukuro is located. Since the early 1950s, this area has been home to many comic artists. "God of manga" Tezuka Osamu, for instance, used to live in the Tokiwa-so apartment building together with a group of talented young disciples who went on to become best-selling manga authors (Fujiko Fujio, Ishinomori Shotaro, Akatsuka Fujio, etc.), while Yokohama Mitsuteru, creator of the manga *Tetsujin 28-go*, lived and worked most of his life not far from Tezuka.

More recently Ikebukuro has further boosted its otaku credentials, as major companies like Animate, K-Books and Lashinbang have opened multiple stores in the area. Ikebukuro is also the main pole of attraction for *otome*, or female fans. The reason is that students attending the many women's colleges in the area find in Ikebukuro a female-friendly environment. The prevalent female presence in the area means that many shops, manga cafes and game centers are geared toward female customers. The otaku cafes are manned by butlers and "high school *bishonen* (pretty boys)" instead of maids, and many manga and dojinshi on sale belong to the BL (Boys Love) genre that otaku girls love so much.

This district is definitely worth checking out, and now, after the huge success of the 2010 TV anime series *Durarara!!*, which takes place in Ikebukuro, it may have finally landed on the Cool Tokyo map once and for all.

The JR station splits central Ikebukuro into an East and West side. Luckily for you almost all the otaku places of some interest are concentrated east of the station. For many tourists and first-comers, navigating the neighborhood or even finding your way out of the chaotic station can be a nightmare. Regardless of the line you use, the best thing to do once you get off the train is to remain underground and walk all the way to Exit 35. Once you surface to street

IKEBUKURO IS A NEIGHBORHOOD FULL OF SURPRISES.

level, keep walking in the same direction until you see two streets on your left. Take Sunshine 60 Street—the one with a Lotteria on the left corner and a Sanrio Gift Gate store on the right side. In this street there are two of Ikebukuro's best game arcades, **Game Adores** and **Sega Ikebukuro GIGO**. Apart from the usual features, on the sixth and seventh floors of GIGO you'll find Studio Sega, an area entirely devoted to purikura (sticker picture booths). You can actually rent a costume for free and use their makeup rooms before taking those memorable photos with your friends. But men (either alone or in groups) are not allowed unless they are with a female companion.

You can continue along this street and go all the way to Otome Road— the epicenter of female otaku fandom—but if you turn left past Game Adores, you can see **Animate**'s blue and white sign. That's where we are going first. Since opening this shop in Ikebukuro in 1983, Animate has become Japan's largest retailer of anime, manga and video games, with branches everywhere in Japan and even abroad. Still, this nine-story building remains its flagship store. Noteworthy floors are the fourth, shared by dojinshi (mostly new titles by popular circles) and BL/shojo manga, and the eighth, where you can find Animate's limited-edition versions of new manga and DVDs that come with extra freebies and/or alternative covers. Also, the Animate Hall on the ninth floor often has special events. This is by no means the cheapest place in Ikebukuro, but the range of goods being offered is hard to beat.

This short stretch actually features three more shops. Next to Animate but on the third floor, there's **Lashinbang Female Dojin Goods**, whose selection is smaller than K-Books but relatively cheaper (don't forget the name of your favorite artists and circles so you can ask for help in case you can't locate them). Across the street, apart from a Yellow Submarine card shop, you find instead the tiny **K-Books Character Store** and the equally small **Lashinbang Store #5**. Both sell lots of character goods (toys, accessories, figures, stationery), with K-Books specializing in *Kuroko's Basketball*, *One Piece*, *Haikyu!!* and other popular manga published in the *Jump* magazines.

Now turn left at Family Mart. Inside the tall WACCA building across the street, cosplayers will find **Yuzawaya**. This popular chain of craft shops has no less than 38 outlets in the Tokyo area. Unfortunately most of them are scattered in the suburbs, so this Ikebukuro branch is particularly convenient. While Yuzawaya is not especially geared toward those who love dressing up (most customers are housewives and grannies), they do have fabrics, buttons, and thousands of different decorations and materials you may need to create your costumes.

Continue in the same direction, take the narrow street opposite McDonald's, cross the main avenue keeping Parco to your left and arrive at P'Parco, the annex that houses the **Evangelion Store Tokyo-01**. Evangelion's official store in Tokyo has enough merchandise to drain any fan's wallet, from toys and figures to designer clothes, accessories, and many other items (badges, key holders, stickers, etc.).

Watch for special events when they sell limited-edition goods.

When you are finished here, be sure to check out the third floor (ikebukuro. parco.jp/page/shop/floorlist/?floor_ type=floor2&floor=3F) where you can find other otaku-friendly shops. **Rejet shop** specializes in female-oriented video games and CDs, while **Namco CharaPop Store**, and anime shop **Myu** (as well as **B★Point** on the first floor) have an incredible array of manga- and anime-related goods which make for great souvenirs.

IKEBUKURO HOT SPOTS

2 **Animate**
Opening times *daily 10:00–21:00*
animate.co.jp/shop/shop_east/ikebukuro

23 **Evangelion Store Tokyo-01**
Opening times *daily 11:00–21:00*
evastore2.jp

8 **Game Adores**
Opening times *daily 10:00–24:00*
adores.jp/tenpo/sunshine.html

12 **K-Books Character Store** キャラ館
Opening times *daily 11:00–20:00*
k-books.co.jp/company/shop/chara.html

19 **Lashinbang Female Dojin Goods** ら
しんばん池袋本店　4号館　女性同人館
Opening times *11:00–20:00*
lashinbang.com

22 **Lashinbang Store #5**
らしんばん池袋本店　5号館
Opening times *daily 11:00–20:00*

24 **Sega Ikebukuro GiGO**
Opening times *daily 10:00–24:00*
tempo.sega.jp/am/ikebukuro

29 **Yuzawaya** ユザワヤ
Opening times *daily 11:00–21:00*
yuzawaya.co.jp

LIVE INN ROSA

B2F Rosa Kaikan 1-37-12 Nishi-Ikebukuro, Toshima-ku
live-inn-rosa.com
One of the best otaku-friendly live houses in Tokyo, this cozy little space is home to such exotic combos as electro-pop duo Bespa Kumamero and anison/vocaloid cover band Tronies. Especially recommended are its "Ano Uta" (That Song) nights when the hardcore fans' choreographed dances alone are worth the admission price.

Ikebukuro

OTOME ROAD AND SUNSHINE CITY See map on page 95

In the last few years, Otome Road has become the new Mecca for many (female) otaku pilgrims. While at first sight it is only an unassuming 200-meter-long stretch, some of the most popular shops and cafes in Ikebukuro can be found along or near this street.

When you reach Sunshine 60 Street (see page 94), turn right past Sega, then take the first left. You'll soon arrive at the **K-Books Cast Store** (キャスト館), **11** see map on page 95. This shop covers the increasingly popular 2.5-D musical scene. So if you are into *Prince of Tennis* (see page 57) and other manga-inspired musicals, here you can find lots of pictures and photo books, show programs, DVDs, etc.

Now cross the street under the overpass and go left past Family Mart. You will see Animate Sunshine Bldg. at the southern-most end of Otome Road. Inside there are cafes on the first and top floors but the rest is entirely devoted to cosplay. **ACOS Main Store** on the second and third floors sells costumes (both new and classic anime characters),

THE ANIMATE SUNSHINE BUILDING WELCOMES YOU TO OTOME ROAD.

wigs, cosmetics, weapons and other accessories, while on the fifth and sixth floors there is **HACOSTADIUM** cosset (cosset.jp), a photo studio providing everything you need for your cosplay shoot, from different kinds of sets and props to photo gear (SL camera, tripods, reflection boards, etc.). Sandwiched between these Animate joints, second-hand chain store **Lashinbang** runs its own costume store which sell doll costumes too.

All these shops are open every day 11:00–20:00. Here's a list in "order of appearance."

4 **ACOS Main Store/HACOSTADIUM cosset**
acos.me (Animate Sunshine Bldg.)
4 **Lashinbang Cosplay** らしんばん池袋本店 衣装館
lashinbang.com
21 **Lashinbang Store #2** らしんばん池袋本店 ２号館
lashinbang.com/cont/stores.html
This store is all about audio and video items: anime CDs, DVDs and Blu-rays; voice actor CDs; video game soundtracks; BL drama CDs; video game software and consoles; and PC games for girls.

20 **Lashinbang Main Store** らしんばん池袋本店 本館
lashinbang.com/cont/stores
This "moe convenience store" sells comics, novels and assorted publications, with BL and other female-oriented titles on the first floor, and men's manga (including dojin games, CDs and other items) on the second.

10 **K-Books Anime Store** アニメ館
k-books.co.jp
The closest thing to a K-Books general store sells manga, anime, video games and toys including things for kids (lots of plushies too!). This said, the second floor has lots of otome and BL games. This is Ikebukuro after all.

17 **K-Books VOICE Store** VOICE館
k-books.co.jp
All about male voice actors. This shop has plenty of anime CDs/DVDs/Blu-rays, of course, but also photos, fan magazines, concert programs and T-shirts. Many of the drama CDs are actually special editions that are hard to find elsewhere.

16 **K-Books Live Store** ライブ館
k-books.co.jp
From CDs and DVDs to other assorted items (badges, figures, stickers, etc.), this store covers *Love Live!*, *The Idolmaster*, the Vocaloid genre, and other music- and idol-related anime and characters.

13 **K-Books Comic Store** コミック館
k-books.co.jp
Mainstream comics, light novels, magazines and picture books. Many of them, of course, with female readers in mind.

15 **K-Books Dojin Store** 同人館
k-books.co.jp
This is, according to some people, the jewel in the crown of the Tokyo K-BOOKS chain, and if you are into BL and other manga for women you absolutely have to pay it a visit. The third floor sells new works, while upstairs (second-hand shop) is where you can find the real bargains including whole sets. On the third floor they even have independently published novels and dojin goods (badges, cups, cell phone straps, tote bags, etc.).

14 **K-Books Cosplay Store** コスプレ館
k-books.co.jp
More than 2,000 second-hand cosplay-related items, from costumes and wigs to accessories and even cosplay magazines.

If you walk to the end of Otome Road and turn left, at the end of the second block you will find **Café 801** (cafe801.org), **6** see map on page 95. This stylish BL manga cafe is also nicknamed "otome's library" because it has 1) a 13,000 volume-strong collection of ladies and BL comics, novels,

LEFT ACOS Main Store mainly caters to female cosplayers.

And now, for something completely different, let's go to Sunshine City proper to have some fun. On the second floor, **Namco Namja Town** is a huge amusement park that though run by Namco, is not strictly otaku-themed. Some of the attractions are modeled after popular manga and anime but most of the space is taken by a Showa-period town set (for that nostalgic feeling the Japanese like so much) and two large food areas respectively devoted to gyoza and some of the strangest ice creams (garlic, curry, grilled eel) you will ever eat. Then climb upstairs to find **J-World Tokyo**. Based on stories featured in *Weekly Shonen Jump* and *Jump Square* magazines, this amusement park is divided into several thematic areas. *One Piece*, *Dragon Ball* and *Naruto* are the main stars but there are also attractions for *Haikyu!!*, *Prince of Tennis*, and other stories, with constant new additions depending on what's popular in those magazines. The voices and animation in every attraction are in Japanese, but guidelines written in English are provided. When you are finished blasting baddies with Kamehameha shots, you can relax at the J-World Kitchen and choose among more than 300 Jump-related goods at their gift shop. As in other amusement parks, you can either choose between a one-day passport ticket (2,600 yen; 2,400 for 4–15 year olds) that gives you unlimited access to all the attractions, or an 800 yen entrance ticket (600 yen for younger kids), in which case you need to pay extra for each attraction (400–800 yen).

26 **Pokemon Center Mega Tokyo**
pokemon.co.jp/gp/pokecen/megatokyo
26 **Namco Namja Town**
namco.co.jp/tp/namja/
26 **J-World Tokyo**
namco.co.jp/tp/j-world)

etc.; 2) and is off-limits to men most of the time (guys are allowed in for just one week every month; check schedule online). Besides the open reading area, it has a few small rooms in case you need some privacy. One hour costs 500 yen (plus one drink order) while if you want to stay more than four hours you can choose the "free time" plan (1,800 yen including two drinks of your choice). Private rooms cost an additional 200 yen.

You may have noticed the very tall building next to Otome Road. That's part of the **Sunshine City** complex, another place worth your time. If you are not done shopping yet, head to the Alpa mall's West Wing (all the shops are open 10:00–20:00). On the basement floor, besides a Toys-R-Us, a Sanrio Vivitix and a Disney Store for women, you will find the **Donguri Republic/MOE Garden** collaboration shop. The Republic sells Studio Ghibli merchandise while the Garden is run by Gekkan MOE magazine and is all about picture books. Next climb to the second floor to find **Pokemon Center Mega Tokyo**. This is Japan's largest Pokemon Center. If, like many other people, you can't resist the charm of Pikachu and friends, bring lots of money because this place has 2,500 different officially licensed items on sale (plushies, toys, key chains, clothes, cell phone straps) including limited-time exclusives.

ABOVE AND LEFT Otome Road is home to the K-Books empire, with six stores catering to all (mainly female) otaku needs.

STUDIO DWARF AND DOMO-KUN

A JAPANESE DWARF IS CONQUERING THE WEST, ONE COUNTRY AFTER ANOTHER, WITH ITS ARMY OF CUTE MONSTERS AND ANIMALS. THE DWARF IN QUESTION IS GODA TSUNEO'S ANIMATION STUDIO. SINCE THE LATE 1990S, GODA HAS CREATED A NUMBER OF POPULAR CHARACTERS WHOSE FAME HAS CROSSED THE BORDERS, REACHING EUROPE AND AMERICA. I MET GODA-SAN AND CHIEF ANIMATOR MINEGISHI HIROKAZU AT DWARF'S STUDIO IN TOKYO'S WESTERN SUBURBS.

Goda-san, you are especially famous for creating Domo-kun, a beady-eyed, furry creature that keeps its jaws constantly open but turns out to be just a clumsy and kind-hearted monster. How was Domo born?
Goda: In 1998, when I was working in the Creative Department of TYO Productions Inc., NHK was looking for a commemorative character to celebrate the 10th anniversary of its satellite channels. I remember I stayed up all night trying to come up with an idea. I was just drawing simple shapes at random—circles, triangles. Then I drew a rectangle and suddenly

Domo-kun materialized in front of my eyes. I was there, at three in the morning, staring at that thing, and little by little I came up with a story. The first vision I had was this monster in a dark cave that stares blankly at a TV set.

How did you come up with Domo-kun's name?
Goda: Well, I was racking my brain, trying to think of something good, and then I heard the guy next to me talking on the phone. He was like "Domo, domo… domo, domo… domo, domo!" which would be something like "Yes, yes, yes… okay,

okay… thank you, bye!" And I thought, okay, Domo (laughs)! *Domo* in Japanese can mean many things, like 'thank you,', 'I'm sorry' or even 'goodbye' so it's a very useful word.

Since creating Domo-kun you seem to have wholeheartedly embraced the world of animation.
Goda: That's right. I began to use these characters more and more often until I left my CM production company, began to write children's books and supervise character goods production, and finally in 2003 I launched dwarf. In the beginning I worked alone but I soon realized I couldn't do everything by myself, so I began to call some of the people with whom I had been collaborating since 1998. Minegishi, for example, officially joined dwarf in 2006.

Differently from Goda, Minegishi studied animation in college and has worked in this genre since the mid-1970s. Minegishi-san, has stop motion technology changed a lot since when you began 38 years ago?
Minegishi: Yes, indeed. First of all, the passage from film to digital has been a big change. Besides, when I started we didn't have a monitor to check what we were doing so we had very little control on the making process. However, now we do everything by computer. For example, we can work on the next frame while checking the

previous one, so we can move our dolls with a high degree of accuracy. In this sense our work has become much easier.

How do you come up with Domo-kun's story plots? What inspires you?
Goda: As Domo is a child, he's constantly daydreaming and everything is new and interesting to him. He reminds me of my childhood, when I used to explore the world around me, constantly living in the present. So every time I create a new story I always think about my childhood memories.

Domo-kun has become famous worldwide, but I find him very Japanese in character, don't you think so? What is so Japanese about him?
Minegishi: It is true that his gestures are never exaggerated and he seldom overeacts. Like many people in Japan, his intentions are often not very clear and remain open to interpretation. This requires the viewer to fill in the blanks, so to speak. It is a very Japanese thing.

Do you think Domo attract different audiences in Japan and abroad?
Minegishi: In the US, for instance, they treat Domo like a friend and he seems

to be popular with all kinds of people. In Japan he is regarded very much as a child. Children treat him like a friend, and adults treat him like a weirdly cute kid. As a character, he is somewhat undeveloped and the only word he speaks is "Domo!" This leaves a lot of space for audience interpretation, because you have to figure out what he really means. This is one of the things I like most about him. I also like the fact that he has very simple needs. Basically he just wants to be happy.

Your works have become synonymous with stop-motion animation, which are a throwback to an older, somewhat romantic approach to story-making. How does it feel to work like this in the digital age?
Minegishi My mentor and teacher, Kawamoto Kihachiro, was an internationally famous doll animation director. He created a whole world with his stories, and I found his vision very fascinating. He taught me the fun and joy of expressing my own feeling through the dolls. The process itself of creating the illusion of movement through little changes is something I really like.
Goda It surely is a very labor-intensive way to work. Just think that in order to

create a one-second sequence we need to take 24 photos. We usually work from 10:00 am to 11:00 pm, and in one day we usually manage to produce a five-second segment, which means on average we need one week to create a 30-second story. Stop motion animation goes all the way back to the origins of cinema. As Minegishi-san said, there has been an evolution, but it still remains a rather "primitive" style. Both the characters and the background are handmade, and in order to simulate movement we have to move them by hand. So you get that analog feel. There's nothing new or cutting edge to it, so it never gets old. In this sense it's like a children's book. They never lose their charm even after ten or 50 years. On the other hand, a film like *Transformers* looked amazing when it came out, but in a few years will probably look shabby. Then there's the team work involved. Now if you have a computer you can create many different things by yourself, but what we do at dwarf cannot be achieved without collaboration. Working with other people toward a common goal is something I particularly enjoy.

Goda Tsuneo (OPPOSITE) is the creator behind Domo-kun (LEFT) the cute and clumsy monster that has conquered the hearts of many people even in the West.

IKEBUKURO FESTIVALS AND EVENTS

ANIMATE GIRLS FESTIVAL

While otakudom is inhabited by many ladies—who go by the name of *otome*—it is true that most geek events in Japan are overwhelmingly attended by guys. Girls may be a sizeable percentage of the cosplay and dojinshi crowd but, at big conventions like AnimeJapan and Japan Amusement Expo, they are a distinct minority. The notable exception to the rule is the Animate Girls Festival where all the manga, anime, games and figures on display were made with female fans in mind. First organized in 2010, the festival has grown so much that the current location's capacity has reached its limit. Everybody would probably gain from a move to a larger place (e.g. Tokyo Big Sight) but Ikebukuro is the otome capital of the world after all. The two-day program is filled with a variety of stage events like voice actor appearances, but what really attracts the huge crowds are the 100-plus booths scattered around several floors of Sunshine City and selling tons of exclusive merchandise like otome games, *bishonen* manga, *yaoi* fiction and hobby products. All the main players of the otome game industry (e.g. Broccoli, Rejet, etc.) are present and are literally assaulted by an army of hungry ladies with lots of cash to burn. And outside it's the same thing, with scores of cosplayers—many sporting male character costumes—roaming the designated areas between Sunshine City and the station.
Admission fee *1-day ticket: 1,500 yen (advanced ticket 1,200); 2-day ticket: 2,200 yen (advance ticket only). Cosplay: 1-day ticket*

2,100 yen (advance ticket 1,800); 2-day ticket: 3,400 yen (advance ticket only). You can also buy a "bundle pack" which includes a special CD or DVD (see website for details). Be warned that tickets sell out several months in advance. **Dates** *Nov.* **Opening times** *9:00–16:00 Ikebukuro Sanshine City and Funsui Hiroba (Fountain Square), 3-1-1 Higashi Ikebukuro, Toshima-ku.* **How to get there** *3-minute walk from Higashi Ikebukuro Station (Tokyo Metro Yurakucho Line), or an 8-minute walk from Ikebukuro Station (JR Yamanote Line, Tokyo Metro Marunouchi and Fukutoshin Lines). From Higashi Ikebukuro, walk toward Exit 6 or 7 and a sign should direct you to the "Underground Passage" to Sunshine City. From the JR station, go to Exit 35, then walk down Sunshine 60 Dori. The underground entrance (escalator) to Sunshine City will be visible on the right-hand side next to Tokyu Hands.* animate.co.jp/special/agf

JAPAN COSPLAY FESTIVAL

If you are looking for a cosplaying experience with a twist there might be nothing better than this bi-monthly event which takes place in an amusement park not far from Ikebukuro. It sure feels special to cosplay outdoors

A TRIO OF RUROUNI KENSHIN COSPLAYERS. THIS CHANBARA (SWORD FIGHTING) MANGA HAS SOLD MORE THAN 70 MILLION COPIES WHILE ITS ANIME VERSION IS AMONG THE 100 MOST WATCHED SERIES IN JAPAN.

AT MANY COSPLAY EVENTS IT IS TYPICAL TO SEE FANS PRESENT DIFFERENT VERSIONS OF THE SAME CHARACTERS, LIKE THIS "ARMY OF *NARUTO*."

while taking advantage of the many different environments and photo backgrounds Toshimaen offers (gardens, a merry-go-round and Western-style buildings). As usual, everybody is very friendly. Just remember that the JCF is held during regular business hours and many other people are here only to enjoy the rides and attractions. So there are a few rules you have to follow, like avoiding costumes that reveal too much as you don't want to shock all the little kids who run around the park. As in other public places in Japan, tattoos are a no-no, and video recording is not allowed. Also, you are supposed to come to the park in your regular clothes and change in the dressing room, so remember not to show up at the gate in your full regalia.

Admission fee *1,800 yen (high school students: 1,500 yen, junior high students: 1,000 yen). Discounts for groups (minimum 6 people).* **Dates** *twice a month (see website for schedule).* **Opening times** *10:00–17:00 Toshimaen, 3-25-1 Koyama, Nerima-ku.* **How to get there** *1-minute walk from Toshimaen Station (Seibu Ikebukuro Line) or a 2-minute walk from Toshimaen Station A2 Exit (Toei Oedo Line).*
takama.ne.jp/jcf

NERIMA ANIME CARNIVAL

Nerima is, together with West Tokyo, famous for anime production. Some 80 studios are spread around the north-eastern ward, including some of the more storied companies like Toei Animation and Mushi Production (Tezuka Osamu worked for the former before creating the latter one and making *Astro Boy* and *Kimba the White Lion* among others) and recent additions like Goda Tsuneo's dwarf (see interview). It is here that a Carnival has been held since 2007 around Nerima Station. Like Kichijoji Anime Wonderland this is a rather laidback affair with plenty of interesting things going on: special screenings and events for upcoming movies produced by

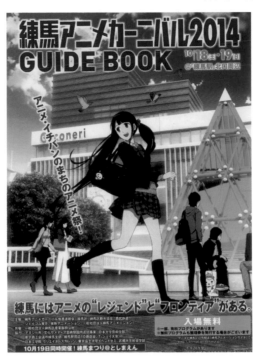

Nerima-based studios; workshops where you can experience different aspects of anime production; anison live performances; character shows; voice actors' and creators' talk shows; and the Nerima Marche' stalls selling anime goods.
Admission is free (except some charged events). **Dates** *Oct.* **Opening times** *10:00–21:00. Nerima Culture Center, Coconeri Plaza, and Heisei Tsutsuji Park are in front of Nerima Station.* **How to get there** *1-minute walk from Nerima Station North (Kita) Exit (Seibu Ikebukuro Line, Tokyo Metro Yurakucho and Fukutoshin Lines, Toei Oedo Line).*
animation-nerima.jp

ULTRAMAN FESTIVAL

Japanese guys of every age have been in love with Ultraman since it first appeared on TV in 1966. Since then the 50-meter-tall superhero has become a major pop culture phenomenon, creating a major *kaiju* boom and going on to star in almost 30 TV series. This festival features a number of exhibitions (displaying old and new models, scripts, equipment, etc.), attractions and live stage performances that always prove very popular with kids. If you are a fan, don't forget to pack

Nerima Anime Carnival is another good chance to meet other fans and experience different aspects of anime production.

your wallet because the huge gift shop carries everything from toys, figures, glasses, sake (!) T-shirts and more limited-edition merchandise.
Admission fee *same-day tickets: 1,900 yen (elementary school students and younger 1,300 yen). Advanced tickets: 1,700 (1,100).* **Dates** *Aug.* **Opening times** *10:00–17:30. 4F Bunka Kaikan, Ikebukuro Sanshine City, 3-1-1 Higashi Ikebukuro, Toshima-ku.* **How to get there** *see Animate Girls Festival*
ulfes.com

THE MIGHTY ULTRAMAN IS ONE OF THE MOST BELOVED SUPERHEROES IN JAPAN.

FOR A QUICK SNACK, THE ANIMATE CAFE KITCHEN CAR CAN BE USUALLY FOUND IN FRONT OF ANIMATE'S FLAGSHIP STORE.

IKEBUKURO EATERIES

See map on page 95

ANIMATE CAFES

Opening times *daily 11:00-21:30*
cafe.animate.co.jp/shop/ikebukuro/
Giant manga/anime/game retailer Animate keeps opening always new cafes both in and outside Tokyo, and three of them (plus a kitchen car!) can be found in Ikebukuro, the company headquarters. They all are collaboration cafes, which means their theme and menu change once every month or two. Apart from food and drinks inspired by the anime or game characters, fans can enjoy related items displayed throughout the cafes and buy character goods. As with Akihabara's Good Smile x Animate Café you have to 1) become a member of Club Animate; 2) make a reservation online; and 3) hope your name will be chosen, as seats are assigned according to a lottery system. In rare cases (check their website) they allow people to get a seat on the same day, but only if the cafe is not sold out.

2 **Animate Café Ikebukuro #1**
Opening times *daily 11:00–21:30*
cafe.animate.co.jp/shop/ikebukuro/
3 **Animate Café Ikebukuro #2**
Opening times *daily 11:00–21:30*
cafe.animate.co.jp/shop/ikebukuro_2/

2 **Animate Café Shop Ikebukuro**
Opening times *daily 11:00–20:00*
cafe.animate.co.jp/cafe_shop/ikebukuro/

2 **Animate Café Kitchen Car**
Opening times *daily 11:00–19:00*
cafe.animate.co.jp/kitchen_car

5 **Café and Bar Characro**
B1F 1-32-4 Higashi-Ikebukuro
Opening times *11:30–22:30. Closed on the third Wed of the month*
namco.co.jp/cafe_and_bar/characro_gin-tama/
As explained on their website, this is a "character cross-over site," or "a place where reality and fictional characters meet." Or, to put it differently, welcome to another eatery with changing themes, this time run by amusement park operator Namco. Recent popular anime and games include *THE IDOLM@STER*, *Macross Frontier*, and *Tiger & Bunny*. Compared to similar enterprises, each theme usually lasts longer and the staff seems to be made of hardcore fans who know their anime and games inside out. Admission is via advance reservation only, and visits are limited to 100 minutes each, with four or five admission periods each day.

7 **Dagashi Bar** 駄菓子バー
2F 1-24-9 Nishi-Ikebukuro
Opening times *17:00–24:00 (Mon–Thu, Sun & holidays), 17:00–04:30 (Fri–Sat & day before holiday)*
dagashi-bar.com/shoplist.html
For many Japanese, the words "Showa Retro" and *dagashi* (the kind of cheap sweets kids munch on in older manga and anime) conjure up nostalgic images of a carefree childhood and "the good old days." This bar chain has cleverly combined the two concepts into a place where, for a 500-yen table charge and one drink order, you can eat as many dagashi as you want. They have other typical kids' favorites on the menu (curry and rice, croquettes, etc.) but the main draw remains feasting on cheap junk food while admiring the retro 60-style interior.

18 **Kamen Rider The Diner**
4F 1-21-9 Nishi-Ikebukuro
Opening times *11:30–22:00 (Mon–Fri), 11:30–23:00 (Sat–Sun & holidays)*
paselabo.tv/rider
Black and red colors abound in this secret Shocker base… I mean, official restaurant that was opened to celebrate the 40th anniversary of the original TV series. Diners are surrounded by life-size Rider suits and bikes, and monitors showing old TV episodes, while the display area has so many figures and gadgets (including many of the Rider's belts) that it feels like a

Even more than the food, customers of Kamen Rider The Diner (LEFT) drool over the army of figures and other original gadgets on display.

hall. The "witches" wear original uniforms and perform their magic tricks. First-time visitors must pay 500 yen to get their point card issued but if you don't plan to return, you can just say you don't need it. There's a table charge (700 yen for men, 400 for women) for every hour you stay. You are also expected to order something from the menu during the first hour and again each extra 30 minutes, otherwise the witches are going to slap an extra 350 yen on your bill and your wallet will magically empty.

9 **Ikebukuro Danshi BL Gakuen**
池袋男子BL学園
2F 3-9-13 Higashi-Ikebukuro
Opening times *15:00–22:30 (Mon–Fri), 12:00–5:00 (Sat), 12:00–22:30 (Sun)*
blcafe.jp
The Boys' Love (BL) genre has a strong following among female fans. If you too are a so-called fujoshi (but men are welcome as well) you will enjoy this naughty Boys BL Academy. The place looks like a school during recession, including a blackboard, clock and high school uniform-wearing staff who spendtime playing around with each other and chatting up customers. You can also put them into risqué situations. If, for instance, you choose the Moso Coupling Pocky from their game menu, for 980 yen you can pick up two students and make them eat one of those chocolate-

museum. There is also a Shocker throne where you can actually sit and get your photo taken. The non-stop high-octane BGM is a little bit loud and in the long run can be rather annoying. Advance reservation (either online or by phone) is not strictly necessary but recommended, especially if you want to go on a weekend.

BUTLER, STUDENT, AND MAID CAFES
1 **Afilia Grand Lodge**
王立アフィリアグランドロッジ
5F 1-26-2 Minami-Ikebukuro
Opening times *11:00–14:30 & 15:30–23:00 (Mon–Fri), 11:00–23:00 (Sat–Sun & holidays)*
afilia.jp
Mahou Gakuin (Magic/Witchcraft Academy) currently has four "schools" in Tokyo and two more in Nagoya and Osaka. This Grand Lodge is the chain's original site and its main feature is a dining room with special U-shaped long tables witch give the place the appearance of a school dining

THE STAFF AT DANSHI BL GAKUEN ARE ALWAYS EAGER TO INDULGE THEIR FEMALE CUSTOMERS' BOYS' LOVE FANTASIES.

Omelet and ketchup over rice is the most common dish in many otaku diners.

coated biscuit sticks until they meet in the middle and kiss each other. It's very silly or incredibly exciting, depending on your tastes.

25 St. Giuliano Music Academy

7F 1-12-11 Higashi-Ikebukuro
Opening times *15:00–23:00 (Mon–Fri), 13:00–23:00 (Sat–Sun & holidays)*
st-giuliano.com

There seem to be a lot of people in Japan who wish they could go back to their high school days. If you are like them, you may want to pay a visit to this cafe. The atmosphere is very informal and relaxed until the school-boys start singing and dancing on stage like it was the annual culture festival. On weekdays there are three performances in the evening, while on week-ends there are five. First-time visitors are issued a point card (300 yen). After that the same rules as Afilia Grand Lodge apply with slightly different prices.

27 Swallowtail

B1F Showa Bldg., 3-12-12 Higashi-Ikebukuro
Opening times *daily 10:30–21:20*
butlers-cafe.jp (the menu and reservation pages have an English version)

AT SWALLOTAIL, FEMALE CUSTOMERS ARE TREATED LIKE ROYALTY.

Maid, Butler and Danso Cafes

Tokyo is famous for its many theme bars and restaurants, and maid, butler and *danso* cafes are a popular form of otaku entertainment dining. On one side, they are a typical example of how the Japanese manage to think out of the box and come up with seemingly outlandish but ultimately successful enterprises. On the other side, they not only cater to the Japanese love for uniforms but follow in the long local tradition of customer service. After all Japan is famous for its *ochaya* (traditional establishments where patrons are entertained by geisha) and hostess and host clubs.

Maid characters first appeared in anime in the 1980s but definitely captured the otaku imagination in the 1990s with PC dating simulator game *Welcome to Pia Carrot!* In 1998 a temporary cafe was opened to promote the game's sequel, while the first permanent maid cafe (Cure Maid Café) appeared in 2001. This novel idea became so successful that according to business news website SankeiBiz, in the following decade 282 similar establishments opened in Akihabara only. Many of them didn't survive the intense competition but maid cafes are still one of Akiba's more recognizable features. In the process they have somewhat broken out of the Moe stereotype and now many places are frequented by women, students, couples and tourists.

While each place strives to be different, a typical maid cafe is a small room with simple chairs, small tables and decor that, though minimal, often manages to be garish and over the top. Some even have a tiny stage for singing and dancing performances. The maids will welcome you with a high-pitched *okaerinasaimase goshujinsama/ojosama* (welcome home, master/mistress). You can order a la carte (typical dishes are *omu*-rice (omelet rice), curry, and cakes) but they usually recommend a set menu which may include one dish, one drink and a photo with a maid of your choice. On average the food is unremarkable and quite expensive compared to regular eateries Then again, many people don't come here for the food. Also, don't be disappointed if the maids look overly childish and unskilled. In Japan being hapless and sloppy is a sure sign of

This is by far one of the best-looking themed cafes in Tokyo, from its elegant furniture (including two massive crystal chandeliers) and attention to detail to its beautiful selection of tea cup and graceful displays. You will also get the royal treatment from highly trained butlers with perfect manners and warm voices. It's the kind of place where you want to wear something smart. The menu features lunch, dinner, tea, and dessert sets for you to choose from. Although it's especially popular with ladies, the cafe is open to everybody except children under five.

28 Wonder Parlour Café

3-9-15 Higashi-Ikebukuro

Opening times *14:00–22:00 (Mon–Fri), 12:00–22:00 (Sat–Sun & holidays)*

wonder-parlour.com

More than other maid cafes, this place aims to achieve an authentic Old England ambience, with its European-looking interior and classical background music, while the maids wear originally designed long costumes. This being Ikebukuro, most of its clientele are women who are both attracted by the exotic atmosphere and brand-name teas. Advanced reservation (by telephone only, 03-3989-8224) is optional.

WHEN IT COMES TO OTAKU DISHES, THE CLEVER PRESENTATION OFTEN OUTSHINES THE FOOD ITSELF.

In gender-confused Otakuland, *danso* (girls dressed as boys) are only one of many possible permutations.

cuteness. A sophisticated, articulate hostess can be intimidating, but a young and inexperienced girl is the epitome of moe-ness. They will lead you in singing a "spell" that will make your food taste better (something like *Moe-moe kyuuuun!* or *Pyoko-pyoko pyonpokorin!*) while shaping

your hands into a heart, or play (for a fee) some innocent game like *Paper, Scissors, Stone* or *Pop Up Pirate*.

While maid cafes enjoy the lion's share of the costumed cafe industry, they have been joined by places where impeccably dressed and mannered butlers mainly wait on female clients, and *danso* cafes whose staff is made of girls dressing and behaving like boys. Both of them have a rather different character. While some maid cafes frankly look a little tacky, butler and danso cafes feature a more restrained and elegant décor. Also, the maids' (feigned) inexperience is replaced by highly trained butlers who wouldn't look out of place in an English country house, while danso (according to many the most witty and talkative of the lot) play their androgyny with a mix of aloofness and tongue-in-cheek humor in order to attract clients of both sexes.

A lot has been said about the appeal of these places—especially the kind of ritualized, mediated intimacy which prevails in maid cafes—while media reports often hint at their potential erotic nature. The important thing to remember, though, is that the maids are just waitresses and their main job is to sell food and beverage—albeit in a weirdly fantasy setting. While, for instance, a hostess bar is a place where you are supposed to playfully flirt with sophisticated-looking women, you cannot do that with a maid or ask for her personal contact, let alone touch her. You can't even take pictures inside the cafe except for the food you have ordered. Break these rules and they are going to kick you out. This said, these are all spaces of fantasy and play that reward open-minded people, so just relax and have fun.

All these bars and cafes welcome foreigners. Some places now even hire foreign girls who can speak Japanese (probably for that added exotic touch) but almost all maids are Japanese and they will go out of their way to overcome any communication problems (because, yes, most of them don't speak English). Anyway don't worry because you won't need to speak Japanese to have fun and enjoy the experience.

CHAPTER 5

ROPPONGI

AND ODAIBA

EXPLORING ROPPONGI

MINATO WARD HAS BEEN, FOR MANY YEARS, ONE OF TOKYO'S MORE COSMOPOLITAN AREAS DUE TO A HIGHER-THAN-AVERAGE FOREIGN PRESENCE. MANY EMBASSIES, FOR INSTANCE, ARE CONCENTRATED IN THE ROPPONGI, AZABU AND AKASAKA DISTRICTS. LIKEWISE, A GOOD NUMBER OF FOREIGN COMPANIES AND INTERNATIONAL SCHOOLS ARE LOCATED HERE, CREATING AN ENVIRONMENT WHERE A LOT OF BUSINESSES ARE GEARED TOWARD SERVING THE EXPAT COMMUNITY. AT TIMES ENGLISH IS MORE OFTEN HEARD IN THE STREET THAN JAPANESE.

THOUGH NOT SPECIFICALLY AN OTAKU SHOP, DISCOUNT STORE DON QUIJOTE CARRIES MANY OTAKU GOODS.

The ward's love/hate affair with the foreign contingent began soon after WWII, when Roppongi, after being flattened by aerial bombing raids during the war, was occupied by the US army. This in turn led to the area's rise as an entertainment and nightlife district, with many bars, restaurants and cafes sharing space with an ever-expanding nightclub scene so much that in the 1970s and '80s Roppongi had the city's greatest concentration of discos. After the '90s recession and police crackdown on many yakuza- and foreign-run establishments, the area has been revived at the turn of the century by several major corporate investments which have resulted in the construction of the Roppongi Hills, Izumi Garden Tower, and Tokyo Midtown high-rise complexes that combine apartments and offices with highbrow art and entertainment spaces.

A GIANT BRONZE SPIDER WORTHY OF THE BEST JAPANESE B-MOVIES WELCOMES YOU TO ROPPONGI HILLS.

While Roppongi and the surrounding districts have very few otaku shops and eateries, it has become one of the most interesting locations in Tokyo for cultural events including anime- and manga-related festivals as well as a favorite pilgrimage destination for fans who are eager to visit the places where many anime take place.

Our exploration starts from Roppongi Station. Let's take Exit 3, the closest one to Roppongi Crossing, traditionally considered the center of the neighborhood. From there we can go either left or right. Let's go left first, along Roppongi-dori and the elevated Shuto Expressway. After about 300 meters we see a long flight of stairs, on top of which we find the 238-meter-tall Roppongi Hills Mori Tower guarded by Maman, a bronze sculpture of a giant spider by French-American artist Louise Bourgeois. While in this huge "New Urban Center," we won't find any otaku shops or eateries, a number of pop culture-oriented events take place in the plaza and, most importantly, the **Mori Arts Center Gallery** on the 52nd floor often holds blockbuster anime and manga exhibitions, particularly in summer. It is in this building, by the way, that the Pokemon Company has its headquarters.

Now back to Roppongi Station's Exit 3, this time let's go right to Roppongi Crossing past Almond, a rather unremarkable cafe that the locals for some reason pronounce

AROUND TOKYO TOWER

TOKYO TOWER IS ONE OF TOKYO'S FEW RECOGNIZABLE LANDMARKS AND ONE OF THE CITY'S BEST OBSERVATION POINTS; FROM THE EARLY '60S IT WAS THANKS TO ITS ANTENNAS THAT THE MAIN NATIONAL TV CHANNELS BROADCASTED ANIME AND TOKUSATSU SHOWS TO MILLIONS OF VIEWERS, AND FOR MANY YEARS IT'S BEEN A REGULAR FEATURE IN MANY ANIME AND MANGA STORIES AND MONSTER MOVIES (SEE PAGE 8).

Apart from *Sailor Moon*, where it appears almost in every episode because the characters live not far from it, the tower is the first thing we see in *Air Gear*'s opening title sequence (with Air Treks-wearing Ikki sitting on the roof of the first observation deck) while the three junior high school girls who star in *Magic Knight Rayearth* are taken to another world while visiting the tower on a school field trip (a traditional excursion for many out-of-towners). Then there's the 1980s hit manga *Please Save My Earth* featuring seven-year-old Rin trying to use the 333-meter-tall communications tower to broadcast radio signals to the moon where she thinks a group of alien scientists live. The list is long and includes *Cardcaptor Sakura*, *Digimon*, *Burnup-Up Excess* (in the first episode, a similar-looking Neo Tokyo Tower is attacked by a swarm of robotic insects), *Death Note* and—arguably the top of the crop—best friends Kamui and Fuma battling it out at the end of the apocalyptic *X/1999*.

While the tower itself is definitely worth a visit, many otaku these days are actually more attracted by the **Tokyo One Piece Tower** amusement park located in the Foot Town underneath. The many attractions include a tour of the pirate ship conducted by Chopper; a mirror maze; and a training camp where you become a swordsman and help Zoro fight off an attack from the sea. There's also a live show with lots of special effects, and of course two gift shops (one outside the park), a restaurant and the Café Mugiwara.

TOKYO ONE PIECE TOWER (LEFT) IS LOCATED ON THE THIRD FLOOR OF THE TOKYO TOWER (RIGHT).

"amando" and most people use as a meeting spot (without ever going inside). At the intersection many people turn left to reach the Tokyo Midtown complex, but we prefer to go in the opposite direction. This street (Gaien Higashi-dori) is full of shops and restaurants. Our next destination is the Roa Building where the **Kaidan Live Bar Thriller Night** is located. Finding the place is easy because across the street we can see a bright yellow ド ン・キホーテ sign. That's **Don Quijote**, of course, and this branch of the popular discount chain is full of kitschy junk including costumes, masks, toys and other otaku goods. But back to **Kaidan**, this bar is a must for fans of Japanese ghost/horror stories. The place itself is decorated with skeletons, skulls, chains and cobwebs hanging from faux-grimy walls, but the real attraction is the storyteller who comes out every hour and scares the bejesus out of the customers with his tall tales of the macabre. The 15-minute performance is included in the 60-minute 3,500 yen all-you-can-drink menu, and don't worry if you don't understand Japanese because the spooky atmosphere (heightened by the screams of terrorized customers) makes up for the language barrier.

ROPPONGI HOT SPOTS

2 Kaidan Live Bar Thriller Night
B1F 5-5-1 Roppongi, Minato-ku
Opening times *19:00–5:00 (Mon–Sat),*
19:00–23:00 (Sun)
thriller-tokyo.com

4 Mori Arts Center Gallery
52F 6-10-1 Roppongi, Minato-ku
Opening times and Admission Fee *see website for details*

roppongihills.com.e.nt.hp.transer.com/museum (English)

5 Tokyo One Piece Tower
3F 4-2-8 Shiba-Koen, Minato-ku
Opening times *19:00–5:00 daily 10:00–22:00 (last admission 21:00).* **Admission fee** *same-day tickets: 3,200 yen (1,600 for children 4–12 years old) Advance tickets: 3,000 yen (1,500) onepiecetower.tokyo/en (English)*

ROPPONGI EATERIES

3 Luida's Bar
5-16-3 Roppongi
Opening times *14:00–22:15 (Mon–Fri), 12:00–22:15 (Sat–Sun & holidays)*
paselabo.tv/luidas_bar
If you know where the name of the bar comes from, you are probably a *Dragon Quest* fan, in which case you absolutely have to check the place out. The interior calls to mind the popular RPG's medieval style, with swords hanging from the wall. Monitors show previews of upcoming games and even the BGM is *Dragon Quest* game music. Food and drinks of course are

inspired or named after the game's characters and magic spells, and are served by costumed waitresses. Each customer can choose among four or five 90-minute slots. Reservation (only by phone) is optional but recommended

6 Tsubakiya Coffee Roppongi
2F 6-2-35 Roppongi
Opening times *9:00–5:00 (Tue–Sat), 9:00–23:00 (Mon, Sun & holidays)*
tsubakiya-coffee.com
Maid cafes are cute and playful (and a little kitsch) but if you want the real deal you may want to try one of the many branches

(23 just in Tokyo's central 23 wards) of this retro coffee house. Modeled after the cafes that were so popular in Ginza during the Taisho period (1910s–20s) Tsubakiya offers chic interiors, a relaxed atmosphere (complete with classic background music) and traditionally dressed waiters and waitresses who serve your coffee (or tea) in porcelain cups. It's like a maid and butler cafe rolled into one!

SOUTH TOKYO FESTIVALS

I.Doll

Very similar to the Tokyo Doll Show, this event is held in Tokyo, Osaka, Nagoya and Fukuoka several times a year and typically features about 50 pro and 500 amateur booths displaying and selling dolls, clothes accessories, stationery, etc.
Admission fee *1,000 yen including program.* **Dates** *check website for schedule.* **Opening times** *11:00–16:00/17:00 depending on site. For many years this event was held at the Tokyo Metropolitan Industrial Trade Center (1-7-8 Kaigan, Minato-ku) but in the last few years it's been all over the place, including the Big Sight (Odaiba), Makuhari Messe (Chiba) and most recently the Tokyo Ryutsu Center (6-1-1 Heiwajima, Ota-ku).*
idollweb.net

Japan Media Arts Festival

Organized by the Agency for Cultural Affairs, this festival is a must-see for whoever is interested in the connections between art and technology and their social value. Divided in four categories (art, entertainment, animation, and manga) each edition attracts thousands of installations, graphic and interactive art, games and gadgets from around the world, the best of which can be enjoyed for free at a number of locations in Roppongi. The huge National Art Center, Tokyo is where the award-winning works from the four divisions are exhibited. The film screenings are held at a nearby movie theater. It is also here that all the prize-winning manga can be freely read at a specially created Manga Library. The manga division, by the way, is open to both mainstream publications and dojinshi, making this a unique place where visitors can compare the work of professionals and amateurs. Likewise the animation division often features popular anime from Japan like *Crayon Shinchan*, *Evangelion*, *Puella Magi Madoka Magika* and Production I.G's movies. The festival is rounded out by a rich program of symposia, workshops, performances and presentations by the award-winners. Did I mention it is completely free?
Dates *Feb.* **Opening times** *daily 10:00–18:00. National Art Center, Tokyo, 7-22-2 Roppongi, Minato-ku Cinem@art Roppongi, 3-8-15, Roppongi, Minato-ku. Super Delux, B1F 3-1-25 Nishi-Azabu, Minato-ku.* **How to get there** *The National Art Center, Tokyo is directly connected to Nogizaka Station Exit 6 (Tokyo Metro Chiyoda Line). From Roppongi Station Exit 4a (Hibiya Line) it's a 5-minute walk j-mediaarts.jp (excellent website with lots of useful information in English)*

Tokyo International Film Festival

For many years the Tokyo International Film Festival has struggled to find a clear identity. Now, otaku fans will be glad to know that Kadokawa Pictures executive and current TIFF director-general Shiina Yasushi finds Japanese animation one of the country's best cultural assets, and the last couple of editions had plenty of classic and new English-subtitled anime screenings to offer, including a 50-film-strong retrospective of director Anno Hideaki, Araki Tetsuro's *Attack on Titan: The First Part* and *Appleseed Alpha*, Oshii Mamoru's *Garm Wars: The Last Druid* and episodes of *The Next Generation: Patlabor.* It's always worth checking out the TIFF schedule to see what anime are on offer.
Admission fee *1,300 yen (standard tickets) available at mobile ticketing service (portal.tickebo.jp/pc/en/). Tickets sell out very quickly, especially for special screenings and events.* **Dates** *end of Oct.* **Opening times** *see website for schedule. TOHO Cinemas Roppongi Hills, 6-10-2 Roppongi, Minato-ku. TOHO Cinemas Nihonbashi, COREDO Muromachi2 3F, 2-3-1 Nihonbashi Muromachi, Chuo-ku. For other venues, check the website.* **How to get there** *Roppongi Hills complex is a 3-minute walk from Roppongi Station Exit 1c (Tokyo Metro Hibiya Line) or a 6-minute walk from Roppongi Station Exit 3 (Toei Oedo Line). Nihonbashi's theater is a 1-minute walk from Mitsukoshi-mae Station Exit A6 (Tokyo Metro Ginza and Hanzomon Lines).*
tiff-jp.net/en

EXPLORING ODAIBA

WHILE TOKYO IS NOT CONSIDERED A BEAUTIFUL CITY (AT LEAST IN THE TRADITIONAL WESTERN SENSE OF THE TERM), IT SURELY IS FULL OF SURPRISES AND INTERESTING SPOTS, AND ODAIBA IS DEFINITELY ONE SUCH PLACE. THIS ARTIFICIAL ISLAND LITERALLY DIDN'T EXIST UNTIL LAST CENTURY, WHEN THE METROPOLITAN GOVERNMENT DECIDED TO CREATE A NEW FUTURISTIC SUBCENTER THAT WAS MEANT TO PROVIDE THE CITY WITH A NEW FRONTIER AND ITS ONLY PEDESTRIAN ACCESS TO THE SEASHORE. VISITING ODAIBA IS LIKE AN ADVENTURE, AND THE FUN STARTS WITH RIDING YURIKAMOME, THE AUTOMATED, COMPUTER-CONTROLLED TRAIN LINE THAT CROSSES TOKYO BAY AND CONNECTS THE ISLAND TO THE CITY CENTER THROUGH THE 918-METER-LONG RAINBOW BRIDGE (A POPULAR ANIME PILGRIMAGE SITE FOR "DIGIMON" FANS). YURIKAMOME, BY THE WAY, MUST BE ONE OF THE MOST OTAKU-FRIENDLY TRAIN LINES IN THE WORLD AS ALL THE STATIONS USE THE RECORDED VOICES OF DIFFERENT VOICE ACTORS FOR THEIR ANNOUNCEMENTS (SEE THE LIST ON WIKIPEDIA—EN.WIKIPEDIA.ORG/WIKI/YURIKAMOME). FROM THE TRAIN ONE CAN EVEN SEE TWO OF THE ORIGINAL ISLAND FORTS (*DAIBA* IN JAPANESE) THAT WHERE BUILT IN 1853 BY THE SHOGUNATE TO DEFEND THE CITY FROM SEA ATTACK.

For years Odaiba was considered a waste of money, with only a few giant buildings dotting the otherwise desert island. Luckily for us a new wave of developments at the turn of the century has transformed the area into one of Tokyo's major shopping and entertainment centers, and today there are plenty of things to see, starting with the iconic Fuji TV building and its stunning huge metal sphere (while a massive 18-meter tall RX-78-2 Gundam that alone was worth the visit has been recently removed). Speaking of remarkable architecture, Tokyo Big Sight is another important pole of attraction for manga and anime fans as many of the dozen Odaiba-based otaku festivals and events take place inside this cavernous convention center.

Take the Yurikamome at Shinbashi and get off at Odaiba Kaihin Koen's North (Kita) Exit. Keep the street on your left and after 50 meters you will see the **DECKS** building. A lot of the otaku action on the island goes on inside this shopping mall. First of all, if you want to upgrade your Tokyo gaming experience from a simple arcade to a full-blown amusement park, **Joypolis** has about 30 attractions many of which use the latest 3D and interactive technology besides a few "extreme rides" like Initial D (driving simulator) and Halfpipe Tokyo (snow-

Odaiba is especially famous among anime, manga and game fans for hosting many otaku festivals and events such as the Comic Market (ABOVE) but this man-made island has actually much more to offer, like the nostalgic Daiba 1-chome Shotengai (OPPOSITE) where you can even enjoy quirky performances by improbable B-movie masked heroes (TOP).

boarding) and the ever-popular House of the Dead 4 SP zombie shooter. Just remember that some of the games are Japanese-language only.

When you get tired of the 3D games and the noise, you can find some respite at the **Daiba 1-chome Shotegai**, a clever reproduction of a Showa-period shopping street. The whole fourth floor is completely devoted to the good old times, with several retro game arcades, traditional junk food shops and assorted souvenir shops adding to the general feeling of nostalgia. All the shops and venues are open daily 11:00–21:00. Some of the best are:

1-chome Play Land 一丁目プレイランド
Tel. 03-3599-3765
A veritable treasure land of 80–100 retro arcade games, ranging from 10-yen-per-play old favorites like the *Shinkansen Game*, tabletop *Space Invaders* and other wonders from the '80s, beautifully preserved in their dedicated cabinets (*Hang-On*, *OutRun*, *Tokyo Wars*, etc.). Some of these games can now be found only here.

Daiba Yugijo 台場遊技場
Tel: 03-3599-1698
Retro crane games from the '80s.

Daiba Kaiki Gakko
台場怪奇学校
Tel. 03-3599-1664
obakeland.net
Put a scary twist on your old (or current) student memories by challenging this haunted school. But not before signing an agreement dispensing the "horror planner" from any responsibility in case you wet your pants.

ALL INDOOR OTAKU EVENTS IN ODAIBA TAKE PLACE INSIDE THE FUTURISTIC TOKYO BIG SIGHT.

Yamaguchi Bintaro no Yokai Hakubutsukan 山口 敏太郎の妖怪博物館
Tel. 03-3599-5052
Writer Yamaguchi Bintaro is famous in Japan as an occult scholar and this museum explores his interest in yokai (traditional ghosts, monsters and goblins) through a hodgepodge of displays that run the gamut from the funny to the downright creepy.

Haikara Yokocho ハイカラ横丁
Tel. 03-3599-5052
Tons of cheap sweets, traditional junk, and toys.

Edoya 江戸屋
Tel. 03-3599-6778
More junk food!

Walk about 200 meters in the same direction. The next block is occupied by AQUA CITY (here you will find a Toys-R-Us and a Disney store) but we are going to cross the street instead to pay a visit to the **Fuji TV building**. Fuji

DOJINSHI FANS AND COSPLAYERS (**LEFT**) PATIENTLY WAIT IN LINE HOURS BEFORE THE DOORS ACTUALLY OPEN.

DOJINSHI FAIRS

Independent publishing is alive and well in Japan, and this being the Land of the Otaku, the great majority of small-press titles is devoted to manga, anime and video game stories and characters. In fact, while zines (or fanzines), as we conceive them in the West, are relatively few and mostly circulate in underground circles, thousands of so-called *dojinshi* are produced everywhere and openly sold online, in dedicated stores and at dojin fairs. The dojinshi market, in fact, is so big that is nearly as large as the official manga industry.

To be sure, the dojin community encompasses all kinds of independent productions, from video games, DVDs and illustrations to music CDs, clothes and accessories, but the overwhelming majority of dojin works are comic books and magazines. This category, in particular, is further divided in two groups: 1) original stories and 2) *niji sosaku,* or parodies of mainstream anime, manga and video games. This latter subgenre is by far the biggest and most popular among fans. To give you an example, at the biannual Comiket in Tokyo, six halls are devoted to parodies against two for original titles.

The problem with niji sosaku is that most of them are technically illegal, as they rework copyrighted stories, creating alternate plots and using their characters in unorthodox ways—even going so far as to put, say, *Naruto* and *Dragon Ball's* Goku in the same adventure. Then there's the problem with pornography, as many dojinshi feature very explicit art. Surprisingly,

though, all the buying and selling goes on undisturbed while publishers and the authorities look the other way—the exception being the tax office which once in a while gets curious about the rare artist who actually makes big money out of his work.

The artists themselves, with a few exceptions, seem to be mostly flattered by the obvious popularity their works enjoy among fans. It must be added that dojinshi artists are very discreet and don't want their parodies to be known outside their community of fans. Apart from this unspoken rule, the prevailing laissez-faire is generally explained as a win-win situation for the manga industry. On one side, the dojinshi community is seen as a hotbed for new talent, with the best artists eventually signing for major publishers and going on to create their own original stories. Also, dojin fairs and events fuel fans' interest for certain genres and series, creating a virtuous cycle in which fans keep buying both official and independent works, thus supporting the whole otaku publishing industry.

There are so many dojin fairs in Japan that nearly every week one or more take place in and/or around Tokyo. If you can read Japanese, the best way to keep yourself updated is to sign up with the dojin portal Circle.ms (circle.ms) so you can automatically get news on any upcoming events. In this guide you will find detailed information on three of them: Comic Market (whose web-catalogue can be freely consulted at Circle.ms), COMITIA and Super Comic City.

Many dojinshi events require that you buy their catalogue as a sort of entrance fee.

If you don't have the time or are too intimidated to brave the masses of hardcore dojin fans in Odaiba, you can still get your fair share of zines in the many specialized dojinshi stores. These shops have so many titles that making sense of the way in which they are organized is not easy. They may be arranged by genre and/or circle. Popular series are further divided by Character Pairing (CP). Of course everything is written in Japanese, so unless you know the katakana syllabic system you will hardly find anything on your own. Better ask the staff, so don't forget the artist's or circle's name and the zine's original Japanese title.

Most new dojinshi are priced between 500 and 900 yen depending on size (A5 or more commonly B5), page count (30–40 pages), author's popularity, and artistic level. Compilations are more expensive (1,000–2,000 yen). Also, the same publication can be priced differently depending on the shop. Ideally you will want to check a few of them before making your purchase. In this respect Ikebukuro's Otome Road is the perfect place as all the dojinshi stores are bunched up in the same area.

I earlier mentioned pornography. If you are interested in this genre, be sure to take a valid ID with you because you may be asked to show proof of your age. Apparently Toranoana is particularly strict in this sense.

One last word of warning: All dojinshi are sealed, so if you find an interesting-looking zine by an unknown circle there's no way you can check its content out. Unfortunately the front and back covers are usually not very helpful in giving a cue about what's inside. Still, you better not try to tear open the clear bags because (as every shop makes clear) if caught you will be kicked out for good.

ODAIBA HOT SPOTS

1 **Daiba 1-chome Shotegai**
odaiba-decks.com/floorguide/f4f.php

1 **Tokyo Joypolis**
Opening times *daily 10:00–22:00. Admission for people over 17 is 800 yen but if you plan to play a lot your best choice might be the 3,900 yen passport (2,900 after 17:00) which gives you unlimited access to all the attractions.*
http://tokyo-joypolis.com/language/english (English)

4 **Fuji TV building**
Opening times *10:00–20:00 (Tue–Sun). Closed on Mon.*
fujitv.co.jp/en/visit_fujitv.html

Hotel Grand Pacific Le Daiba Project Room-G
2 *grandpacific.jp/lp/gundam*
Girls and young kids might dream of spending one night at the Disneyland Hotel, but a true otaku can't pass a chance to stay in one of these special Gundam-themed rooms. That is, if they can afford to pay a minimum of 15,900 yen (one night, standard room). The filthy rich can then upgrade to the Jaburo Room or the Special Room (34,800 yen) featuring the reproduction of the cockpit.

TV is one of Japan's major private broadcasters. It's famous for the Noitamina late-Thursday-night anime programming block, and dominates Sunday's anime lineup with such heavyweights as *Dragon Ball* and *One Piece* (9:00-10:00), *Chibi Maruko* and *Sazae-san* (18:00-19:00). Its headquarters is also one of the most recognizable and best-looking buildings in Tokyo. Inside you will find a lot to enjoy, including the Hachitama character goods shop, One Piece Restaurant Baratie and Japan's only Sazae-san shop.

Until 2016 our otaku walk would have ended at Diver City (another big shopping mall right behind Fuji TV) where we would find **Gundam Front Tokyo**, an amazing place offering an in-depth experience of the world of the Gundam series. Unfortunately it was closed in April 2017, but Bandai has announced that it will be replaced by a new project.

STRIKER IS ONE OF MANY RETRO GAME THAT YOUNG KIDS CAN PLAY AT DAIBA 1-CHOME SHOTENGAI.

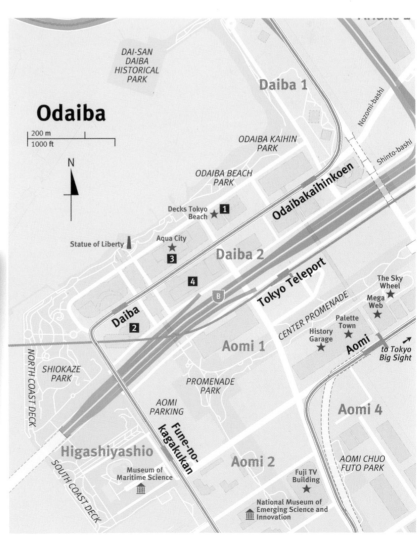

ODAIBA EATERIES

See map on page 115

4 One Piece Restaurant Baratie
Opening times *daily 10:30–22:00*
op-bt.com
This *One Piece*-themed eatery was inspired by Baratie, Chef Zeff's sea restaurant where Sanji worked as a sous-chef before joining the Straw Hat Pirates. Its menu (based on the *East Blue*, *Grand Line*, and *New World* story arcs) is more elaborate than similar otaku restaurants (hence the higher prices) and changes every few months.

3 NOITAMINA Shop & Cafe Theater
Opening times *daily 11:00–21:00*
noitamina-shop.com
For fans of Fuji TV's late-night anime program, this cafe features large screens where you can watch new episodes of their works (sometimes even before they actually air on TV) while enjoying their anime-inspired food and drinks. Be careful, because seating is limited on Saturdays when they do their special Cafe Theater video screening.

REBECCA KOGA AKA CELESTIAL SHADOW

REBECCA KOGA IS AN AMERICAN COSPLAYER WHO HAS LIVED IN TOKYO SINCE 2009. ORIGINALLY FROM SEATTLE, WASHINGTON, SHE HAS BEEN MAKING HER OWN COSTUMES SINCE 2000. phantomlegacycostumes.com

Where does this passion for cosplaying come from?

It started about 15 years ago. In Washington, we have a Renaissance Faire where people can dress like knights or princesses. That was my first kind of cosplay event. Then in 2004 I went to my first animation convention, Sakura-con in Seattle, and the level of the costumes was way beyond what I had seen at the Renassaince Faire. From there my interest snowballed out of control. I decided I wanted to be a cosplayer and make that kind of beautiful costumes.

Did you go to Sakura-con because you wanted to see the cosplay scene there?
Actually I was already into anime and manga at the time, so I wanted to learn more about animation. But when I saw everybody wearing those gorgeous costumes I thought it was perfect; like the Renaissance Faire, but it was about something I actually liked.

So you started making your own costumes from the beginning, didn't you?
Yes, I hardly had any money to buy a costume, so I would get the materials from recycled clothes, curtain fabrics, whatever I could get my hands on.

What did your parents think about your passion?
They liked it! From the start they were very supportive because at least in Washington handmade things are really special, so my parents thought there was money to be made in it (laughs). Which is true, by the way.

You moved to Tokyo in 2009 after marrying your Japanese husband. How was the transition between the

two countries cosplay-wise?

My husband is very supportive of my hobby, so he found me some events I could go to and helped me make some friends. I think my first event in Japan was only two or three months after moving here.

Is cosplaying in Japan really as different from the US as they say?

I guess so. In the US it's more common to see a lot of variations. Some people do "gender-bended" versions, turning a boy character into a girl. Others do crossovers, like putting Disney and Star Wars together. You don't see that here. In Japan cosplayers want to do the original character as accurately as possible. Then I would say the level is also different. I've seen a lot more elaborate costumes here than in America. People here spend a lot of money on their costumes. If they can't make one themselves, they will spend thousands of dollars buying one. In the US many people seem to be on a budget, so they just throw something together.

You told me you know other foreigners who cosplay in Japan. Do you find the local scene is open to foreigners?

I think so. You are definitely not going to see a lot of foreigners, but Japanese cosplayers are very curious if they notice a foreigner is doing the same series as them because they feel a connection, so it's a way to make friends.

Have you ever had any problems while cosplaying in Japan?

Well, it's pretty common for guys to try to take up-skirt shots, but I'm always straightforward with people. If they do something I don't like I simply tell them to go away. But in America, people will actually try to touch you. In Japan nobody would ever dream of doing that. They know if they get physical they are going to be in trouble. So they are more into sneaky things.

Japan is a veritable cosplay paradise and there are events held in and around Tokyo pretty much every week. How often do you cosplay now?

I'd say every other month. When it comes to bigger events like New Layers Paradise, Cosplay Festa TDC (both of them take place at Tokyo Dome City) or the Japan Cosplay Festival I go once every two or three months, but I also go to studio events every month just to take pictures with a group of friends

How can I find about these events?

I think the best way is to check out the Cure website (ja.curecos. com). They have an event listing which shows you what's going on in the Tokyo area.

And what shall I do to join one of these events?

For public places like the ones held at Tokyo Dome City, you can just show up at the door and buy your ticket on the same day. They usually give you an entrance ticket or something you can stick on your costume, and then direct you to the changing room. After that you are free to do whatever you like—as long as you are not breaking any rules. As for studio events, you need to make an advance reservation. You send them an email saying something like, it's going to be three cosplayers and a photographer; we need the studio for three hours; things like that. They charge you a fee based on that.

Speaking of taking pictures, have you been to HACOSTADIUM in Ikebukuro?

Yes, twice! It was fun. The sets are very clean and well put together. The only problem is that it's a little small and on weekends it gets incredibly busy, so I only go on a weekday.

Back to costume-making, where do you shop for materials?

The best place in Tokyo is Nippori [four stations north of Akihabara on the Yamanote Line]. There's a street called Sen-I Gai (Fabric Town) (nippori-senigai.com/free/2016map) with some 80 shops. Anything you can possibly imagine textile-wise you can get there. I'm sure most Tokyo cosplayers shop there.

How about when you want to make accessories or weapons?

For that I usually go to Tokyu Hands. It's a huge DIY chain store with three big branches in Shibuya, Shinjuku, and Ikebukuro and many others in and around Tokyo.

Do you have any advice for people who are thinking about cosplaying in Japan?

First of all they should really research the event they are going to because each one has different rules. For instance, at the JFC in Toshimaen, they don't allow girls to show their stomach at all because it's an amusement park with lots of little kids around. And secondly, do not wear your costume on your way to the event because you will get in trouble. This is a big taboo in Japan.

VETERAN COSPLAYER REBECCA KOGA MAKES HER OWN COSTUMES.

ODAIBA FESTIVALS AND EVENTS

UNLESS NOTED OTHERWISE, ALL THE EVENTS LISTED BELOW TAKE PLACE AT TOKYO BIG SIGHT (3-11-1 ARIAKE, KOTO-KU) WHICH IS DIRECTLY ACCESSIBLE FROM KOKUSAI TENJIJO SEIMON STATION (YURIKAMOME LINE) THROUGH A CONNECTION BRIDGE OR A 7-MINUTE WALK FROM KOKUSAI TENJIJO STATION (RINKAI LINE).

ANIMEJAPAN

The days between the end of March and the beginning of April signal the start of many activities in Japan, from the business and fiscal year to the school year, and AnimeJapan is where the anime industry shows off its new products and sets up new projects and collaborations. It is also one of the more internationally inclined events in Japan with the declared ambition of becoming the world's best anime event. One of the newest additions to the festival season, it was born in 2014 when two competing events, Tokyo International Anime Fair (TAF) and Anime Contents Expo (ACE), agreed to join forces. The alliance seems to have worked out fine as the festival regularly exceeds 100,000 visitors. The different character of the two original events is evident in AnimeJapan's hybrid character. On one side, the family-only area (with its special entrance) features activities like games and sing-alongs and is a reminder of TAF's kid-oriented approach. On the other hand, ACE represented the cool hardcore side of anime fandom and this is often reflected in more adult-oriented limited-edition collaboration goods and other exclusive and preorder

merchandise for sale. AnimeJapan features film screenings and a variety of stage events, talk shows and live performances from voice actors. Among the more popular features are displays of original illustrations from many anime movies and their creators' signature boards. Of course such a festival wouldn't be complete without a cosplay area. This one actually features a variety of settings from recent popular anime and even costumes that the visitors can try on. The big difference with other otaku events is that here cosplayers are free to step out of their area and walk around the booths.

Admission fee *2,000 yen (free for elementary school student). Advance tickets: 1,600 (see website for details). Only the owners of advance tickets can apply to view the stage events. The lucky ones are chosen by lottery.* **Dates** *Mar.* **Opening times** *10:00–17:00. anime-japan.jp/en*

ANIME JAPAN (**RIGHT AND BELOW**) FEATURES BOTH STAGE EVENTS AND SPECIAL BOOTHS LIKE TRANSFORMERS ADVENTURE.

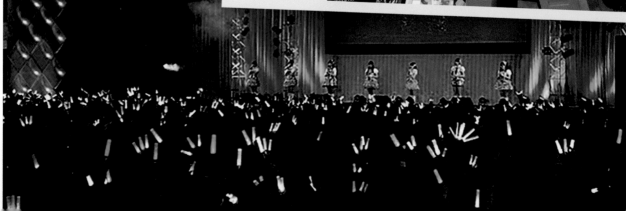

charge and craziness. The first time there can be quite overwhelming, so if you need help or information you can go to the International Desk on the second floor of East Hall 1. Last but absolutely not least, Comiket is famous for the huge number of cosplayers who gather in the plaza outside. Cosplayers must register in advance and pay a fee. As it is now custom everywhere, you cannot come or leave the fair already wearing your costume, and can only change clothes at designated dressing rooms (i.e. don't do it in the toilet!).

Most otaku festivals in Odaiba (and other places in and around Tokyo) now devote special areas to cosplay.

Free admission. Registration fee for cosplayers: 800 yen for each day. **Dates** *mid-Aug & end Dec.* **Opening times** *10:00–16:00 (company booths are open until 17:00) comiket.co.jp/index_e.html (English site—fewer information but useful if you can't read Japanese)*

COMIC MARKET

Comiket, as this event is usually called, is the world's biggest dojinshi (fanzine) fair and arguably Japan's largest otaku gathering, visited by more than half a million people twice a year. It is so big that even the huge Tokyo Big Sight convention center's ability to absorb big crowds is put to the test every time the dojinshi makers and their fans take possession of its six halls in the East Wing and Halls 1 and 2 in the West Wing (corporate companies are relegated in Halls 3 and 4) creating security problems. Differently from similar but much smaller fairs like Super Comic City and COMITIA Comiket can only be organized twice a year as more than 3,000 volunteers are needed to make sure that everything goes smoothly. Besides the corporate booths in the West Wing (PC game software makers, manga publishers, music producers, etc.) the 35,000 dojinshi circles (often consisting of only one person) sell everything, from games, illustrations and anime to more eccentric stuff (e.g. military goods and sports items), but

most fans are after the zines. The market's latest editions have typically featured more than 11 million publications on sale, nearly 9 of which are sold in three days. Comiket is especially famous for *niji sosaku*, or publications that parody existing mainstream manga, sometimes putting together characters from different manga and anime in strange (even risqué) situations. These works make the lion's share of the zines for sale and can be found in the East Wing while original publications are in Halls 1-2 of the West Wing. If you are hunting for a specific title and want to get it by any means necessary you will have to plan your visit carefully (get the telephone book-sized catalog), endure hours of waiting and very long lines. Otherwise you will be much better off arriving in the early afternoon after the initial

THE NUMBER OF COSPLAYERS IS MATCHED BUT THAT OF CAMERA-WIELDING FANS.

DOLLS PARTY

Volks is a manufacturer of mecha and garage kits but is particularly famous worldwide for its Dollfie, Super Dollfie and Dollfie Dream lines of dolls. In 1999 the Japan-based company began to organize an event where collectors could meet and share their love for dolls. Dollfies (short for doll and figure) are realistic and anatomically correct ball-jointed dolls made of porcelain-like hard plastic and can be fully customized (their body parts can be easily changed, including the wigs they use for hair and even their eyes). Therefore Dolpa—as the event is called by fans—is also an opportunity for many dealers to sell their clothes and exquisitely detailed accessories. As for the dolls themselves, other companies are featured, including fashionable Pullip and long-time fan favorite Licca-chan, but this is first and foremost a Dollfie paradise. Dolpa is currently held three times a year—twice in Tokyo and once in Kyoto, where Volks headquarters are located.

Admission fee *you need to buy the Japanese-language Official Guide Book (2,000 yen). The guide can be bought on the same day but if you want to get in line to buy limited-edition or pre-sale items you need to buy it in advance.* **Dates** *early May & Dec.* **Opening times** *10:00–17:00.* *volks.co.jp/jp/dolpa_portal/index.html*

ALL JAPAN MODEL AND HOBBY SHOW

This long-running event was born in 1963 during the Golden Age of Japanese toys, and even today, after more than 50 editions, it remains an excellent window on the local industry, displaying over 10,000 hobby-related items. All the major manufacturers show their new and upcoming products, from plamodels and figures to radio-controlled models, trains and dolls. Among the side-attractions there are demonstrations of radio-controlled (rajikon) toys (helicopters, multicopters, cars, etc.), gunpla-building classes, and kids can try their hand at flying rubber band-powered planes. The latest editions even featured a "junk market" where model builders could dig through thousands of assorted model parts, and of course the limited-edition models booths never fail to draw long lines.

Admission fee *1,000 yen (free for junior high school students and younger).* **Dates** *end of Sep.* **Opening times** *9:00–17:00.* *hobbyshow.co.jp*

COMITIA

This is another important event in the busy dojinshi schedule. Though smaller than the Comic Market and Comic City, COMITIA has a wider geographical reach, as it is held in Tokyo, Osaka, Nagoya, Niigata and Sapporo. The other noteworthy peculiarity is that *niji sosaku* (manga parodies) are banned so only original productions can be sold—not only manga but CDs, accessories and other items as well. Following the same logic, even cosplaying is not allowed. On the other hand, professional artists can sell their works along with the amateur circles but only as individuals (i.e. company booths are not admitted). Traditionally at the end of COMITIA a smaller event takes place. It's called "Sample Reading Club" because fans can read the sample dojinshi that were submitted to the main fair.

No admission ticket but you need to buy the catalogue (1,000 yen). **Dates** *Feb, May, Aug, Nov.* **Opening times** *11:00–16:00.* *comitia.co.jp*

EVEN THE INTERIORS OF MANY ITASHA ARE LOVINGLY DECORATED BY THEIR OWNERS.

ITA-G FESTA

In the 1980s, when Japan was threatening to become the world's No. 1 economic power and people were more than happy to show off their newfound wealth, more and more luxury cars began to roam Tokyo's streets. The ultimate status symbol was an Italian sports car that became known as an *itasha* (*ita* for Italy, while *sha* means car). The good times were rather shot-lived, but otaku car fans have recently appropriated the nickname for their manga-, anime- and video game-character decorated vehicles. Only in this case the prefix "ita" is short for *itai* (painful) to show the amount of time, energy and money these people have put into beautifying their four-wheeled lovers. Of course every scene must have its own magazine, so Ita-G (short for Itasha Graphics) came along and since 2008 has organized a sort of itasha motor show. They claim this is the world's largest gathering of itasha and we have no reason to doubt it (even because, let's face it, such things could only happen in Japan). Ita-G Festa has already celebrated its tenth anniversary and each time attracts vehicles from all over Japan to Odaiba's open spot not far from Fuji TV's futuristic-looking building. Apart from some 1,000 heavily decorated cars—some even sporting huge stereo systems pumping out anison and other otaku music from their giant speakers—there are plenty of *itansha* (motorbikes) and even a few scooters and *itachari* (bicycles). But Ita-G Festa is not only about motors. In fact one stage is exclusively devoted to idol group performances while another one features voice actor talk shows and comedy stage performances. And yes, cosplayers are welcome here too.

Admission fee *1,500 (5,000 yen to enter your itasha; 4,500 for a bike; 3,500 for a bicycle). Cosplay event: 500 yen.* **Dates** *first Sun in Oct (sometimes twice a year; check website for schedule).* **Opening times** *9:30–16:30. Odaiba Rainbow Town.* **How to get there** *next to Fune-no-kagakukan Station (Yurikamome Line) or a 5-minute walk from Tokyo Teleport Station (JR Rinkai Line)*

ita-g.jp/event

CULTURE JAPAN'S DANNY CHOO IS ONE OF MANY PROUD ITASHA DRIVERS.

TOKYO INTERNATIONAL COMIC FESTIVAL

This young but promising festival showcases comics by more than 50 artists from around the world. As the organization committee led by Frenchman Frederic Toutlemonde states on its home page, their hope is to eventually "become as significant as the U.S. International Comic-Con or France's Angoulême International Comics Festival" and to provide a platform "where people all around the world, who have an interest in manga

culture, can freely exchange their opinions and ideas." For the last few years they have partnered with COMITIA (see). This means that while the festival itself is free of charge, you will have to pay the entrance fee to the dojinshi market.

Admission fee *1,000 (COMITIA entrance fee).* **Dates** *Nov.* **Opening times** *11:00–16:00.*

kaigaimangafesta.com/en (English)

Akanuma Madoka is one of the indie manga artists who have been showcased at the Tokyo International Comic Festival

DESIGN FESTA

While not strictly an otaku event, there are so many things going on during the two days of the festival that you will surely find some booths for bishojo art, toys, illustrations and other anime- or video game-inspired things. Created in 1994 by designer and stylist Usuki Kunie in order to support artistic creativity "regardless of age, nationality, talent or language," Design Festa's main ambition is to help both professional and amateur artists display and sell their works, and more generally to put them in direct contact with interested fans. With 3,400 booths and 12,000 exhibitors (including designers, craftsman of any kind, musicians, performers, etc.) this is arguably the single largest art festival in Asia and it's so varied that it's literally impossible not to find something that will amaze, surprise or move you. Check their excellent English-language website out to know more about this crazy and unpredictable festival.

Admission fee *1,000 yen (two-day ticket 1,800 yen). Advanced tickets respectively cost 800 and 1,500 yen.* **Dates** *May & Nov.* **Opening times** *11:00–19:00.*

designfesta.com/en (English)

SUPER COMIC CITY

Akaboo is a printing company that mainly caters to dojinshi makers. Every year it sponsors about 20 dojinshi fairs in Tokyo, Osaka and Fukuoka, the biggest of which is Tokyo's Super Comic City (SCC). Though much smaller than the two Comikets, this is still the third largest fair in Japan. Like Comiket, you can find any sort of independently produced works here (manga, illustrations, music, games, character goods, etc.) and cosplayers are allowed in certain areas, while the main differences are that 1) SCC has a stronger corporate feeling; 2) it only lasts for five hours; 3) original works are less that 10% of the total; and, 4) most importantly, this event is predominantly oriented to female audiences. So if you are a guy you will be surrounded by thousands and thousands of girls without any male geeks in sight—which makes for a surreal, delightful and scary experience.

Admission fee *you can either buy a simple admission ticket (1,000 yen) or the event booklet (1,200). Registration fee for cosplayers: 1,000 yen for each day (cloakroom: 500 yen). Registration fee for cosplay photographers: 1,000 yen.* **Dates** *beginning of May.* **Opening times** *10:00–15:00.*

akaboo.jp/beginner_eng.html (English-language guide for beginners)

TOKYO IDOL FESTIVAL

Japan's (and arguably the world's) biggest idol festival has been around since 2010, a product of the Tokyo Idol Project's tireless work to spread idol culture around the globe. This event has rapidly achieved big numbers, with the last few editions averaging over 100 idol groups and 30–40,000 fans. The good and bad thing about this festival is that it packs so many concerts in just a couple of days. In 2014, for instance, 138 groups were spread around seven stages, with performances starting every few minutes, so it is virtually impossible to see all your favorite idols. However it's a good opportunity to confirm that not all idols look and sound alike, with some groups stretching their muscles with rock and heavy metal tunes and even a few weird sounds. TIF is known for its collaborations between members of different groups. It is also the right place to witness the birth of new idol sensations. On the other hand, some groups choose this stage to perform for the last time before disbanding or morphing into different combos. All in all there's a lot of stuff going on including the usual talk shows and (… drum roll…) handshake sessions!

Admission fee *5,500 yen. Two-day ticket 9,500 yen (advanced tickets are 5,000 and 8,800 yen respectively). In order to gain access to the stages, you need to exchange your ticket with a wristband (see website for details on place and time). Ticket sales typically start a few months before the festival and they sell out very quickly. In its drive to attract more foreign visitors, TIF is planning to make ticket purchases possible from anywhere in the world. Check the English page for details.*
Dates *first weekend in Aug.* **Opening times** *9:30–22:00. Different stages around Odaiba and Aomi (see website for map and details).*
How to get there *to reach Odaiba either take the Yurikamome or Rinkai Lines. The concerts area stretches between Kokusai Tenjijo Seimon Station and Telecom Center Station. Check website for details.*
idolfes.com
fes.tokyoidol.jp

INTERNATIONAL TOKYO TOY SHOW

The dean of otaku festivals was born in 1962 and is still going strong, with an average of 140 exhibitors and 140,000 visitors. Unsurprisingly it is more mainstream and child-oriented than other toy shows. This is after all the industry's most important event. It is co-organized by the Japan Toy Association (JTA) and the Tokyo Metropolitan Government and even enjoys the support of the Ministry of Economy, Trade and Industry. As the JTA states on its website, one of the Show's main purposes is to "provide a venue for announcing new products to markets inside and outside of Japan and for conducting business negotiations," and indeed, access to the event in the first two days is limited to registered traders (almost 19,000 in 2014). No problem, for there is plenty to see and enjoy in the last couple of days. In 2014, for instance, a grand total of 35,000 items were on display. 35 of these won the Japan Toy Award that every year honors the best products in seven different categories including boys and girls toys, educational and innovative toys, and even "high target" toys which are mainly designed for grown-up kids (i.e. adults). All the industry's heavy-weights are here peddling their games, models, dolls, robots and gadgets of any kind, and this being Japan, no toy show would be complete without an army of character-based "enterTOYment" (as the rather cheesy event motto says)—not only the usual suspects (Hello Kitty, Pretty Cure, Ultraman and One Piece, just to mention a few) but also the increasingly popular *yuru-chara* and even characters from Internet-based apps and games like *LINE* and *Puzzle & Dragons*. The show includes demonstrations of the latest products, Super Sentai stage shows, and exhibits illustrating the history of Japanese toys and even the opportunity to take a picture with your favorite character!
Free admission. **Dates** *Jun.* **Opening times** *9:00–17:00.*
toys.or.jp/toyshow

CHAPTER 6

OTHER OTAKU HOT SPOTS

OTHER OTAKU AREAS AROUND TOKYO

ASIDE FROM AKIHABARA, THE EASTERN STRETCH OF THE JR YAMANOTE LINE FEATURES A FEW MAJOR OTAKU SPOTS AND AT LEAST ONE HIDDEN JEWEL. FROM SHINBASHI TO NIPPORI IT ONLY TAKES ABOUT 15 MINUTES, BUT IF YOU PLAN TO SEE THEM ALL IN ONE GO IT WILL LIKELY TAKE THE WHOLE DAY.

IN TOKYO CHARACTER STREET YOU CAN FIND LOTS OF OTAKU GOODS FOR BOTH BOYS AND GIRLS.

This Eye Monster from Ultraman is one of the gazillion toys sold at Yamashiro-ya.

SHIMBASHI STATION

Tamiya Plamodel Factory

Opening times *12:00–22:00 (Mon–Fri), 10:00–18:00 (weekends & holidays)*

tamiya.com/english/ info/080819factory/index.htm (English)

If you are into plastic models, you'll obviously love Shizuoka-based manufacturer Tamiya, and a pilgrimage to its showroom is a must. Besides 4,000 of their famous Scale Model, Radio Controlled, and Mini 4WD series, they sell about 500 tools, paints and publications. The place doubles as a sort of Tamiya museum as many of their completed tanks, ships and cars are on display throughout the store. Last but not least, there's a 150-square-meter Event Floor, where they host seminars, workshops, and Mini 4WD and Radio Controlled car races.

TOKYO STATION

Tokyo Character Street

Opening times *daily 10:00–20:30*

tokyoeki-1bangai.co.jp

The first basement floor beneath Tokyo Station has arguably the highest concentration of manga/anime/TV-character shops in Tokyo. Some of the 26 stores lining up the station's Ichiban-gai (First Avenue) are devoted to Hello Kitty, Pokemon, Ultraman, *Jump* magazines' characters (One Piece, Naruto, Bleach, etc.), and a few TV broadcasters including NHK (for a complete list check tokyoeki-1bangai.

co.jp/pdf/floorMap_foreign.pdf). They are ideal for souvenir-shopping. First Avenue is directly connected to the Yaesu Exit on the east side of Tokyo Station and is next to other themed areas specializing in sweets and ramen.

UENO, OKAMACHI & NIPPORI

4 Yamashiro-ya

Opening times *daily 10:00–21:30*

e-yamashiroya.com/info/

With six floors full of every toy you can think of, a visit to Yamashiroya is going to take you several hours. They are particularly well-stocked with main-stream, big brand goods, but also have an interesting selection of indie toys and even a few exclusive items you will find only here. It's not the cheapest store in Tokyo, but many of their toys and models are beautifully displayed in glass cabinets, so even if you buy nothing (I dare you!), you can always take it as a visit to a toy museum.

3 Ueno-ya 上野屋

Opening times *10:00–19:30. Closed on Wed.*

gangu-uenoya.jp/html/company.html

Not really a must-see place, but if you happen to be in the area and like dusty old-school shops this one's for you. They sell party goods and the kind of toys kids used to play with in the '60s, but their forte is natural latex masks. They have a huge stock (Godzilla, Gegege no Kitaro, Ultraman, Star Wars, just to name a few) and are priced 2,500–4,500 yen.

2 Kyushoku Toban

Opening times *11:30–14:00 (lunch), 18:00–23:00 (dinner). Closed on Sun & national holidays*

kyusyokutoban.jp/place.html

If you are curious about the food Chibi Maruko and Sazae-san's little siblings eat at school, check out this diner a short distance from Akiba. Kyushoku Toban means "school lunch duty" and the waitresses here don the same kind of smock elementary school kids wear when they take turns serving lunches to their classmates. The menu (served on metal trays) is typical Japanese school lunch fare and includes deep fried whale, while *agepan* (sweet deep fried bread coated with sugar, cinnamon, etc.) is one of their more popular items. The main difference from school lunches is that you can actually order alcohol. The second floor is made to look like a classroom and can be reserved for dinner parties (4–20 people).

1 Kondo RoboSpot

Opening times *14:00–18:00 (Mon–Fri), 10:00–19:00 (Sat). Closed on Sun & holidays* robospot.jp/sys/access

While Akihabara has some nice robot shops, this off-the-beaten-path multi-space is the only one where you can actually touch and play with them. Apart from selling Kondo robots and spare robot parts, Robospot features practice facilities, a training school, and robot soccer and battle events. The good news is that while the place is usually reserved to Kondo robot users (1,080 yen/day (Mon–Fri) or 540/hour (Sat)), first-time visitors are given a chance to try their hand for free.

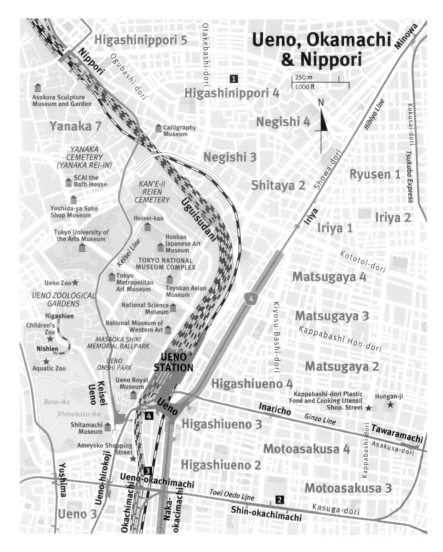

Koiwa

KOIWA

Though Edogawa is the easternmost ward in Tokyo, and Nishi Koiwa is just a few minutes away from Chiba Prefecture, Koiwa Station is only a 15-minute train ride from Akihabara. This is a quiet suburban neighborhood, free of famous landmarks and tourists, but hardcore collectors should definitely check it out. Here's why.

1 Manga Yado / Shirakuna

シラクナ・工房

1-10-4 Nishi Koiwa, Edogawa-ku

Opening times *13:30–19:00 (Tue–Sun)*

In Japan even the blandest-looking neighborhoods can hide a treasure. Take this shop. It used to sell tin toys, then in 2008 its owner began to manufacture vinyl toys under the Shirakuna brand. Today his original kaiju figures share space with a wide range of antique toys from the 1950s, all the way back to the prewar years. This cluttered place functions as a studio as well. Pay it a visit and if you are lucky you will have a chance to watch the artists while they are working on their new creations. You may want to call in advance (03-3659-1990) to make sure it's open.

2 Third Uncle / Character Toy
さあどあんくる
3-34-8 Nishi Koiwa, Edogawa-ku
Opening times *13:00–21:00 (Tue–Sun)*
third-uncle.com
Serious collectors with fat wallets can forget about the other shops in this book and head directly to Third Uncle. They can be sure to leave the store with their hands full and a much lighter wallet. From monsters, action figures and robots to mini cars, plamodels and everything in between, they have a huge stock, all in mint conditions and beautifully displayed.

HACHIOJI
Haunted Restaurant
daily 17:00–24:00 (Mon–Fri), 16:00–24:00 (Sat–Sun & holidays) lock-up.jp/haunted
This ghost-themed restaurant from the same company that runs The Lockup in Shibuya features dark rooms, skulls and other spooky tricks. You can choose between a Phantom Manor Course (2,800 yen) and a Nightmares Course (2,300) while cocktails are served in syringes and test tubes. Online reservation required.

Toybox 1102
Opening times *daily 18:00–1:00 (Fri–Sun & holidays)*
ameblo.jp/toybox1102
facebook.com/toybox1102
The highest-located retro game "bar" in Tokyo can be found on the eleventh floor of a common apartment building in Hachioji. As soon as you step inside

Featuring a restaurant, a food court and other shops, Sanrio Purolando (ABOVE) offers plenty of character-inspired and shaped food.

you are surrounded by toys, indie figures and manga (they are in the toilet too!). Literally thousands of video games are neatly sorted out in several boxes in the living room together with a few monitors, a table-top game cabinet and even a pachinko machine. The place is reservation only (mail the guy at least one week ahead. He will tell you how to find his house). It costs 500–1000 yen for one hour, depending on the number of people going. You can either bring your own food and drinks or ask your host to prepare something.

TAMA CITY
Sanrio Puroland
Opening times *10:00–17:00 (Mon–Fri), 10:00–20:00 or 10:00–18:00 (Sat–Sun). Irregularly closed on Thur and, more rarely, on Wed. (see monthly schedule for details) en.puroland.jp*
This indoor theme park is an uber-cute celebration of Sanrio's most famous creations (Hello Kitty, Little Twin Stars, My Melody, etc.) and while mainly geared toward children, can be enjoyed by adults too. Popular attractions include a roller coaster train, a boat ride, and Kitty's house, while several live performances take place at different theaters around the park. Just remember that the waiting lines in the weekends and during the holidays can be very long. If you visit during the month of your birthday you can get a birthday card at the information desk on the third floor. Wear it around your neck and you will be able to celebrate your birthday by taking commemorative photos with the house characters. As usual there are several restaurants selling mediocre overpriced food, and a big gift shop where you can overdose on cute merchandise. Ticket prices are rather steep—3,300 yen on weekdays (2,500 yen for 3–17-year-olds) and 3,800/2,700 yen on weekends and holidays (including school holidays) —but you can get discount coupons on their website. There are versions of the goddess Benzaiten (goddess of art and music) and Kishibojin (goddess of birth and children) that you can admire on a couple of signs at the entrance. Since then the dynamic moe-temple has added a theme song featuring words from the Lotus Sutra (check out its website), cute hand towels and even a 21-cm-tall figure.

OTHER SHOPS IN TOKYO

Billiken
Opening times *12:00–19:00. Closed on Mon*
billiken-shokai.co.jp
This gallery-cum-shop is very well regarded by local toy collectors, and with good reason: This is one of the best places to look for plastic monsters by the likes of Pico Pico, Sunguts and Yomomark and the kind of indie toys you can find at such events as Super Festival. They have art and children's books, paintings and illustrations as well.

Monstock
4-13-5 Kami-Jujo, Kita-ku
Opening times *16:00–20:00 (random holidays; call before going)*
geocities.jp/monstock_tokyo/home.html
Small shop and quite off the beaten track but definitely worth your time if you are into indie toys. They sell figures by such makers as Toumart and Atelier G-1.

Real Head 真頭玩具
6-4-15 Aoto, Katsushika-ku
Opening times *18:00–21:00 (Mon–Fri), 12:00–17:00 (Sat–Sun & holidays). Irregular holidays*
realxhead.jp
For some people this is the Holy Grail of indie vinyl toy stores and it's totally worth the trip. Mori Katsura has been making and selling his original takes on fight figures and mutant monsters since 2004 and today RealxHead is one of the most revered and sought after brands in the universe. The shop itself, lost in Tokyo's deep eastern suburbs, is a sort of museum. Just remember to call (03-3690-9353) before you go as its schedule is irregular to say the least.

Sofubi Cruiser Cosmo Night Alpha
25-17 Ekoda, Nerima-ku
Opening times *12:00–20:00. Closed on Tue and other irregular days (call before going, 03-3557-4616)*
sofvi.com/news/

The grannies who frequent the narrow shopping street where this store is located are regularly startled by the parade of monsters on display. Inside it's soft vinyl figures and other toys (vintage items too) floor to ceiling, including the Yusei Majin figures created by the shop itself.

Tokyo Solamachi
Opening times *daily (10:00–21:00)*
tokyo-solamachi.jp/english/
The 634-meter-tall Skytree is the latest addition to the admittedly short list of internationally famous Tokyo landmarks. While you are there, don't forget to explore Solamachi, the huge shopping mall at the base of the tower which has lots of character-based and toy shops (e.g. Takara Tomy's model cars and railroad toys, Studio Ghibli's Donguri Kyowakoku shop, etc.). The only downside is that unlike Tokyo Station's compact Character Street, they are scattered over different floors.

GAME CENTERS
Game In Ebisen
2F 1-75-12 Asahigaoka, Nerima-ku
Opening times *daily 12:00–24:00*
ebi-cen.com
Now that Shibuya Kaikan Monaco has closed down, for a genuine retro game experience you will have to track all the way to this independent arcade in Nerima Ward. Most of the collection is made of extreme shooting games, and 90 percent of the clientele are hardcore gamers with extraordinary skills hell-bent on improving their already stratospheric scores. One thing that sets the place apart is that it features a showcase displaying all the games available, and if you find something of your liking they will gladly install the circuit board for you (last order 23:00) and, for a fee, will even record your play on DVD (reservation required). All games are only 50 yen.

EATING AND DRINKING ESTABLISHMENTS
Batta Mon バッタもん (Itabashi-ku)
B1F 28-6 Ooyama Higashicho, Itabashi-ku
Opening times *17:00–23:00. Closed on Mon & Tues*
nigohkai.com/shop.html
For many devoted *Kamen Rider* fans, just hearing the name Sasaki Takeshi is enough to make them faint. Since Sasaki played Ichimonji Hayato, aka Kamen Rider 2, in the original TV series, he has become one of the most beloved actors in the tokusatsu genre. If you are a fan, you may actually have a chance to meet him (in Japanese, of course). Just pay him a visit at the izakaya (pub) he opened a few years ago not far from Ikebukuro. The place is decorated with many original gadgets and illustrations, and the food (typical izakaya fare) is prepared by the man himself. You can freely take pictures, while an autograph will cost you 1,000 yen. Just call in advance to reserve your seat and make sure Sasaki is in the house, as he's often busy with talk shows, performances, etc.

Café Saya
3-37-1 Kamiya, Kita-ku, fax 050-3737-4575
Opening times *13:00-18:30 (Sat only)*
cafesaya.net/access
Tokyo is a city where you can find interesting things in unlikely places, like this doll-friendly cafe in the middle of nowhere. The owner is a doll fan herself and apart from selling hand-made goods (e.g. miniature books), she has created an environment where doll owners can share their passion. After each Doll Show they organize a Doll Festa where dolls can be displayed in specially prepared sets and get them photographed. As seats are limited, the cafe is reservation only. Check its online schedule because it's not open every Saturday.

OTHER MUSEUMS AND LIBRARIES

(1) Gallery of Fantastic Art

GoFA is a tiny commercial gallery exhibiting and selling manga-, anime- and game-related art, postcards, T-shirts, and other goods. They usually have book and artist signings, and sometimes the cafe on the first floor turns into a "collaboration cafe" with a character-themed menu. Check their schedule online because they are closed between shows.

Free admission. **Opening times** *12:00–18:00. Closed on Mon except when it is a national holiday*

gofa.co.jp; gofa.co.jp/access.shtml

Meiji University Contemporary Manga Library (Naiki Collection)

In the first 20 years after WWII, many people in Japan didn't buy books and manga; they used to rent them the same way they would later rent videotapes and DVDs. *Kashihon* (rental) manga became popular in the early '50s and continued to flourish until the early '60s when they were gradually replaced by weeklies like *Shonen Sunday* and *Shonen Magazine*. Naiki Toshio was a comic lover who in 1955 opened one such store in Shinjuku when he was still in high school. His passion for manga was such that in 1978 he turned his 20,000-volume collection into a library. Currently the Gendai Manga Toshokan has grown to 180,000 books and magazines and is part of the Meiji University manga library system. Among them there are many rare publications from the '50s through the early '60s, when manga culture began to spread across Japan. All this stuff can be read in loco for a small fee (100-yen per item) but only members of the Tomo no Kai who pay an annual 6,000-yen membership fee have access to the publications from 1970 and older.

2F 565 Waseda Tsurumakicho, Shinjuku-ku **Admission fee** *300 yen (200 yen for junior high school students and under).* **Opening**

times *12:00–19:00. Closed on Tue and Fri. sites.google.com/site/naikilib*

(1 • 5) Hasegawa Machiko Art Museum

There is literally nobody in Japan who doesn't know Hasegawa Machiko (one of the first female manga artists) and her mega-successful manga and anime *Sazae-san*. This museum, however, mainly displays paintings and other artworks collected by Hasegawa and her sister Mariko through the years. Only once a year, during the summer holidays, Fuji TV sponsors an exhibition entirely devoted to *Sazae-san*. The rest of the year, only a small space on the second floor (Machiko's Corner) is devoted to her manga art. Probably the best thing for *Sazae-san*'s fans is the small but well-stocked shop on the first floor selling a seemingly infinite array of original goods (toys, cups, file folders, towels, memo pads, snacks, etc.). Ironically you have a better chance to see Hasegawa's work outside the museum, as the area features 12 statues of the Isonos besides assorted banners and wall art.

1-30-6 Sakura Shinmachi, Setagaya-ku **Admission fee** *600 yen (high school and university students 500 yen, junior high*

students and under 400 yen).* **Opening times** *10:00–17:30. Closed on Mon (Tues when Mon is a national holiday)*

hasegawamachiko.jp

(1 • 2) Matsumoto Katsuji Gallery

This tiny gallery in posh Setagaya Ward is devoted to the work of another manga pioneer, Matsumoto Katsuji, a children's book illustrator who was mainly popular between the 1930s and '50s and is best remembered for his American comic-inspired shojo manga *Kurukuru Kurumi-chan*. He was an inspiration to several future manga greats and is considered one of the original creators of the kawaii style. On display in this gallery are a few paintings and other works, and a collection of magazines and books featuring his illustrations.

4-14-18 Tamagawa, Setagaya-ku **Admission fee** *300 yen.* **Opening times** *visits by appointment only. You need to call (03-3707-3503) or mail (kurumifriend@gmail.com) at least 7 days beforehand.*

katsudi.com

Meiji University Yonezawa Yoshihiro Memorial Library of Manga and Subcultures

Yonezawa Yoshihiro was a writer and manga critic who in 1975 founded Comiket with two college friends. He was also a collector of anything related to manga, dojinshi and pop culture and when he died in 2006 his huge collection (more than 4,000 boxes and over 140,000 items) was donated to Meiji University's School of Global Japanese Studies that opened this library in 2009. Though the place is a university facility,

MORE THAN JUST A MANGA CHARACTER, SAZAE-SAN IS ONE OF JAPAN'S MOST BELOVED CULTURAL ICONS.

THE MEIJI UNIVERSITY YONEZAWA YOSHIHITO MEMORIAL LIBRARY IS ARGUABLY TOKYO'S BEST-STOCKED MANGA LIBRARY.

it is open to anybody over 18 through a membership system. One-day members can only view open-stack materials, which means they don't have access to materials published before 1979. You can photocopy many of the items in the library but borrowing is not allowed. For details on how to use the library, read the detailed English-language page on their website. The place is highly recommended to people who are interested in manga history and rare materials. There is also a free exhibition space on the first floor. The grand plan for this institution is to eventually become the (temporarily named) Tokyo International Manga Library.

1-7-1 Sarugaku-cho, Chiyoda-ku
Admission fee *1-day membership: 300 yen. 1-month: 2,000 yen. 1-year: 6,000 yen.* **Opening times** *Mon & Fri: 14:00–20:00. Weekend & holidays: 12:00–18:00. Closed on Tue–Thu.*
meiji.ac.jp/manga

(1・2・4・5) Nurie Museum

Nurie is Japanese for coloring book and this museum is completely devoted to this particular children's pastime. In Japan nurie were one of the many cultural imports from the West during the Meiji Period. The practice really took off in the first 20 years of last century but nobody became as good or famous as Tsutaya Kiichi, who elevated a simple hobby into an art. His cute young girls (a mix of Shirley Temple and Kewpie doll) were particularly popular between 1945 and 1965 and the museum's collection (put together by his niece) is particularly

strong for these two decades. At the entrance one finds the museum shop and the temporary exhibits which change monthly. Another exhibition space is mainly devoted to Tsutaya's works. They even provide a corner where visitors can try their coloring skills and maybe feel a little like when they were kids.

Admission fee *500 yen (junior high and up), 100 yen (elementary school).* **Opening times** *12:00–18:00 (Mar–Oct), 11:00–17:00 (Nov–Feb) only on Sat, Sun & national holidays.*
nurie.jp; nurie.jp/foreign/index_eng

(1・2・5) Yayoi-Yume-ji Museum

People in search of a bargain will be happy to know that here you can see two museums with a single ticket. The Yayoi Museum mainly displays the works of illustrators from the end of the Meiji Period until the postwar era (1890–1945). The Yumeji Museum is dedicated to the works of illustrator Yumeji Takehisa, one of the foremost artists and poets of

the Taisho Period (1912–1926), when girl's culture flourished in Japan. Indeed, he was especially famous for his portraits of beauties that he published in girls and ladies magazines like Shojo no Tomo. At the time it was in these publications that most manga artists had a chance to hone their skill. Exhibitions are rather small but still worth a visit if you are into early 20th-century art, older comics and shojo manga. There are also a cafe and a shop selling many goods featuring Yumeji's distinct style.

2-4-2/3 Yayoi, Bunkyo-ku
Admission fee *900 yen (high school and university students 800 yen, junior high and younger 400 yen).* **Opening times** *10:00–17:00. Closed on Mon (Tues when Mon is a national holiday)*
yayoi-yumeji-museum.jp

MANY WORKS BY ARTIST YUMEJI TAKEHISA CAN BE ADMIRED AT THE YAYOI-YUMEJI MUSEUM

KANAGAWA PREFECTURE

(4•5) Yokohama Anpanman Children's Museum and Mall

For many years now, Anpanman has been the undisputed darling of all Japanese children. According to Bandai's annual survey, for the last 13 years in a row it's been the favorite character among kids aged 0 to 12 years. The bread roll-headed superhero has sold over 50 million books so far, while the ubiquitous franchise has become a one-trillion-yen business. So it's not a surprise that this place is yet another money-making machine. To be sure, though it is called a museum, it's closer to an amusement-park-cum-shopping-mall. The rather expensive "museum" side of the impressive-looking building is divided into three floors featuring the usual kids-friendly attractions besides a small exhibition room and a diorama. Anpanman Square, on the other side, is a typical mall providing many chances to spend your money with nine souvenir shops, 10 eateries and even a hair salon and photo studio! Sore ike! Anpanman!!

Admission fee *1,500 yen (1 year and older).* **Opening times** *10:00–18:00 (last admission 17:00). Closed on New Year's Day. Shopping Mall: 10:00–19:00. Anpanman & Pecos Kitchen: 10:00–20:00 (last order 19:00)* *yokohama-anpanman.jp/main.html*

In 2002 *Time* magazine included Doraemon in its *Asian Hero* special issue

(1•4•5) Fujiko F. Fujio Museum

Fujimoto Hiroshi and Abiko Motoo created many unforgettable characters under the pen name Fujiko Fujio (Perman, 21emon, Kiteretsu Daiyakka, Esper Mami, etc.) but there's no doubt the one for which they have become world-famous is Doraemon. Since their first appearance in 1969, the stories featuring the robot cat from the 22nd century and his children friends have sold more than 100 million copies, making him one of the most recognizable symbols of Japanese pop culture. So it's no surprise that he gets the lion's share in the museum devoted to Fujiko F. Fujio's work (Fujimoto's adopted name after he ended his 40-year partnership with Abiko). Indeed, this place is often called by manga fans Doraemon Museum.

The facility's centerpieces are the two big galleries displaying Fujimoto's

THE YOKOHAMA ANPANMAN MUSEUM IS ONE OF FIVE MUSEUMS IN JAPAN DEVOTED TO THE POPULAR CHARACTER.

original works on a rotation basis. This is one of the very few manga museums in Japan whose main purpose is to collect, preserve and display a particular author's work. The useful English audio guide (included with admission) has a lot of commentary on his life and work. Children, on the other hand, are definitely more attracted by the playroom, manga-reading room, and the rooftop garden featuring "life size" statues of Doraemon & Company together with some of the story's most recognizable places and gadgets (the playgound's earthen pipes, the Dokodemo Door, etc.), while a 100-seat theater displays original short films.

If you are a fan, be sure to pack your wallet with loads of money because you will hardly resist a visit to the cafe selling Doraemon-themed dishes and the well-stocked museum shop. Both food and some of the goods are quite expensive (figures and dolls typically goes for 4–5,000 yen).

Don't forget that tickets are not sold at the museum

and must be purchased in advance. The quickest and cheapest way to get them is at a Lawson convenience store through a Loppi ticket machine. A tutorial on how to do this can be found at tokyogigguide.com/tickets. You will be required to make a reservation, choosing a date and time slot (10:00, 12:00, 14:00 or 16:00). If possible, try to avoid weekends and school holidays as the museum gets packed with kids.

Admission fee *1,000 yen (adults), 700 yen (high school and junior high school), 500 (4 years and older).* **Opening times** *10:00–18:00. Closed on Tue (except Apr 29th–May 5th and Jul 20th–Sep 3rd) and Dec 30th–Jan 3rd* *fujiko-museum.com/english*

(1 • 5) Tin Toys Museum

Japan used to be the major exporter of tin toys in the world. From the 1910s (when it replaced Germany) all the way through the mid-'60s, tin toys consti-tuted about 60 percent of Japanese toy exports before they were gradually replaced by plastic. Apparently now there is only one tin toys craftsman left in Japan. Kitahara Teruhisa is one of the major collectors of tin toys in the world. While a small place, his museum packs some 3,000 toys ranging from cars and trains to aircraft and dolls. The collec-tion is arranged roughly by era and goes all the way back to the late 1890s. It includes foreign characters like Mickey Mouse and Popeye but otaku fans will be particularly delighted to find

many Japanese examples of space rockets, Ultraman toys, several rarities like those wonderful '50s robots (in mint condition!), and even early examples of Astro Boy. If you are into old tin toys this is a must-see place.

Admission fee *200 yen (junior high school and under 100 yen).* **Opening times** *daily 9:30–18:00 (–19:30 on weekends & holidays).* *toysclub.co.jp/muse/tintoy.html*

CHIBA PREFECTURE

(4 • 5) Toei Hero World

Toei is world famous for its *tokusatsu* live-action superhero TV shows and movies, like *Kamen Rider* and the *Super Sentai* series. In 2013 the film studio partnered with amusement park and game center operator Namco to open a hybrid park/museum in Chiba. The amusement park side of the place is mainly geared toward children (some

attractions are actually off-limits unless you are really small) but the museum is a must-see if you are a special-effect movie fan. Most of the costumes and props on display were used for the actual productions, adding one more thrill to the visit. Overall the exhibition space is rather small but it feels much larger thanks to the clever layout, with battle dioramas and full-sized heroes surrounding you from everywhere. Last but not least, the shop sells not only the usual exclusive goods (cups, cookies, T-shirts, etc.) but even some Premium Bandai merchandise that is generally sold only online.

Admission fee *museum only 1,400 yen (1000 yen junior high students and younger). Museum + unlimited access to attractions: 2,000 yen.* **Opening times** *9:00–20:00 (last admission 19:00). Closed only few days a year (check the website before going)* *toei-heroworld.jp*

SAITAMA PREFECTURE

(2 • 4) Saitama Manga Kaikan/Saitama Municipal Cartoon Art Museum

When debating the origins of manga, people's opinions tend to differ. However everybody seems to agree about the role Kitazawa Rakuten played in its development. The Saitama-born artist was in fact the first professional cartoonist in Japan and is considered one of the founding fathers of modern manga. Now the site where he lived has been turned into a memorial museum—arguably the very first manga-related institution created in Japan. The first floor features an exhibition space devoted to works by Kitazawa himself and other artists, together with the reproduction of his work room, while the second floor is a manga library. While rather off the beaten track, this museum is worth a visit especially if you are into manga history.

Free admission. **Opening times** *9:00–16:30. Closed on Mon (Tues when Mon is a national holiday).* *city.saitama.jp/004/005/002/003/001/ index.html*

Other Festivals and Events

@Jam Project

The Tokyo Idol Festival now has a strong rival in the @Jam Project (at-jam.jp) which is behind a string of music concerts that have featured such groups as JKT48, Tokyo Girls' Style and even boy groups. Each event has a similar format but differs in size, from the monthly more intimate performances in Akiba (@Jam Next) to the mega concert in Yokohama at one of the largest venues in the Kanto region (**@Jam Expo**) and the two-day festival in Odaiba. The bigger events include multiple stages (seven at the Arena in 2015), talk stages, DJing and meet-and-greet areas.

@ Jam Next

Admission fee *2,500 yen (either part one or two), 4,000 yen (all-day ticket). Advanced tickets only.*
Dates *every month on the second Sun.*
Opening times *Pt.1: 13:00–; Pt.2: 17:00–. Akiba Cultures Gekijo, Akiba Cultures Zone B1F 1-7-6, Soto-Kanda, Chiyoda-ku*

@ Jam the Field

Admission fee *5,000 yen. Advanced tickets only.* **Dates** *check schedule online.* **Opening times** *13:00–20:00 Different venues in or around Shibuya (check website)*

@ Jam

Admission fee *5,000 yen (two-day ticket 8,800 yen).* **Dates** *end of May.* **Opening times** *14:00–.*
Zepp DiverCity Tokyo, Diver City Tokyo Plaza, 1-1-10 Aomi, Koto-ku

@Jam Expo

Admission fee *reserved seat: 8,000; standing only: 7,000 (both come with a CD). VIP ticket: 35,000 (private box and lot of amenities).* **Dates** *end of Aug.* **Opening times** *10:30–20:00 Yokohama Arena, 3-10 Shin-Yokohama, Konan-ku, Yokohama*

Cosplay Festa TDC

The oldest one-day event in Japan has been held since 1997 at Tokyo Dome City, attracting an average of 6,000 people each time, from veteran cosplayers to beginners.

The area devoted to cosplaying is 30,000 square meters wide. This is also the only event of this size which offers cloakroom service. Last but not least, all attractions in the amusement park that is part of the Tokyo Dome City complex are included in the entrance fee.

Admission fee *2,300 yen (advance tickets 2,100 available at Lawson's).* **Dates** *several times a year. Check the website for upcoming dates.* **Opening times** *10:00–21:00. Tokyo Dome City, 1-3-61 Koraku, Bunkyo-ku cosplayfesta.com*

New Layers Paradise

Basically it's like Cosplay Festa TDC. You can attend even if you are not a layer (cosplayer) and only want to take pictures, but you need to register your camera for a fee.

Admission fee *2,300 yen (advance tickets 2,100 available at Lawson's). Camera registration fee for non-cosplayers: 500 yen.* **Dates** *4 times a year. Check the website for schedule.* **Opening times** *10:00–21:00. Tokyo Dome City, 1-3-61 Koraku, Bunkyo-ku laypara.jp*

Super Festival

First launched in 1992 and run by toy maker Art Storm (they own the Fewture shop in Akihabara), this is one of toy fans' favorite events in Tokyo. Here, new and old (i.e. collector's items) toys, models and figures are both exhibited and sold by

manufacturers, shops and private dealers. Established companies like Marusan and Bullmark, new emerging brands and boutique makers display a vast array of shokugan, alloy and tin toys, plamodels, garage kits, dolls and bishojo figures. There is also a special area for mini cars, model trains, airplanes, etc., and a bunch of other items including T-shirts, CDs, LDs, books, magazines and cards. Equally popular with the toy-loving crowd is the Tokusatsu Archive stage which hosts talk shows and signing events by popular creators, actors and industry veterans. This festival is very laidback and full of friendly people, and stiff corporate PRs are nowhere to be seen.

Admission fee *1,500 yen (elementary school students 800 yen).* **Dates** *Jan, Apr & Sep.* **Opening times** *10:30–16:00. Kagaku Gijutsukan, 2-1 Kitanomaru-koen, Chiyoda-ku artstorm.co.jp/sufes.html*

Tokyo Anime Award Festival

TAAF's stated aim is to support both the artistic and business side of animation and its main attraction is the international lineup of works (both feature and short films) they show during the five days of the event, divided between two sections: the Competition Grand Prize (featuring Japanese and foreign films that have not been screened in Japan for commercial purposes) and the Anime of the Year Award (films that attracted local fans' attention during the past year). In recent years the organizers have mostly played it safe by recognizing the "usual suspects" (e.g. Disney, Studio Ghibli) which have proved to be winners at the box office. Let's hope they will come up with more daring choices in the next few years. Still, for anime fans this is yet another great chance to see some good stuff.

Admission fee *1,000 yen (3,000 yen for all-night screenings).* **Dates** *Mar.* **Opening times** *see website for schedule. Ikebukuro. animefestival.jp/en/*

Tokyo Doll Show

Since 1998 the Tokyo Doll Show has been a chance for both manufacturers and hobbyists to show and sell their dolls and doll accessories. Not only all the major brands (Volks, Pullip, Licca-chan, etc.) are present but smaller companies as well. Perhaps the most fascinating aspect of the show is seeing the care with which the dolls' "parents" prepare and proudly show their dolls, often dressing them like famous manga and anime characters. Taking pictures is usually okay but you should always ask for permission.

Admission fee *The catalog/brochure costs 1,000 yen (junior high and high school students: 500 yen; free for elementary school students). If you want to be among the first to enter, you also have to buy a numbered ticket (500 yen). Otherwise you must wait at the end of the line.* **Dates** *scheduled irregularly three times a year (see website for details).* **Opening times** *11:00–16:00. Sunshine City Hall D, 3-1-1 Higashi Ikebukuro, Toshima-ku dollshow.net*

CHIBA

All the festivals in Chiba take place at Makuhari Messe (2-1 Nakase, Mihama-ku, Chiba City) which is a 2-minute walk from Kaihin Makuhari Station (JR Keiyo Line). From Tokyo Station it takes 30–40 minutes (550 yen). The Makuhari Messe site provides useful information in English: m-messe.co.jp/en/index.html

Japan Amusement Expo

The world of Japanese arcade games is ruled by two powerful groups, the Japan Amusement Machine and Marketing Association and the All Nippon Amusement Machine Operators Union. They used to run two competing events until in 2012, when they decided to merge them into a giant fair, the Japan Amusement Expo. Visiting JAEPO is like stepping into a huge game center where all the machines on display are brand new. This is in fact where Japan's main arcade game makers unveil their latest creations. The main exhibition area is chockfull of some 1,000 machines. The next bigger area is the Prize Zone (*UFO Catcher* gadgets) while other smaller areas

FESTIVAL, CONVENTION AND FAIR CALENDAR

January
Akiba Daisuki Festival (Akihabara)
Next Generation World Hobby Fair (Chiba)
Super Festival (Kitanomaru Park, Chiyoda-ku)

February
Wonder Festival (Chiba)
Japan Amusement Expo (Chiba)
COMITIA (Odaiba)

March
AnimeJapan (Odaiba)
Tokyo Anime Award Festival

April
Nico Nico Chokaigi (Chiba)
Super Festival (Chiyoda-ku)

May
Super Comic City (Odaiba)
Dolls Party (Odaiba)
Design Festa (Odaiba)
COMITIA (Odaiba)
@ Jam (Aomi, Odaiba)

June
International Tokyo Toy Show (Odaiba)
Next Generation World Hobby Fair (Chiba)

July

August
Tokyo Idol Festival (Odaiba)
Comic Market (Odaiba)
Animelo Summer Live (Saitama)
@Jam Expo (Yokohama)
Akiba Daisuki Festival (Akihabara)
Ultraman Festival (Ikebukuro)
COMITIA (Odaiba)

September
Japan Media Arts Festival (Roppongi)
Tokyo Game Show (Chiba)
All Japan Model and Hobby Show (Odaiba)
Super Festival (Chiyoda-ku)

October
Kichijoji Anime Wonderland (Kichijoji)
Ita-G Festa (Odaiba)
Nerima Anime Carnival (Nerima, near Ikebukuro)
Anime Manga Festival in Saitama (Saitama)
Tokyo International Film Festival (Roppongi, etc.)
Wonder Festival (Chiba) [Summer 2016 was held in July]

November
Animate Girls Festival (Ikebukuro)
Design Festa (Odaiba)
Tokyo International Comic Festival (Odaiba) (or end of October)
World Mascot Character Summit in Hanyu (Saitama)
COMITIA (Odaiba

December
Jump Festa (Chiba)
Dolls Party (Odaiba)
Comik Market (Odaiba)

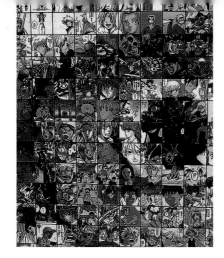

are respectively devoted to publications covering the amusement and entertainment industry and the few foreign exhibitors (usually from China). And let's not forget the ever-present army of cosplayers who descend on Makuhari Messe to show off their skin-revealing outfits even in February's cold temperatures

Admission fee *1,000 yen (free for elementary school kids and over-60s).* **Dates** *Feb.*
Opening times *10:00–17:00.*
jaepo.jp/index_en.html (English)

Jump Festa

What sets this event apart from similar conventions is that Jump Festa is sponsored by giant manga publisher Suiheisha, and focuses on the content of four titles of its best-selling *Jump* series of *Shonen* manga magazines. Traditionally each festival showcases new movies, games and merchandise for the upcoming season. From goods to live performances and even food, everything follows the same theme. Jump Super Stage gives fans an opportunity to meet popular voice actors as well as current and former Jump artists, while in the Genga World they can admire original art and signed illustrations. Recent editions have averaged nearly 150,000 visitors, many of whom are lured by the limited-edition goods on sale.

Free admission. Dates *third weekend in Dec.*
Opening times *10:00–19:00.*
jumpfesta.com

Next Generation World Hobby Fair

The biggest game and hobby event in Japan is organized by publishing company Shogakukan (one of the major peddlers of manga in the country) and is held in four different cities. The Tokyo meeting takes place in nearby Chiba twice a year. Compared to other otaku events, many of the latest toys and video games showcased are geared to younger kids (elementary and junior high school) but everybody is invited to try them all day long for free. There are also a market area where you can get limited-time goods, stage events devoted to the hottest items, and even sign sessions where kids up to 15 years old can get an autograph from one of their favorite artists.

Free admission. **Dates** *Jan & Jun.*
Opening times *9:00–16:00.*
whobby.com

Nico Nico Chokaigi

This Super Meeting (Cho-kaigi) is a hodgepodge of events, mixing together typical otaku favorites (anime, video games, cosplay, vocaloid, etc.) with the mildly weird (UFOs, dinosaurs, pro wrestling and… sumo?!) and the frankly disturbing (a Japan Self-Defense Forces booth doing some PR work for hawkish Prime Minister Abe Shinzo). The anime area features hands-on attractions from a number of popular works that will give you a chance to try your hand at voice acting, idol producing or replicating the characters' exploits. Festival organizer Nico Nico Douga is Japan's answer to YouTube and has developed the biggest video community in this country. Videos uploaded on this site feature an original (shall we say "only-in-Japan?") commenting system where comments posted by viewers appear directly on the video screen allowing users to interact in real time. Depending on your tastes and inclinations, the effect can be cute, exhilarating or just plain annoying. The site, by the way, is particularly famous for home-made videos creatively mixing anison and images, and the festival indulges Nico Nico users' interests with plenty of amateur singing, dancing, and performances. Each edition largely exceeds 100,000 attendees over two days while the online live broadcast is followed by more than 7.5 million people. And those who have some energy left can even attend the Nico Nico Cho Party in the late hours.

Admission fee *2,000 yen (advanced ticket 1,500 yen). Two-day pass 2,500 yen (advanced purchase only).* **Dates** *last weekend in Apr.*
Opening times *10:00–18:00.*
chokaigi.jp

Tokyo Game Show

In the world of supposedly "international" otaku festivals, the Tokyo Game Show (Japan's biggest video game exhibition) seems to be one of the few events with a true global appeal, as in 2014 nearly half of the record 412 exhibitors came from outside Japan. Gaming has recently entered a new dimension with different technological supports like smart phones and tablets offering fans novel ways to play, and this festival has a Social Game Area showcasing the hundreds of titles specifically created for iOS, Android and other such platforms. The Family Area is off-limits to "kids" older than 11 years old (unless they are their parents) and features the usual character-related events while on the other end of the spectrum the Romance Simulation Game Area is all about dating-simulation PC games that otaku of both sexes love so much. Other

favorite areas are devoted to independent developers, merchandise sales, game hardware, live music events and the usual cosplay area.

Admission fee *1,200 yen (advanced tickets 1,000 yen), free for kids younger than 12.* **Dates** *Sep.* **Opening times** *10:00–17:00.*
expo.nikkeibp.co.jp/tg

Wonder Festival

Garage kit fans and collectors are a rabid bunch who can hardly wait to see their favorite products vis-a-vis. To help quench their thirst, figure manufacturer Kaiyodo brings all the best figures and models under one roof twice a year, making WonFes the best event in Japan for showing and selling prototype figures by both amateur and professional creators, with an average of 1,800 dealers and 50,000 fans in attendance. Many companies now showcase limited editions especially produced for this festival, while for amateurs this is one of the few chances they have to show off their manga- and anime-inspired PVC and cold-cast creations without violating copyright laws thanks to the "one-day-copyright-waiving" system. So if you are hunting for works by some garage kit superstar like Bome, this is definitely the go-to place. Just be prepared to fight with thousands of other fans, as these works sell out immediately.

P.S.: Since 1999 the festival hosts a parallel event called Wonder Showcase where a selected number of gifted sculptors chosen by the planning committee are given the royal treatment by displaying (and selling) their works in special glass booths. Wonder Showcase is also WonFes's official label and the pieces featured in each edition are later available at Kaiyodo Hobby Lobby Tokyo in Akihabara and Kaiyodo Online Shop.
Admission fee *2,000 yen.* **Dates** *Feb & Oct.* **Opening times** *10:00–17:00.*
wf.kaiyodo.net

SAITAMA

Anime Manga Festival in Saitama

Saitama is famous as the site of a number of popular manga and anime and in 2013 the local authorities decided to start a festival that would help further promote the prefecture as an otaku Mecca. The operation seems to have been very successful as the first two editions have attracted about 60,000 visitors. The festival features idol stage shows, concerts by anison performers, talk shows, and even an itasha (anime-decorated cars) exhibition and cosplay event.
Admission fee *500–600 yen for market, cafe and tourism exhibitions (free for high school students and younger). Concert: 6,800 yen. All other events are free.* **Dates** *Oct.* **Opening times** *10:00–18:00.*
Sonic City, 1-7-5 Sakuragicho, Omiya-ku, Saitama City, Saitama Prefecture.
anitamasai.jp

Animelo Summer Live

Anisama, as the Japanese fans like to call it, is the most important music festival devoted to songs featured in anime, video games and tokusatsu TV shows, and most performers are singers and voice actors specializing in these genres. The three-day event features more than 100 performers and is particularly famous for its artist collaborations and typically reaches its climax in the theme song (different each year) that is sung by all performers at the end of the concert.
Admission fee *8,700*
yen (for ticket details check anisama.tv).* **Dates** *end of Aug.* **Opening times** *16:00–21:00. Saitama Super Arena, 8 Shin-Toshin, Chuo-ku, Saitama City*
anisama.tv

World Character Summit in Hanyu

Yuru-chara (from the English "character") are cute mascots which are mainly used as promotional tools. Most of them (the so-called *gotochi-chara*) represent cities and regions around Japan—to help stimulate tourism and sagging economies) What makes them so popular in Japan is their being *yurui* ("loose" in a gentle, laid-back way). Often created by amateur artists, their unsophisticated, oversimplified design and naïveté add to their kawaii appeal. Indeed, their popularity is such that the combined mascot army now commands character-driven sales worth 2 trillion yen.

One of the unlikely centers of yuru-chara activity is Hanyu, a small city in the northernmost part of Saitama Prefecture where every November hundreds of mascots converge from around Japan and even a few foreign countries.

The two-day event attracts more than 400,000 visitors. On each stage the mascots take turn in doing their gags and performances while the rows of booths lining up the event location are continually assaulted but thousands of goods hunters. All in all it's a veritable only-in-Japan experience.
Admission fee *100 yen.* **Dates** *third weekend of Nov.* **Opening times** *9:00–15:30 Hanyu Suigo Park, 751-1 Mitakaya, Hanyu City, Saitama Prefecture*
gotouchi-chara.jp/hanyu2014/index.html

TRAVEL TIPS

WHEN TO GO

Nearly every month there are some interesting otaku events and festivals going on in Tokyo, and the shops in particular are open all year round. Summer, though, can be brutal, as the rainy season goes from mid-June to mid-July, and temperatures often exceed 33℃ from July to August, and humidity averages 80%—not the ideal conditions to explore the city while dragging around a backpack and bags full of manga and toys. Unfortunately if you are into idols you will have to brave the heat waves and the biblical crowds and come in August because all the main festivals take place during this month. Spring is fine (and you may have a chance to see the fabulous cherry blossoms during the few days between March and April) but the weather can be quite unstable. Winter, on the other side, is cold and often windy but very dry, with mostly blue skies. The first two-three days of the year is also the one period when (almost) all shops and museums are going to be closed. Weather-wise, fall is probably the best time to go, with a good range of otaku festivals to choose from.

LEARN SOME JAPANESE

Communicating effectively in Tokyo can be a challenge as most signs are in Japanese and only a few people can speak decent English. While learning kanji (the Chinese characters) takes a lifetime, I recommend you take the time to learn the katakana alphabet because many shops' names and other useful information (things they sell, product names, restaurant menus, etc.) are often written this way. Being able to read this information will make your stay in Japan much easier.

PACKING

1) A backpack is essential for moving around Tokyo. 2) It would be good to bring a spare foldable bag too. Considering all the things you surely want to buy, it will come handy on your return trip. Just remember not to exceed total luggage weight or the check-in people at the airport may charge you an extra fee. 3) Unless you plan to attend a formal event or go somewhere fancy, casual clothes are okay, but try not to look too shabby. In Japan, people are going to judge you by the way you look. 4) You are going to walk walk walk. Better bring a change of shoes. 5) Don't forget your prescription medication and other medicine you may not find in Japan.

GETTING TO TOKYO

Tokyo has two airports: the main one in Narita and another one in Haneda. While an increasing number of international flights now arrive at Haneda, you will probably land at Narita, more than 60 km east of Tokyo. To reach the city center, your best options are a limousine bus or a train. A very good deal is buying a round-trip ticket for the Narita Express train (N'EX) that connects the airport to all major stations in the Tokyo metropolitan area. At 4,000 yen, you can save 33 percent on the normal fare.

JET LAG

When you arrive in Japan you will probably be severely jet-legged, which means by 9:00 pm you won't be able to keep your eyes open while the day after you will be staring at the ceiling at 3:00 or 4:00 am. So try to stay up as long as you can. The sooner you manage to get back to a normal cycle the better, because in Japan there's not much you can do early in the morning, and the shops usually open between 10:00 and 11:00.

GETTING AROUND

Trains are the best way to go anywhere. They are safe, clean, reasonably cheap, and show up every 4–5 minutes (even more frequently during rush hour). You are definitely going to use the JR system and the Tokyo Metro subway (each line is color-coded), and maybe even some other private train lines. The good news is that you can pay all your rides with a Suica or Pasmo smart card. These cards can be purchased at every ticket vending machine (just follow the English instructions) and are recharge-able. While they are issued by different companies, they can be used on every train line. Just swipe them on the sensor when entering and exiting. These cards are so handy you can even use them at convenience stores and vending machines. When taking a train, if you are not sure about which track number your train is, you can ask in Japanese: *Sumimasen, (place name) wa nanban desu ka?* As for train etiquette, talking loudly (especially on your cell phone) and eating on trains is frowned upon. Just don't do it.

When on foot and looking for an address, if you get lost just ask the police. People in Japan use police boxes as information centers.

MONEY

While more and more places now accept credit cards, Japan is still very much a cash-only country (particularly the smaller independent shops). So get some yen before leaving, or exchange some of your currency at the airport when you arrive in Tokyo (rates are good).

Remember to call your credit card company before leaving and tell them you are going to use it abroad. You can use your ATM card only at an international ATM. The best places where you can find them are at Citibank branches and especially at the many post offices.

SHOPPING

Non-resident foreign customers can take advantage of the duty-free shops (there are many in Akiba) provided they spend at least 10,000 yen. Just remember to take your passport with you. If you buy appliances, be sure to get overseas multi-lingual models.

Many local stores specialize in used games, manga and DVDs. They make for excellent deals as they are often discounted around 50%. No need to worry because they are always handled carefully and could easily pass for brand-new items. This said, if an item is sold at an incredibly cheaper price than other stores, chances are some parts are missing or it's not in mint condition (look for red writing on the price sticker).

If you can't find the price on a particular item, it's usually okay to ask "how much?" in English, but if the clerk doesn't understand you, try the Japanese *ikura desu ka?* and keep paper and pen ready so they can write it down for you.

Prices are pretty much fixed, so don't bother asking for a discount. Haggling is just not part of Japanese culture. However at shows some sellers are willing to give you a 10% (more rarely 20%) discount. You may also have an outside chance at a small independent second-hand store, especially if you buy a lot of things.

In restaurants and cafes, you don't have to tip, even because in certain places you are going to pay a table or seat charge.

FOOD AND DRINKS

All the cafes, bars and restaurants included in this guide are otaku-themed eateries, but this doesn't mean you have to eat every day in such places—even because they are far from cheap. Many of the common restaurants have plastic food displays which make ordering much easier. Eating in Tokyo is not particularly expensive (as long as you stay away from the high-end fancy restaurants) and, unless you are exceptionally unlucky, on average the food is very good. The ubiquitous convenience stores (*conbini* in Japanese) sell lots of food and drinks too. Most of the food is not particularly healthy (it's full of preservatives) but a cheap rice ball or some chocolate can help you fill a hole in your stomach between meals. The added bonus for otaku hunters is that at every conbini there are often anime tie-ins with snack food—a cheap way to boost your collection of toys and character goods. And don't forget all the vending machines selling all kinds of drinks (stay away from English tea and coffee unless you like them extra sweet) and even some snacks.

MOBILE PHONES

If you have a mobile phone with 3-G technology, you can use it in Japan (ask your telephone carrier how much you will be charged). Otherwise you will need a SIM card that you can get from a vending machine at Narita Airport or Odaiba's Aqua City. It costs about 3,700 yen for one week and around 5,000 for two. They both offer a maximum

download speed of 150 megabits per second and 50 Mbps as an upload speed. If the data amount exceeds 100 MB a day, the network speed will slow down. You can even buy a smartphone and SIM card together for 13,000 yen. You will need to 1) choose your SIM card size (don't forget to check this information before you travel); pay with your credit card (sorry, no cash); activate your SIM card by scanning your passport at the vending machine, then typing in your email address and contact number in Japan (your hotel phone number will do); go to the "mobile networks" setting and then "access point names." If you have never done this before it might be a little confusing. WARNING: you can't make voice calls with this SIM card purchased this way.

TOILETS

Public toilets are rare (most of them can be found in public parks and gardens), often old style (squat type) and rather smelly. On the other hand, you can freely use those at the many convenience stores you find everywhere. On average they are quite clean, and you don't have to buy anything in order to use them.

CRIME AND SAFETY

Tokyo (and Japan in general) is one of the safest cities on Earth, even considering how crowded it is. You can go anywhere at all times of day or night without fear of being mugged or attacked by angry hooligans. However, always use your judgment whenever you sense you may find yourself in a bad situation. Most importantly, by no means get into a fight, especially with a local. The last thing you want to do is to deal with the police. Cops here have a lot of power and can detain you for up to three days without charging you.

HENTAI (PORNOGRAPHY)

Pornography is part of otaku culture and Akihabara is Hentai Central. Erotic images are everywhere, with scantily-clad teenagers smiling from posters, pillows and mug cups. This is typical otaku stuff and is generally accepted or even actively sought out. This does not mean, though, that mainstream shoppers will not be offended by some of the more hardcore stuff. The Japanese moral police have a weird approach to censoring pornography and even the ubiquitous convenience stores are allowed to sell magazines with stories featuring incest, rape and sex with junior high girls. So you have been warned.

TAKING PHOTOS AND VIDEOS

Taking pictures and videos in certain stores and particularly inside game centers and maid cafes is prohibited (even the Akiba maids who are out in the street advertising their cafes usually don't like to be photographed). In a store, if you want to be on the safe side, ask beforehand (*shashin totte mo ii des ka?*). In a game arcade, be very discreet. The first time you get caught, they usually ask you politely to stop. If they catch you again, they will ask you to leave.

MEETING PEOPLE

There are a few Meetup groups in Tokyo devoted to all things otaku starting with Tokyo Otaku Unite! (meetup.com/TokyoOtakuUnite). Check out if they are up to something when you are here.

USEFUL WEBSITES

(Planning your trip)
jnto.go.jp
essential-japan-guide.com/plan
(Flights)
kayak.com (lets you compare different online travel sites)
(Hotels)
hotels.com
expedia.co.jp
(Train routes and timetables)
hyperdia.com/en
trains.jp

OTAKU GLOSSARY

Akiba-kei (lit. Akihabara style) slang term dating back to the early 1980s and used as a synonym for otaku.

Anikura anime song club music.

Anison anime song.

Bishojo beautiful girl.

BL/Boys' Love see yaoi.

Bromide commercial photographic portraits of celebrities (e.g. singers, actors, etc.).

Burikko woman or girl who acts cute by playing innocent and helpless.

Butler's cafe cosplay restaurant where well-dressed men cater to a female clientele.

Cameko (short for camera kozo): people who like to take cosplay pictures.

Cheki (lit. small instant camera) a Polaroid picture you can take with a maid.

Chogokin (lit. "Super Alloy," a fictitious material which appeared in Mazinger Z) line of Popy/Bandai-made die-cast metal robot and character toys.

Danso a girl dressed as a boy.

Dojin independent productions (books, music, films, software) not available through standard commercial outlets.

Dojinshi fanzine.

Fujoshi (lit. rotten girl) female fans of manga and novels that feature romantic relationships between men.

Gachagacha see Gachapon.

Gachapon vending machine-dispensed capsule toys.

Garage kit model kits usually cast in polyurethane resin.

Gunpla Gundam plastic models.

Hentai anime and manga pornography.

Itachari bicycle version of itasha (see).

Itasha a car decorated with manga, anime and video game characters (usually cute girls).

Itatansha motorbike version of itasha (see).

Kaiju monster movie.

Layer short for cosplayer.

Light novel short young adult novel mainly targeting middle and high school girls.

Mecha robots controlled by people (e.g. Mazinger Z, Grandizer, Gundam).

Menko game of slapping cards down to overturn opponent's.

Moe (neologism) affective response to fictional characters from anime, manga and video games.

Niji sosaku fanzine that parodies existing mainstream manga.

Otagei see Wotagei.

Otome (lit. maiden, young girl) female otaku.

OVA (Original Video Animation) animated films and series made specifically for release in home video formats without prior showings on television or in theatres.

Plamodel (pla-mo) plastic model.

Purikura (short for Print Club) photo stickers.

Rajikon radio-controlled model.

Shojo manga manga aimed at teenage female readers.

Shokugan small toy that comes packaged with candy sold at convenience stores and supermarkets.

Shonen manga manga aimed at young male readers.

Situation CD CDs featuring audio dramas where storylines from anime, video games, TV series, etc. are continued or expanded.

Sofubi toy figure made from soft vinyl.

Super Sentai costumed superhero-team TV shows.

Tokusatsu live-action film or TV drama featuring considerable use of special effects.

V-Cinema straight-to-video movies.

Visual novel interactive fiction game featuring static, anime-style graphics, multiple storylines and multiple-choice decision points.

Wota fans of idol singers.

Wotagei Aakiba-style dancing and cheering routines.

Yaoi genre of male-male romance narrative.

PHOTO CREDITS

All photos © Gianni Simone except following:

Front cover top right, 12 bottom left © Charles; **Front cover bottom left, 18** © Doug Kline; **Front cover bottom right, Back cover 2nd row right, 113 top, 123 top left, 123 right middle and bottom, 126 top right** © Danny Choo; **Front cover left below, 3 bottom right, 136 bottom,** © @ Jam Project; **Front flap, 8 bottom** © Eugene Flores; **Back cover, top left** © aluxum/istockphoto.com; **Back cover, top row right** © Makoto Kojima; **Back cover, top row 3rd left, Inside back cover, 5 bottom left, 5 middle right, 29 bottom middle, 29 bottom right, 31 bottom right, 33 top left, 37 top left, 49 bottom left, 54 left, 67 top middle, 90 bottom left** © Guilhem Vellut; **Back cover, top right, 28 top left, 55 right** © Alberto Carrasco-Casado; **Back cover, top row 2nd right, 49 top middle** © tenaclousme; **Back cover, top row 2nd left, 4 bottom left** © Taichiro Ueki; **Back cover, 2nd row left, 22 bottom below, 24 top, 25 bottom, 42** © Karl Baron; **Back flap, 120/121 left below** © CrunchyLens; **Inside front cover, Inside back cover, 5 top left, 14 bottom, 34 right, 37 middle and bottom, 104 top, 118 left top and bottom, 140 bottom, 141 top** © Antonio Tajuelo; **Inside back cover, 2 top right, 88 top** © Ajari; **Inside back cover** © klondike. Hagii Kaoru; **2 top left, 22 top, 23 top left, 120 top, 121 top right** © Hikaru Kazushime; **2 bottom left, 73 top right, 74 bottom** © Eddy Milfort; **2 bottom right, 49 bottom right** © Moyan Brenn; **2/3 top middle** © LeLe Junie Moon; **2/3 bottom middle, 49 top right, 53 top** © Roxanne Ready; **3 top left, 19 below, 20/21 top middle, 122 top** Kana Natsuno; **3 top right, 54 top, 64/65 bottom middle** © Cory Doctorow; **3 bottom left** © eerkmans; **4 bottom middle** © Zengame; **4 bottom right** © James Dennes; **5 top right** © isa_adsr; **6 above** © Frances Delgado; **6 below, 116 top left, 123 right top, 124 top right** © Steve Nagata; **7 bottom left and right, 133 top left** © Meiji University Yonezawa Yoshihiro Memorial Library of Manga and Subcultures; **9 top left** © Tokyoship; **9 top right** © Tom; **9 bottom** © Bobak Ha'Eri; **10 top right** © sora; **11 bottom** © Fedup Muraletik; **12 right bottom** © Takahashi Hideyasu/Shogakukan; **13 top left** © yukishana; **13 top middle** © Suginami Animation Museum; **14 top** © Hey-Rocker; **15 top** © 2014 LEVEL-5 Inc.; **15 bottom left** © j bizzie; **15 bottom right** © Marcin Wichary; **16 top left** © LEVEL 5; **16 top right** © 2013 LEVEL-5 Inc.; **17 right** © erocsid; **20 left below** © hslo; **22 bottom above** © Omarukai; **23 top middle** © Takashi Nishimura; **23 bottom** © Jeelee Cuizon; **24 bottom** © Volks; **25 middle** © Dennis Amith; **28 bottom** © Yuichi Kosio; **30 bottom right** © Jim; **31 middle, 95 bottom left, 102 top and bottom** © Carter McKendry; **31 bottom left** © Hikosaemon; **32 bottom left** © ciry2; **33 top right** © Ian Muttoo; **35 right bottom, 127 bottom middle, 137 middle below** © demiurgo; **Inside back cover, 29 top right, bottom left, 38 bottom, 44** © Ryo FUKAsawa; **39** © Pasela Resort Akiba; **43 top left** © panina.anna; **43 top right** © Final Fantasy Eorzea Café; **45 top** © Momochi Minami; **45 bottom** © Kyle Hasegawa; **48 top left, 59 middle below** © Amy Jane Gustafson; **49 top right** © puamella; **Inside back cover, 50 top** © beibaoke/Shutterstock.com; **50 middle** © Siraanamwong/Dreamstime.com; **51 top left** © kazamatsuri; **Inside back cover, 51 top right** © Helen Cook; **54 bottom** © Taco Ekkel; **Inside back cover, 57 top** © KT/S·N·STP, KT/S·TM; **59 right** © Cherrie Mio Rhodes; **61 top right and bottom left, 62 top** © Guwashi999; **64 top left** © Struggle Gen; **64 bottom left, 69 top left, 69 right below** © Re-animation; **65 top right** © Tomohiro Ohtake; **65 middle right** © shiranai; **Inside back cover, 65 bottom right** © Nicholas Wong; **66** © ESB Professional/Shutterstock.com; **69 top right** © Japanexperterna.se; **70 top** © Christian Van Der Henst S.; **70 middle** © Connie Ma; **71 middle** © Cozinhando Fantasias; **72 bottom** © Big Ben in Japan; **72/73 top left** © Dan DeChiaro; **Inside front cover, 73 middle** © damon jah; **74 top** © Gary; **75 top** © Armandas Jarusauskas; **77 bottom** © localjapantimes; **79 bottom** © Ken Works Tokyo Times; **81 middle** © yoppi; **82 top and bottom left** © OliOpi/Shutterstock.com; **82 bottom right** © omatsu/japan-photolibrary.jp; **83 right below** © ponsulak/Shutterstock.com; **84 middle** © 2004 Shirow Masamune KODANSHA IG ITNDDTD; **84 bottom** © 2014-2015 Hinako Sugiura MS HS Sarusuberi Film Partners; **86 top** © MIKI Yoshihito; **86 bottom right** © Paul Downey; **88 middle right, 89 top** © hoji/japanphotolibrary.jp; **90 top** © Joe Wu; **90 right above** © Kim Ahlstrom; **90 right below** © Erik; **91 left** © Lucy Takakura; **92 middle above** © Shojo Manga-kan; **92 middle below left and right** © Suginami Animation Museum; **93 bottom left and right** © Tachikawa Manga Park; **Inside back cover, 94 top left, 101 bottom** © Richard Elzey; **94 bottom left** © Farhan Ahmad Tajuddin; **94 bottom above, 106 bottom** © Maid Café Pinafore; **95 top left, 96 top** © Marco Ool; **95 top right** © Yee›s photo; **95 middle** © istolethetv; **30 top, 30 bottom left, 51 bottom, 95 top below, 128 middle** © Stefan; **103 top** © Nerima Anime Carnival; **Inside front cover, Inside back cover, 105 middle bottom and right bottom** © BL Gakuen; **106 top** © Swallowtail; **107 bottom right** © TK Kurikawa/Shutterstock.com; **108 top left, 109 top left, 109 middle left, 109 bottom right, 114 bottom** © Phillip Maguire/Shutterstock.com; **108/109 top middle, 117 top** © IQRemix; **108/109 right below, 112 bottom** © Drew Thaler; **108 bottom** © Sean Pavone/Shutterstock.com; **Inside front cover, 109 bottom left, 137 middle above, 138 bottom** © Kanegen; **110 bottom** © cowardlion/Shutterstock.com; **111 bottom right** © Santanor/Shutterstock.com; **115 top right** © Heiwa 4126; **116 top right, 124 bottom** © Super Comic City; **118 right, 119 bottom left and right** © Rebecca Koga; **120 bottom** © AnimeJapan; **Inside back cover, 120 right middle** 思弦張; **Inside front cover, 120/121 top middle, 121 bottom right** © Reginald Pentinio; **124 middle left** © Akanuma Madoka; **125 top** © International Tokyo Toy Show; **126 top left, 130 top** © Tomohiro Ohtake; **127 right middle, 134 top right** © T.YANASE/FRÖEBELKAN·TMS·NTV; **127 middle left** © Amy Jane Gustafson; **127 bottom right** © Kiichi –Shogakukan; **132 bottom** © Machiko Hasegawa Art Museum; **133 bottom above and below** © Yayoi-Yumeji Museum; **133 bottom left** © Sora; **134 bottom left** © tipwam/Shutterstock.com; **134 bottom right** © Kentaro Ohno; **135 top left** © Tin Toys Museum; **135 bottom** © ISHIMORI PRODUCTION INC. and TOEI COMPANY, LTD.; **138 bottom above** © FlyAway2112; **139 top left** © Nautilus 2014; **139 bottom** © Animelo Summer Live

ACKNOWLEDGMENTS

Although this book is mainly the result of my personal research, and I am the sole responsible for any mistakes, I have been lucky enough to be helped, advised and inspired by several amazing people to whom goes all my gratitude.

I really enjoyed working with editors Cathy Layne and June Chong. Cathy believed in this project from the beginning and patiently schooled me in the fine art of book writing, while June took care of the book in the last stages.

My guru Patrick W. Galbraith is the person to blame for giving me my first tour of Akihabara. Also, the sidebar on maid cafes is partly based on his essay "Maid in Japan: An Ethnographic Account of Alternative Intimacy" (in "Intersections: Gender and Sexuality in Asia and the Pacific," Issue 25, February 2011).

I found a lot of useful information about Tokyo's turbulent relationship with Godzilla in Armand Vaquer's *The Monster Movie Fan's Guide to Japan*, a detailed guide to kaiju movie locations.

While I spent my fair share of time and money in countless game centers, Brian Ashcraft's informative and entertaining *Arcade Mania!* gave me a needed historical perspective on the video game industry.

Rebecca Koga aka Celestialshadow was an endless source of information on cosplay. Learn more about her and her costume-making activity at phantomlegacycostumes.com.

Mayuko Okuno helped me unveil the secrets of Ikebukuro's Otome Road.

Honorable mention to editors Claude Leblanc (Zoom Japon magazine) who sadistically kept giving me story assignments while I was busy working on this guide, thus helping me pay the bills.

I aalso want to thank all the people (too many to mention one by one) who shared their thoughts and opinions, and kindly let me use their photos. In particular Frances Delgado of How a Girl Figures fame (www. howagirlfigures.com) whose old otaku rooms is featured in the book.

Last but not least, I want to thank my folks for letting me watch the Grendizer TV series at dinner time one fateful April 1978; and my lovely wife Hisako for her encouragement, endless patience, and her invaluable contribution to the research for this book.

Published by Tuttle Publishing, an imprint of Periplus Editions (HK) Ltd

www.tuttlepublishing.com

Copyright © 2017 Periplus Editions (Hong Kong) Ltd

All rights reserved. No part of this publication may be reproduced or utilized in any form or by any means, electronic or mechanical, including photocopying, recording, or by any information storage and retrieval system, without prior written permission from the publisher.

ISBN 978-4-8053-1385-5

DISTRIBUTED BY
North America, Latin America & Europe
Tuttle Publishing
364 Innovation Drive, North Clarendon,
VT 05759-9436 U.S.A.
Tel: 1 (802) 773-8930; Fax: 1 (802) 773-6993
info@tuttlepublishing.com; www.tuttlepublishing.com

Japan
Tuttle Publishing
Yaekari Building, 3rd Floor,
5-4-12 Osaki, Shinagawa-ku, Tokyo 141-0032
Tel: (81) 3 5437-0171; Fax: (81) 3 5437-0755
sales@tuttle.co.jp; www.tuttle.co.jp

Asia Pacific
Berkeley Books Pte. Ltd.
61 Tai Seng Avenue, #02-12
Singapore 534167
Tel: (65) 6280-1330; Fax: (65) 6280-6290
inquiries@periplus.com.sg

20 19 18 17   10 9 8 7 6 5 4 3 2 1
Printed in China   1704CM

ABOUT TUTTLE:
"BOOKS TO SPAN THE EAST AND WEST"

Our core mission at Tuttle Publishing is to create books which bring people together one page at a time. Tuttle was founded in 1832 in the small New England town of Rutland, Vermont (USA). Our fundamental values remain as strong today as they were then—to publish best-in-class books informing the English-speaking world about the countries and peoples of Asia. The world has become a smaller place today and Asia's economic, cultural and political influence has expanded, yet the need for meaningful dialogue and information about this diverse region has never been greater. Since 1948, Tuttle has been a leader in publishing books on the cultures, arts, cuisines, languages and literatures of Asia. Our authors and photographers have won numerous awards and Tuttle has published thousands of books on subjects ranging from martial arts to paper crafts. We welcome you to explore the wealth of information available on Asia at **www.tuttlepublishing.com**.

HELEN HALL LIBRARY
100 Walker St
League City, TX 77573
DISCARD